The Routledge Guidebook to Paine's
Rights of Man

Upon publication in 1791–92, the two parts of Thomas Paine's *Rights of Man* proved to be both immensely popular and highly controversial. An immediate bestseller, it not only defended the French revolution but also challenged current laws, customs, and government.

The Routledge Guidebook to Paine's Rights of Man provides the first comprehensive and fully contextualized introduction to this foundational text in the history of modern political thought, addressing its central themes, reception, and influence. The *Guidebook* examines:

- the history of rights, populism, representative governments, and challenges to monarchy from the 12th through 18th century;
- Paine's arguments against monarchies, mixed governments, war, and state–church establishments;
- Paine's views on constitutions;
- Paine's proposals regarding suffrage, inequality, poverty, and public welfare;
- Paine's revolution in rhetoric and style;
- the critical reception upon publication and influence through the centuries, as well as Paine's relevance today.

The Routledge Guidebook to Paine's Rights of Man is essential reading for students of eighteenth-century American and British history, politics and philosophy, and anyone approaching Paine's work for the first time.

Frances A. Chiu teaches history and literature at the New School in New York, USA. She is a graduate of Smith College (A.B.), Northwestern University (M.A.), and Oxford University (Ph.D.).

THE ROUTLEDGE GUIDES TO THE GREAT BOOKS

The Routledge Guides to the Great Books provide ideal introductions to the texts which have shaped Western Civilization. The Guidebooks explore the arguments and ideas contained in the most influential works from some of the most brilliant thinkers who have ever lived, from Aristotle to Marx and Newton to Wollstonecraft. Each Guidebook opens with a short introduction to the author of the great book and the context within which they were working and concludes with an examination of the lasting significance of the book. *The* Routledge Guides to the Great Books will therefore provide students everywhere with complete introductions to the most significant books of all time.

Machiavelli's The Prince
John T. Scott

Augustine's Confessions
Catherine Conybeare

Foucault's The History of Sexuality
Chloe Taylor

The New Testament
Patrick Gray

James's Principles of Psychology
David E Leary

Berkeley's Three Dialogues
Stefan Storrie

Smith's Wealth of Nations
Maria Pia Paganelli

Paine's Rights of Man
Frances A. Chiu

For more information about this series, please visit: https://www.routledge.com/The-Routledge-Guides-to-the-Great-Books/book-series/RGGB

The Routledge Guidebook to Paine's *Rights of Man*

Frances A. Chiu

Routledge
Taylor & Francis Group

LONDON AND NEW YORK

First published 2020
by Routledge
2 Park Square, Milton Park, Abingdon, Oxon OX14 4RN

and by Routledge
52 Vanderbilt Avenue, New York, NY 10017

Routledge is an imprint of the Taylor & Francis Group, an informa business

British Library Cataloguing-in-Publication Data
A catalogue record for this book is available from the British Library

Library of Congress Cataloging-in-Publication Data
Names: Chiu, Frances, author.
Title: The Routledge guidebook to Paine's Rights of man / Frances A Chiu.
Other titles: Guidebook to Paine's Rights of man
Description: Abingdon, Oxon ; New York, NY : Routledge, 2020. |
Series: The Routledge guides to the great books |
Includes bibliographical references and index.
Identifiers: LCCN 2019052685 (print) | LCCN 2019052686 (ebook) |
Subjects: LCSH: Paine, Thomas, 1737-1809. Rights of man. |
Political science--History--18th century.
Classification: LCC JC177 .H5 2020 (print) |
LCC JC177 (ebook) | DDC 320.51--dc23
LC record available at https://lccn.loc.gov/2019052685
LC ebook record available at https://lccn.loc.gov/2019052686

ISBN: 978-0-415-70391-8 (hbk)
ISBN: 978-0-415-70392-5 (pbk)
ISBN: 978-0-203-76247-9 (ebk)

Typeset in Times New Roman
by Taylor & Francis Books

CONTENTS

TABLES

ACKNOWLEDGMENTS

In some respects, this is a book that began prior to my doctoral dissertation on the Gothic at Oxford University when I found myself fascinated by the French revolution debate. As such, proper acknowledgements begin with my late doctoral supervisor, Marilyn Butler, with whom I've had many an enlightened conversation on late 18th-century English reformers and radicals, as well as Jon Mee, whose conversations and writings on William Blake and 1790s radicalism have inspired me over the years. Thanks are owed to Kristine Danowski, a best friend who rekindled my interest in Paine after the completion of my dissertation, in addition to the chairs of the Social Sciences departments at the New School from 2005–2009: namely, Gina Luria Walker, Julia Foulkes, and Gustav Peebles, all of whom granted me permission not only to teach the first-ever course in the U.S. on Thomas Paine and classes on popular democracy but also to organize a symposium on Paine in 2009. There are also many friends, other faculty, graduate students, and my own undergraduates in the U.S. and U.K. who have shared valuable observations in classrooms and private conversations: Gary Berton, Katherine Boyd, Kenneth Burchell, Ed Dodson, Max Fincher, Tammy Green, Erik Hayden, Peter Heap, Juan Melo, Julia Saunders, Martin Screeton, and Koren Whipp.

This book, however, would not have begun without the encouragement of historian and sociologist, Harvey Kaye, who got the ball rolling by recommending me to Routledge. I would also like to thank the wonderful editors at Routledge, beginning with Andy Humphries, who handled the proposal, Rebecca Shillabeer, Iram Satti, Siobhan Poole, Lucy Vallance, Sarah Gore, Gabrielle Coakeley, Adam Johnson, and Tony Bruce, Senior Publisher of Philosophy: all have demonstrated the greatest patience during the completion of the project. I must also mention the wonderful reviewers for their insightful observations and suggestions. Thanks go to the Production editor, Reanna Young, and copy-editor, Richard Cook, for their assistance in the final stages. I would like to give a shout out to the terrific reference librarians of the Noah Webster Library (West Hartford, CT) for tracking down a multitude of books. Many thanks and gratitude go to Martha Spiegelman of Thomas Paine Friends who has combed through my text, spotting howlers and minor errors with equal aplomb. It goes without saying that any remaining errors in the text are completely mine.

Not least are my personal debts during the difficult period of 2014 to 2018. This book is dedicated to the memory of Cecelia H. Chiu—the woman who was not just my mother, but mentor, teacher, and best friend over the decades: it was she who developed my understanding of social and political issues, all while stoking my interests in history and literature from grade school through grad school. Her illness through much of 2014, and her passing in October of that year could not have been a more grievous hardship even though an anticipated one: and I do not know how this book could have been completed without the love, encouragement, and friendship of my cousins and maternal aunts, particularly Christine Chen, Teresa Hogan, Shu-Hwa Lin, Ingrid Lin, and Frances Yang. I must not forget my late father, Huei-huang who funded my education over the years. Nor must I forget the furry and comforting presence of my two Persians, Sir Charles Fox and Duchess Georgiana.

My final acknowledgements go to the progressive movements which have been taking place across the U.S. and in the U.K. since 2015. During what has otherwise been a bleak period of mourning for me, these movements—headed respectively by Bernie Sanders and Jeremy Corbyn—have shone like a ray of light, reminding me that Paine's dream of a more equitable world is still alive.

New York City, 2019

INTRODUCTION

> We need not bother too much about being able to trace a continuous
> pedigree for these ideas. They are the ideas of the underground, sur-
> viving, if at all, verbally: they have little trace. It is unlikely that the
> ideas of the seventeenth-century radicals had no influence on the
> Wilkesite movement, the American Revolution, Thomas Paine or the
> plebeian radicalism which revived in England in the 1790s. Unlikely:
> but such influence is difficult to prove....
>
> Christopher Hill, *The World Turned Upside Down*

"Pain[e]'s wild rebellious burst proclaims her rights aloud." Thus
declared William Wordsworth months after initial sales of
Thomas Paine's *Rights of Man*, Part 1 broke nearly every extant
publishing record: one that would only be superseded by the
publication of Part 2 in February 1792. As the most famous
response to Edmund Burke's *Reflections on the Revolution in
France* (1790), Paine's *Rights of Man* stands as one of the earliest
and most comprehensive British political texts to challenge a
government on the verge of modernization. By directing his
attention to less formally educated readers who had previously
been ignored by political theorists and even pamphleteers, Paine

was able to render a somewhat staid and tame tradition of British Whiggism into a dynamic new philosophy of progressive politics. In short, it was a work that transformed the former corset maker and excise officer into a modern Prometheus—especially after being declared seditious by a fearful British government. Yet regardless of its initial suppression, the ideas propounded in *Rights of Man* continued to reverberate around the world, inspiring causes as diverse as labor rights and women's suffrage in America in addition to Irish and Uruguayan nationhood. Even today, more than two centuries later, this once notorious title remains as relevant—and even controversial—as ever in an age that has become all the more cognizant of the relationship between political and economic power. As Harvey Kaye puts it aptly, "Now, after two centuries, it seems we have all become Painites."[1]

At first glance, a guide to *Rights of Man* may appear superfluous given its acknowledged readability: this was a book, after all, that appealed to the illiterate as well as the literate. So why is a guide to this seminal text necessary? There are several compelling reasons. Firstly, despite the recent spate of scholarship and popular literature on Paine, there is still a need for a general guide that not only introduces Paine's concepts to modern readers, but also situates them in the history of Western liberal thought. Is Paine indeed the "progenitor of our modern understanding of human rights?" as claimed by political philosopher, Robert Lamb?[2] We have yet to grasp just how his ideas on individual rights, social and economic rights, political representation, democracy, and republicanism converge—and diverge—from those professed through the ages. We have also yet to understand why, in turn, these ideas came to generate so much controversy upon its bipartite publication in 1791 and 1792. This dearth is especially unfortunate in light of innumerable misinterpretations accrued over the centuries, with Paine himself variously branded as a libertarian, free-market capitalist, and socialist. Finally, if my own experiences in teaching literature and history are any indication, the sheer obstacle of 18th-century prose can present difficulties not only to the most proficient undergraduates, but also to graduate students.

As such, this guide aims to explicate, first and foremost, the arguments presented in the text itself while showing how Paine's conceptualizations of rights, representative government, and inequality fit into the broader trajectory of liberal and progressive thought in Britain, America, and France. This junction cannot be overemphasized particularly since Paine has been all too often wrongly perceived as an iconoclastic revolutionary. At the same time, however, it is equally important not to run to the other extreme by denying Paine the full extent of his achievements: just because he stood on the shoulders of giants—as so many other thinkers have done—should not mislead us into thinking that he was not a very original visionary,[3] or worse yet, a mere hack who simply popularized certain ideas. In order to appreciate the full extent of Paine's radicalism, then, we must understand how the events and issues of his time informed his thought process and rhetoric; he was, after all, a devout reader of newspapers which took full advantage of the lax copyright laws in late 18th-century England and America. This introduction will sketch the evolving discourse of rights from the Middle Ages through the 18th century in relation to other concepts addressed by Paine in *Rights of Man*: namely, hereditary government, class conflict, political representation, the rise of populist rhetoric, and economic justice. I will also demonstrate how Paine's earlier writings (1772–89) fit into the discourse of rights by examining his ideas on social class and political representation as well as his style and rhetoric. Chapter 1 will focus on the first part of *Rights of Man*, published in 1791: here, I will show not only how Paine interpreted the origins and events of the French revolution but also how he refashioned contemporary arguments on revolution, republicanism, hereditary privileges and government. Chapters 2–4 will delve into the second part of *Rights of Man*, published in 1792, specifically Paine's understanding of constitutions and representative government as well as his schemes for alleviating poverty among the poor and elderly. Both parts will contextualize Paine's ideas to a much further extent than has previously been done, showing how he reinterpreted or at least reconfigured ideas from his contemporaries while diverging from other respondents to Edmund Burke's *Reflections on the Revolution in France*. In many respects, my analysis of Parts 1 and 2 of *Rights of Man* will be as much a survey of late 18th-century British liberal opinion on political representation, taxation, economic injustice, and public welfare, demonstrating the extent to which Paine, in some cases, ventured beyond Whiggism, and in other cases did not. Finally, the Conclusion will examine how Paine's ideas have continued to resonate through the ages—including our own.

I. RIGHTS, REASON, AND REFORM: FROM GRATIAN TO GRANVILLE SHARP

Paine famously claimed that "I neither read books, nor studied other people's opinions; I thought for myself."[4] Whether his words can be accepted at face value remains an unanswered question given the accidental burning of a building that housed many of his manuscripts. Nonetheless, if his contributions to the discourse on rights, popular democracy, and public welfare in *Rights of Man* are to be accurately assessed, some attention must be paid to the historical discourse of rights, from its roots in canonic law to the intertwining discourses of civil and political rights, representative governments, and public welfare—despite the overall accuracy of the epigraph from Christopher Hill: that it is difficult to draw a continuous thread through the 17th-century radicals, the Wilkesite enthusiasts of the 1760s and '70s, or indeed the entire history of English, American, and French populist radicalism from the Middle Ages. After all, as Paine opined in 1805, "the Inequality of rights has been the cause of all the disturbances, insurrections and civil wars that ever happened in any country, in any age of mankind."[5] It is thus important to see how and why certain themes in the history of rights have resurfaced repeatedly, albeit in multiple guises and under different circumstances. How and why did the concept of rights emerge in the 12th and 13th centuries? How did the seemingly disparate contexts of Magna Charta, peasant uprisings, discourses on the limits of monarchical authority, as well as the English revolution of the 1640s, yield an evolving understanding of rights? Such will help us understand how ideas on class inequality and hereditary government intertwined over the centuries while contributing to the valorization of representative governments and universal enfranchisement—and thereby help us assess the extent of Paine's radicalization in his writing of Rights of Man, Parts 1 and 2.

A. "ALL BONDE MEN MAY BE MADE FFRE FOR GOD MADE ALL FFRE"[6]

The idea of claiming a right—whether the right to speak freely, to remain silent, or to bear arms—is one that appears so obvious that we barely stop to think about its history. At first glance, it would appear to be a secular one ushered into the Enlightenment by the Glorious revolution, American revolution and French revolution: the latter two of which are understood to have been determined at least in part by Paine himself. Certainly, the sudden spike in the number of titles featuring the word "rights" during the early 1790s would also seem to offer ample proof. A few historians such as C.B. MacPherson and Leo Strauss have pushed the origins of the concept back to the English Civil War. This concept of rights, however, has a much longer history, going back at least six centuries when the idea of a natural law (e.g., all men and living creatures endeavor to sustain themselves) eventually gave rise to the idea of a natural right (e.g., all men and living creatures have a right to sustain themselves) in texts on canonic laws. Even though the terms "natural law" or "natural order" had existed since the writings of Cicero and Ulpian, the idea of subjective rights did not begin to surface until Gratian published his *Concordia discordantium canonum* (1140), subsequently to be retitled the *Decretum*. Here, Gratian defined *ius naturale* (natural law) as that which one is commanded in the Law and Gospel to treat others.[7] He maintained that the primacy of natural law remained immutable at times, sometimes deviating greatly from human law because, by natural law, "all things are common to all," whereas human law had established private property (59). Such a belief subsequently led other thinkers, for instance, Godfrey of Fontaine, to regard the right to the necessities of life not only as a natural right, but an inalienable one where "By the law of nature (*iure naturae*) each one has a certain right (*ius*) in the common exterior goods of this world, which right cannot be licitly renounced" (cited in Tierney, 59). More notably, Gratian would address the notion of the "iura libertatis, the rights of liberty," which could not be lost even when "held in bondage."

As natural laws slowly came to be differentiated from natural rights, it was not long before commentators on the *Concordia* scrutinized Gratian's uses of *ius naturale* more closely. In 1160, Rufinus defined it as "a certain force instilled in every human creature by nature to do good and avoid the opposite." By the 1180s, it became possible to read "*ius naturale,*" according to Brian Tierney, as "licit and approved, neither commanded nor forbidden by the Lord or by any other statute ... as for instance to eat something or not to eat it...." (67); the right of nature is obviously one that is permitted by "the law of nature" (68). In turn, the next stage in the development of a natural rights discourse came to be shaped by the debate on Franciscan poverty (i.e., particularly in regard to the right to consume without legal property rights since Franciscans disavowed private ownership). In the *Breviloquium*, William of Ockham hinted at a basic right to survive, suggesting God granted man a power "that right reason declares to be necessary and useful to the human race" not only "for living, but living well." Perhaps more importantly, Ockham would stipulate that such rights be duly honored by the emperor and pope, noting that tyrannical rulers could be deposed since God had also conferred the power to establish rulers with temporal jurisdiction on mankind directly. Not less significant is his increased use of *ius* in reference to elections, such as *ius eligendi* (right of electing), *cedere iuri suo* (to cede one's right), *ius instituendi electores* (right of instituting electors).

It is not entirely coincidental that this centuries-long discussion of natural rights in clerical circles was accompanied by a nascent awareness of excessive monarchical power even though the word "rights" was barely in vernacular use. The Magna Charta of 1215, drafted by the Archbishop of Canterbury on behalf of a group of rebellious barons, defended church rights and established habeas corpus. Taxes and other feudal payments to the Crown were to be limited, and subject to baronial consent. It was not until 1297, however, that Magna Charta became part of statute law. While medieval political thinkers were already promulgating the notion that a tyrannical king was no king and therefore not to be obeyed, such works as John Ponet's *A Shorte Treatise of Politike Power* (1556) and George Buchanan's *De Jure Regni apud Scotos* (1579) also imposed limits to monarchical authority.[8] According to Ponet, a Marian exile and Bishop of Winchester, princes were not to be indiscriminately obeyed in all matters, particularly where crime or corruption was concerned: better to suffer "a thousand deaths, than do anything that is evil."[9] Buchanan, whose works were frequently quoted by Algernon Sidney,[10] shared compatible views. Because the origins of government are founded in the origins of society and "the sharing of life," it was necessary for kings to govern by law, not "arbitrary will."[11] Moreover, since it is the people who confer political authority, kings must abide by law. Conversely, when there is a "mutual compact between king and citizens," but the king has broken the compact, he instantly "forfeits whatever rights belong to him under it," thereby ensuring that the people have the right to rebel.

If such texts as the Magna Charta and Buchanan's *De Jure Regni* sought to define the parameters of monarchical authority, the popular disturbances of the 14th, 15th, and 16th centuries would broach the rights of subjects more directly. For Paine, as we will see in Part 2, it was the uprising of 1381 rather than the Magna Charta that warranted greater admiration. Even if it is probably a stretch of the imagination to regard the revolt of 1381 as an immediate consequence of Ockham's claims for the rights of subjects, there is no question that the central issue was one of commoners' rights: namely, the rights of those who were not propertied elites. Indeed, the concept of equal rights would receive even more emphasis in the speech of the St. Albans cleric, John Balle, who famously pondered "When Adam delved and Eve span, who then was the gentleman?"[12] Imprisoned at Maidstone for invectives against the Pope and other prelates, he was later freed by his adoring admirers, "many of the mean people" (Dobson, 371)—perhaps because his ideas on equality were more common than imagined. Although the uprising of 1381 did not bring the desired changes immediately, with Richard II quickly retracting his promises to fulfill the demands of the rebels, the experience of the uprising helped deter the government from levying any more poll taxes. The lords also increasingly began to grant freedom to their serfs, offering more equitable leasehold arrangements. Not least, the limitation on wage increase as stipulated by the Statute of Labourers was also to be abandoned.

Indeed, many of these ideas on equality and democratic representation would resonate in Kett's rebellion of 1549, a reaction to the enclosures of common land by landlords that took place in Paine's native county of Norfolk. Again, the desire to abolish feudalism and curtail the power of the landed elites in their communities was renewed,[13] while a demand for the clergy to become more involved in their communities (e.g., teaching poor children to read their catechisms and primers) also indicated a desire for the clergy to become more useful to their community. There was a demand for "all bonde men" to be "made ffre." It is probably not fortuitous that the idea of "the commons" and "commonwealth" acquired a new significance as rebels in Kent, Sussex, and Surrey were led by a "Captain Commonwealth" while the rebels themselves came to be referred to as "commonwealths" (Wood, 52). Not unlike the rebels of 1381 as Andy Wood suggests, their programme was one which amounted to "a radical reconstruction of society from the bottom up" (Wood, 4).

B "EVERYONE HAS A NATURALL, INNATE FREEDOME TO ENJOY HIS BIRTHRIGHT"

If the uprisings of 1381 and 1549 reveal a dawning consciousness of rights to be enjoyed by Englishmen (and women) as well as a greater inclination to impose limits on authority, the Civil War of the 1640s marked a new stage in the evolution of modern political consciousness. During a period depicted by Christopher Hill as one of "great overturning, questioning, revaluing of everything in England,"[14] earlier notions of rights and representation were canvassed on a larger, more populist scale, giving rise to "a sudden outburst of new civic awareness" that was not only unprecedented in its demand for change and progress, but also intensified by the explosion of print.[15] The arbitrary actions of Charles I, from his demands for ship money to the suspension of Parliament, came to unleash a powerful new political discourse promulgating concepts of equality, civil liberties, and political representation while the consanguineous rise of Christian humanism and Puritan individualism fueled the fire. Not unlike the rebels of 1381 and 1549, radicals wondered why they should be oppressed by other fallible men—the very men who were defying the king? For just as Oliver Cromwell and the gentry opposed Charles I, members of the New Model Army would in turn express frustration with Cromwell's resistance to more thoroughgoing reform a few years later. The difference between the new questioners of the mid-17th century and their medieval counterparts can be grasped from the later generation's more sustained and definitive endeavor to create a new polity that acknowledged the importance of democratic representation, and civil rights (e.g., religious toleration) while celebrating reason and progress—in short, facilitating the rise of what is now referred to as "the Enlightenment." These more radical members were soon to earn the sobriquet of "Levellers"—one which they reluctantly accepted.

What are some of the more meaningful differences between the rhetoric of rights in the 1640s and those of earlier uprisings? First and foremost, there was a belief that a new age was at hand. As Richard Overton put it, "whatever our forefathers were ... we are men of the present age and ought to be free."[16] Under the varied leadership of the charismatic "free-born" John Lilburne, Richard Overton, Thomas Rainsborough, William Walwyn and several others, the Levellers resurrected the issues of natural rights as they proposed a government that would represent the vast majority of those not belonging to either the aristocracy or gentry while decrying the lack of religious toleration.[17] Beginning with their first published tract, *An Agreement of the People*, a work addressed to "the free-born people of England" and long presumed to have influenced the drafting of the U.S. Constitution, the Levellers focused on the theme of equal rights, demanding toleration, suffrage for all propertied males, annual elections, free trade unencumbered by monopolies and trade restrictions, and equality before the law. Some went so far as to claim that men and women were "by nature all equal and alike in power, dignity, authority, and majesty."[18] As Derek Heater rightly points out, the Leveller awareness of freedom as a fundamental human right rather than a mere civic right exhibits a modernized understanding, even if not consistently highlighted in their writings and speeches (Heater, 37). In conjunction with Lilburne's multiple appeals to his "freeborn rights" during his various trials for publishing unlicensed literature in the 1630s and '40s, not to mention his representation of his multiple imprisonments as a threat to all ordinary Englishmen, the more radical Overton would pitch an even more universal claim that "everyone has a naturall, innate freedome to enjoy his Birthright."[19]

So long as suffrage was limited to a few and the right to worship freely sharply curtailed, any semblance of Christian equality was sorely missing. Here too, the Levellers would confront the issue of social, civil, and political injustice more thoroughly than earlier rebels. Just as Walwyn had asserted some few years back that God "regards neither fine clothes, nor gold rings ... nor wealth,"[20] most Levellers agreed that rich and poor should be equal before the judiciary courts because "No true freedom can be established" but one that "hath respect to the poor as well as the rich" ("A Watchword to the City of London");[21] by law, everyone should be "bound alike" and "no tenure, estate, charter, degree, birth, or place do confer any exception from the ordinary course of legal proceedings whereunto others are subjected." Moreover, why should criminals guilty of relatively minor crimes against property receive unduly harsh punishments? Indeed, as the Levellers alleged, Cromwell displayed more than ample hypocrisy with his "arguments against and usurpations of the House of Lords over commons' liberties and freedoms" (*Arrow*, Hill, 56–7). It is worth noting, however, that for all the criticism of Cromwell's elitism or that displayed by "the lords and great men" who "over-rule all as they please" ("Remonstrance," Hill, 45), not all Levellers were prepared to grant universal suffrage to servants and beggars in the belief that their indigence would render them easily corruptible by the wealthy: a prejudice that persisted well into the twentieth century. Yet, even this reservation was not enough to assuage Cromwell and other members of the gentry. Although Cromwell ridiculed the new reformers as a "despicable and contemptible generation of men,"[22] several of their most noted leaders would nonetheless face trials and executions.

In the meantime, other Levellers would pursue even more far-reaching goals, focusing more on economic rights rather than on citizenship and individual rights. Led by Gerrard Winstanley, the "True Levellers"—more familiarly known as the Diggers—harbored few qualms when establishing a number of communitarian colonies throughout England with the purpose of cultivating waste lands: an idea that was also embraced by Peter Chamberlen in *Poor Man's Advocate, or England's samaritan* (1649), and William Goffe in *How to Advance the Trade of the Nation and Employ the Poor*. As if harking back to John Balle's thoughts on equality and taking them to their logical ends, a Digger manifesto of 1649 proclaimed to laborers, servants, and beggars that "all men were to enjoy the creatures alike without property one more than the other."[23] The problem was that government did little for commoners while providing even more for those already well off:

> the government we have gives freedom and livelihood to the Gentrie, to have abundance, and to lock up Treasures of the Earth from the poor, so that rich men may have chests full of Gold and Silver, and houses full of corn and Goods to look upon; and the poor that works to get it, can hardly live, and if they cannot work like Slaves, then they must starve.[24]

Winstanley's new England, was to be nearly a living example of More's *Utopia* even if the latter was not mentioned by name. The Diggers would also lambaste the "Norman Yoke," identifying it as a chief source of oppression in the history of English government, one responsible for the enclosure of land and property ownership ("A Declaration from the Poor, Oppressed people", *CW*, 31) as well as "oppressing Norman laws" ("A Letter to the Lord Fairfax", *CW*, 72). By then, the Norman Yoke had already become a powerful quasi-myth which would continue to resonate strongly more than a century later, according to Christopher Hill, since it "appealed to all the underprivileged" while invoking "far profounder feelings, English patriotism and English Protestantism."[25]

Much of the emphasis on equality and democracy received further expatiation from radical Protestant sects which flourished during the temporary collapse of ecclesiastical authority. If the Puritans who supported Cromwell's revolution had long engaged with their congregations on a much more participatory basis than others while claiming deeper levels of faith, the emerging Ranters and Quakers—the latter a sect to which Thomas Paine's father belonged—came to preach an egalitarian philosophy much akin to that of the Levellers and Diggers. Rejecting assumptions informing common mores and piety, the Ranters were arguably as infamous for their social egalitarianism as for their rejection of sin, their purported nudist colonies, and celebration of free love.[26] This message of compassion for the poor was disseminated by the Ranter preacher George Foster, who claimed he heard the Lord of Hosts proclaim "Equality, equality, equality," promising to "make the low and poor equal with the rich" (cited in Hill, *World*, 223). Since both Ranters and Quakers embraced the idea of resistance with the latter occasionally engaging in nude protests—referred to as "going naked for a sign"—they shared an unsurprising degree of disrepute in the eyes of local and state authorities even if Quakers never quite called for open rebellion.[27] In fact, Quakers would be branded by an M.P. as "all Levellers, against magistracy and property" (cited in Hill, *World*, 239–240). Not unlike the Levellers and Diggers, Quakers demanded the abolition of tithes, religious toleration, and legal reform in addition to voicing concern for the poor:[28] the poor not only had a right to be cared for, but a say in legislation too. As such, it is hardly coincidental that Lilburne and his archenemy Winstanley joined the Quakers late in their lives while the Quaker Edward Billing published a manifesto with Leveller ideas in 1659: all of which led Thomas Comber to reflect back on the 1650s as a period when "Several Levellers settled into Quakers," becoming "Winstanleys disciples" with their philosophy that "none should have more ground that he was able to Till and Husband by his own Labour" (cited in Davies, *Quakers*, 63–5). Nor is it entirely coincidental that the republican Algernon Sidney and John Locke befriended the radical Quaker, Benjamin Furly. It is therefore likely that some of the predominant ideas we associate with Paine—his contempt for hereditary privilege and concern for ordinary people—were passed down through the Quaker teachings from his paternal side as Paine continued to respect and admire them through much of his life; indeed, it is perhaps this Quaker lineage that helps explain certain similarities in his thought to that of the Levellers and Diggers.[29]

Even though Leveller, Digger and Ranter ideals failed to be implemented in the short run with many practitioners eventually retreating altogether from political activity, their activities created a sea change in the understanding of civil and political rights: a change that bolstered more sophisticated conceptualizations of republicanism and representative governments. In certain respects, the continuation of 1640s radicalism through the latter half of the century was anything but unforeseen for just as the Levellers and Diggers execrated Cromwell and his government for their perpetuation of propertied tyranny, others equally deplored his dismissal of the Rump Parliament in 1653. Moreover, even when his autocracy was no longer an immediate issue by 1680, the twin issues of tyranny and absolutism would resonate in the posthumous publication of Sir Robert Filmer's defense of divine right, *Patriarcha.* Despite the more theoretical and less populist orientation of the commonwealth treatises of Marchamont Nedham, James Harrington, Algernon Sidney, and John Locke, the familiar themes of government by consent, resistance, religious and civil liberty, hereditary government, and agrarian law remained prominent—perhaps because of their personal acquaintance with former Levellers such as Lilburne and the latter's associate, John Wildman. Indeed, American revolutionaries, late 18th-century British reformers, and French Jacobins alike would continue to find inspiration in their work. If Thomas Hollis and Richard Brand were later to collaborate in republishing the works of Harrington, Nedham, and Sidney a century later, the famous Whig historian Catharine Macaulay would recommend the works of "Nevil, Sydney, and Harrington" for their "science of policy" while extolling "the keen satire and judicious reflections of Marchamont Nedham."[30] Similarly, the translations of their writings in France played no insignificant role in informing the writing of the revolutionary constitution.[31]

Whatever one makes of the ever changing, if not occasionally downright mercenary nature of Marchamont Nedham's career in journalism, his *Excellencie of a Free State* (1651–2) certainly underscored the Leveller demand for government by consent while probing into the pitfalls of hereditary and oligarchical government. Originally published in the pages of the *Mercurius Politicus*, a newspaper supervised by John Milton, *Free State* maintained that government was designed for the "good and ease of the people" and a "secure enjoyment of their rights." Like the Levellers, of which

Lilburne and Wildman numbered amongst his personal acquaintances,[32] Nedham privileged "the people" as "the only proper judges" of the "behaviour of their governors."[33] This emphasis on choice and consent may also explain why Nedham equally championed religious toleration in *Case of the Commonwealth of England Stated* (1650), opining that world history indicated that a "variety of opinions can be no way destructive of public peace."

By the time that Sidney, another acquaintance of Wildman, commenced work on his *Discourses on Government* in the 1670s, much had already changed: any hopes of Britain remaining a commonwealth had long been vanquished with the abdication of Oliver Cromwell's son, Richard, from the role of Lord Protector in 1659 prior to the restoration of the Crown in 1660. With its championing of consensual government and criticism of monarchies,[34] *Discourses* was an unpublished work that led him to be accused of aiming at "the understanding of the rabble" (cited in Houston, 65). The fact that excerpts from his manuscript were used to incriminate him fatally for his role in the Rye House plot to assassinate both Charles II and his brother James, Duke of York, was to play an equally significant role in the enhancement and romanticization of his ideals over the following century. Here, like Walwyn—and later on, Paine himself—Sidney impatiently brushed aside the veneration of tradition, promoting progress in its stead as he argued that since men were no longer living in caves and hollow trees, why should they "continue under the same form of government" implemented by their ancestors?[35] Just because kings were the first magistrates did not mean they should remain so (456); nor should laws stand without emendations when necessary (461). Indeed, much like the Levellers, as modern historians have noted, Sidney complained that public laws had been transmogrified into instruments of private oppression, given their sheer number and continued use of Latin and Norman French in legal proceedings (Houston, 171). Similarly, like Walwyn and Winstanley, he underscored reason, observing that it would be unnatural for great nations to be governed by "children" or "fools" when there are others possessed of "virtue, experience, wisdom" (94) since "Common sense teaches ... that governments are not set up for the advantage, profit ... off one or a few, but for the good of the society" (91).

In light of the Glorious Revolution of 1688 with its fateful delivery of Protestant England from the clutches of the Catholic James II, the acceptance of monarchy in Locke's *Treatises on Government* becomes less inexplicable when compared to the anti-monarchical texts of the 1650s and '60s. By censuring Filmer for pretending that kings had "a distinct and separate interest from the good of the community," Locke's Whiggish *Treatises* can be read as a culmination of earlier radical thought: perhaps not surprisingly since the events of 1688, much like those of 1649, involved the deposition of a king, namely, the absolutist James II, the younger brother of Charles II; meanwhile, the Tories and Whigs—which had emerged during the Exclusion Crisis of 1678–1681[36]—would now replace the Cavaliers and Roundheads. Like Sidney, Locke was also an associate of the Leveller, John Wildman, holding it necessary to have "one rule for rich and poor."[37] Maintaining that laws ought to be designed exclusively for "the good of the people" (129), he reiterated to his readers, as Brian Tierney has noted, the right of a poor man to the surplus property of the rich because the latter "cannot justly be denied him when his pressing Want calls for it" (Tierney, 75). As Jeremy Waldron also points out, Locke asserted that the natural condition of mankind was one where power and jurisdiction were "reciprocal, no one having more than another."[38] Moreover, even though Locke was generally tolerant of monarchy, he criticized those who allowed undue prerogative to the king—especially those who insinuated that he had "a distinct and separate interest from the good of the community" (138). He would also radically redefine "prerogative" as "whatsoever" shall be done "for the good of the people" (135) while observing that any who encroached on liberty and property deserved to be resisted, if not overthrown—including magistrates. In fact, it was arguably worse given their ingratitude "for the greater share they have by the law" (163).

But perhaps that which brings Locke closest to the Levellers—and farthest from the Diggers—is the privileging of private property and commerce, or "buying and selling." If Locke asserted the right to self-preservation, he equally claimed the very act of labour as a form of proprietorship, explaining

> Was it a robbery thus to assume to himself what belonged to all in common? ... We see in *commons*, which remain so by compact, that it is the taking any part of what is common, and removing it out of the state nature leaves it in, which *begins the property* ... Thus the grass my horse has bit; the turfs my servant has cut ... The *labour* that was mine, removing them out of that common state they were in, hath *fixed* my *property* in them. (88)

In addition, when God "gave the world in common to all mankind," He commanded man not only "to labour" but also to "subdue the earth, *i.e.* improve it for the benefit of life" by means of his "labour" (89). As such, unlike Kett's rebels and the Diggers, Locke did not disapprove of those who enclosed and cultivated land since it "increases the common stock of mankind" (90); that land "should always remain common and uncultivated" (89) was a misguided idea. If anything, it could be argued that overall, Locke elevated the Leveller emphasis on individual rights to a new level. For just as he defended religious toleration, maintaining that civil magistrates had no role in "the care of souls" because God never assigned such an authority to anyone, he likewise maintained that rights to individual property could not be encroached upon by the government such as in the heyday of Charles I.[39] Indeed, throughout much of the following century, the idea of government as a guarantor of individual rights and property would take precedence with the Tories broadly supporting what came to be broadly construed as the "establishments" (i.e. Church and King) and the Whigs liberty and democracy. It was not until the publication of *Rights of Man* that the conceptualization of government as an agent for the collective improvement of society would resurface.

C. "GIVE US OUR RIGHTS!" REFORM, RADICALISM, AND RELIGION, 1760–88

For much of the 18th century, the issues of representative democracy, inequality, and religious toleration that raged during the 1640s through 1660s remained dormant until the accession of George III to the throne in 1760. Indeed, few would have anticipated a tumultuous age of reform to follow so quickly on the quelling of the Jacobite rebellions of 1715 and 1745 (headed respectively by the son and grandson of James II) and a substantial victory in the Seven Years' War (1756–63): especially when the young, recently married George III enjoyed a popularity far beyond his great-grandfather and grandfather as the first monarch since Queen Anne to be born and raised in England.

But with the newly crowned king's attempts to exert control over his government from 1762 through 1783, an unexpected period of instability followed. As George III appointed Lord Bute, his former tutor, as prime minister in 1762, Whig magnates received one unwelcome shock after another since many had grown used to their single-party rule under the Hanoverian-born Georges I and II, neither of whom ever attained fluency in English. If there was a dizzying, unstable succession of Prime Ministers after Bute's brief tenure, with the vast majority—apart from Lord North during much of the American revolution and William Pitt the Younger after 1784—holding office for no longer than two years,[40] the growing number of Tories and Tory-leaning men in George's cabinet was no less disturbing to the Whigs. It was against this backdrop of ministerial uncertainty and rumors of double cabinets that ushered in a wave of popular democracy and a new consciousness of rights. However irrelevant the discomfiture of these Whig grandees may appear in this context, it was nonetheless a crucial element in a brewing political drama featuring a seemingly unprepossessing incoming M.P. of Aylesbury, John Wilkes. At the behest of the Whigs, Wilkes published a newspaper, *The North Briton* (1762–3), in response to Tobias Smollett's pro-Bute newspaper, *The Briton*. Witty and highly popular, *The North Briton* excoriated Bute thoroughly: Bute was accused of winning George's favor by means of an affair with the latter's widowed mother, the Princess Dowager, and of selling Britain short after the Seven Years' War with weak terms laid out in the Peace of Paris. Claiming that "The people have their prerogative too," Wilkes gained even more popularity after being charged with seditious libel for issue number 45 where he criticized George III for praising the Peace of Paris, signed after the conclusion of the Seven Years' War. it is perhaps not surprising that he quickly succumbed to public pressure and resigned from office on April 8, 1763. Moreover, not unlike Lilburne, to whom he was compared by his detractors,[41] Wilkes became a hero of sorts during his trial as he delivered a compelling tale of subverted rights, portraying himself as an oppressed commoner struggling against powerful bigwigs. It was a tale that gained exceptional strength with the sharp rise in the number of newspapers, pamphlets, and journals, not to mention the flourishing of coffee houses, taverns and other public venues, all of which facilitated the discussion of news.[42] Liberty for ordinary people, Wilkes warned, was vanishing—unless his jury at large took action. Declaring his concern for the English liberty of "all the middling and inferior class of the people" which he deemed stood "most in need of protection," Wilkes won considerable sympathy on both sides of the Atlantic during and after his trial at the Court of Common Pleas. Nor did interest subside upon his return to England following a four-year sojourn in France.[43]

The perception of an oppressive state that ignored the needs of the majority was accompanied by an ostensibly different one: namely, the civil and political oversight of the Protestant Dissenters, a minority which comprised only 5–7% of the nation. Despite sporadic attempts at repealing the Test and Corporation Acts throughout the 1730s, it was not until the publication of the final volume of William Blackstone's *Commentaries on the Laws of England* in 1769 that more persistent attempts at repealing the offending Acts were launched. Blackstone's complacent remark that "everything should be as it is" in regard to laws on religion provoked many—including one of the founders of Unitarianism and discoverer of oxygen, Joseph Priestley. Although his widely read *Essay on the first principles of Government* grew out of a slightly earlier publication that was intended as a response to *Dr. Brown's proposal for a code of education*, much of Priestley's discussion was aimed at the lack of political and civil liberty in Britain, particularly for Dissenters. Even if disabilities were increasingly disregarded by the authorities, he noted that a prohibition against Catholics and Dissenters from public office was comparable to that of a man arbitrarily slapped with a fine.[44] It is here too that Priestley ventured beyond Locke in crafting some of the most compelling arguments against state interference in private matters. If political liberty served as "the chief guard" of "civil liberty" (31), the personal nature of religion and education should place them beyond the meddling of the civil magistrate (42, 64).

The issues of rights would receive even greater attention with the collected impact of the American revolution and the beginning of a decades-long struggle for the abolition of slavery in Britain and its empire. At the same time that colonists were protesting the imposition of the Intolerable Acts, two Africans, Jonathan Strong and James Somersett, sought to reclaim their liberty in London in 1768 and 1772: here, despite significant differences in circumstance and cause, the two separate struggles for liberty would be increasingly conflated with domestic concerns. Priestley himself was quick to draw a passing comparison between British oppression of the colonies with slavery in *The Present State of Liberty* (1769), when he exclaimed à la Samuel Johnson, how preposterous it was for colonists demanding freedom to enslave others; elsewhere, in the same pamphlet, he complained of "the folly, if not the iniquity" of the attempts to subjugate the Americans (Priestley, *PW*, 130). Some went further, including Burgh who warned readers of *The Public Advertiser*, that Parliament's attempts to enslave Americans would eventually culminate in attempts to enslave Britons themselves.[45] Although the rhetoric on the rights of slaves and Americans were still predominantly levered around "the rights of Englishmen," the nascent awareness of "others" was one which came to inform issues of human rights for those in the more distant reaches of Britain's growing empire.

Indeed, the conscious conflation of slavery, colonial oppression, and limited enfranchisement within Britain itself, with an emphasis on natural rights, was arguably the most pronounced in the writings of the polymath Granville Sharp, widely acknowledged for his role in the protection and defense of Strong and Somersett prior to his decades-long crusade to abolish slavery: Sharp was no less a champion of the American cause[46] and advocate of parliamentary reform, particularly the extension of the franchise and annual elections. Branding slavery a violation of the "British constitution and liberties," he deemed it a "gross infringement of the common and natural rights of mankind" (*Injustice*, 40), regardless of color or nationality. In terms dating back to Gratian's, Ockham's, and Locke's right to the preservation of life, Sharp regarded the welfare of the people as "the principal end of all *legal* Human Governments" because "*all Men are naturally equals*" (xiv) in *A Declaration of the People's Natural Right to a Share in the Legislature* (1774), a pamphlet that deplored the lack of parliamentary representation for America and Ireland. Declaring that all British subjects from Great Britain to the colonies were "*equally* entitled to the same *Natural* Rights that are essential for their own preservation," Sharp also believed it only proper that the people enjoy "*a share in the legislation*" which was not merely a "*British Right*" but also "a Natural Right."[47] In short, the idea of a comprehensive "human rights" was just beginning to emerge.

II HEREDITARY GOVERNMENT AND INEQUALITY

This new awareness of rights was to be increasingly entwined with a consciousness of social and economic inequality: namely, that some people were more "equal" than others and enjoyed disproportionate power—an idea that runs throughout Paine's *Rights of Man*. An early awareness is already evident in the famous speech delivered by John Balle where he not only demanded "When Adam delved and Eve span, who then was the gentleman?" but also stipulated that there be no distinctions between "villains and gentlemen." Why should some "say or shew that they be greater lords than we be?" And why should others be "bondsmen?" He argued that there was no need to retain an aristocracy "who were tyrants to their subjects, arrogant to their equals and suspected by both" since they lived "in debauchery, violat[ing] the marriage bond and destroy[ing] churches."[48] Many of these ideas would resurface in 1549 during Kett's rebellion. One account, for instance, weighed in on the indignation of the rebels at the greed and power enjoyed by the lords as well as the injustice involved, noting that "Many base and vile persons ... bitterly inveighed against the authoritie of Gentlemen, and of the Nobilitie." Ordinary people felt consumed by labor, doing nothing "but sweatem mourne, hunger, and thirst." They were angry at the enclosure of the common pastures, furious at the "great covetousness excess and pride of the Nobilitie" preventing them from having "the commodities and pleasure of this life, which Nature the parent of us all, would have common." It was time to "take Armes ... then indure so great cruelty" (cited in Wood, p. 96). Much of the antagonism towards the elites remained intact several years later when Thomas More published his *Utopia* in 1551 and Gilpin claimed in a sermon of 1552 that "mightie men, gentlemen and all riche men" intended "to robbe and spoile the poore" (cited in Wood, 35). For More, Utopia would restore justice to a world where present-day nations were "nothing else than a kind of conspiracy of the rich, who are aiming at their own interests under the name and title of the commonwealth."

With resentment roiling against the landed elites, the word "commonwealth" acquired a new importance a little more than a century later. Claiming that as much as two-thirds of England was purposely left for barren waste by the propertied elites, Winstanley declared the necessity of renouncing the Norman yoke that consolidated the power of kings and landlords, thereby destroying the precepts of natural equality as exemplified by Jesus Christ. Kingly power was no more than "the power of self-love," one established "by the Sword" ("A New Yeer's Gift," *CW* II, 109): such violated "the Word of God" by which "whole mankind was made equall" ("A Watchword to the City of London", *CW* II, 85); "every body" was to "frely enjoy their creation rights" (261). It is here that we begin to find criticisms of war as well, with Winstanley decrying the valorization of military prowess when Jesus Christ was "the great Leveller" (*New Yeer's Gift*, 144) who "shall cause men to beat their swords into plowshares ... and nations shall learn war no more" (144). Not unlike the rebels of 1381 and 1549, the Diggers resented the idea of hereditary government; and not unlike Kett's rebels, the Diggers chafed at enclosures and the disproportionate appropriation of land by propertied elites. There were to be no more "tyrant kings, lords of manors" and "exacting landlords" (*Law of Freedom, CW* II, 313) because any government that granted the earth to the gentry "and hunts out the poor commons from enjoying any part" is one of the "self-seeking Antichrist" (II, 149). No title of honour was to be had unless won "by industry" or "by age" or "office bearing." No less did he criticize the practice of primogeniture, by which the eldest son inherited the entire estate, advocating for its termination in order to grant provision for older and younger brothers alike. All had the right to live in "plenty and freedom" (*Law of Freedom, CW* II, 312).

If Marchamont Nedham's *Excellencie in a Free State* (1656) made a case for republicanism, it would also scatter the seeds of the anti-monarchical strain that eventually found its way to Paine's writing: could Paine have encountered Nedham's writings—as well as James Harrington's and Algernon Sidney's in contemporary newspapers during the 1770s when the works of the earlier republicans attained a certain vogue? In *Excellencie*, Nedham claimed that monarchies were less secure than republics: not only were they more prone to war, such as in the wars of succession which dogged the houses of York and Lancaster, but reward and preferment were more likely to derive "the Will and Pleasure of particular Persons" rather than meritocracy. By contrast, republics ensured private fortunes, putting them beyond the reach of any arbitrary power. Indeed, what is intriguing if not provocative, is Nedham's redefinition of "levelling"—reversing it, as it were. Whereas he had complacently alleged in the earlier *Case of the Commonwealth* (1650) that the Levellers were liable to redistribute all property, he now aimed the charge of levelling at the monarchy, alleging that "under monarchs," subjects had "nothing they could call their own"—not even their wives—because no one had recourse "against the levelling will of an unbounded sovereignty":[49] some of the most notorious examples included Charles I, and those who succeeded Louis XI in France. Such men were "the greatest levellers in Christendom."[50] In particular, "levelling" from the top was attributed to the avarice that was likely to accompany riches as the unsatiated demand for luxuries generally raged utmost among the wealthiest. Ordinary people were less likely to indulge in "those oppressive and injurious practices" of "kings and grandees." In other words, luxury entailed a "tendency to tyranny": a very different conclusion from the more conventional assumption that great wealth was a foregone deterrent against greed, partiality, and corruption. Nor could it be denied that most "Hereditary Princes" have either been "Tyrannous and Wicked by Nature, or made so by Education and Opportunity"; if anything, the "power of the sword" was all too often the foundation of English government and titled elites. As such, it is neither coincidental that Nedham, like Winstanley, also dwelled upon Samuel's disapproval of monarchies—nor that he would proffer one of the first arguments for meritocracy, observing that the interests of the state were "best advanced when all places of honour and trust" were reserved for "men of merit, without distinction."

This distrust of monarchy and extreme disparities in wealth is no less apparent in James Harrington's utopian *Oceana* (1656), a text initially censored by Cromwell.[51] Despite Harrington's focus on political stability and the creation of empire rather than government by popular consent, it could be argued that his conceptualization of a republican England as represented by the fictional island, Oceana, and his concern with inequality bear some affinity to Winstanley's ideas. With its Leveller-like skepticism of "the corrupting influence of power" as noted by J.C. Davis,[52] Harrington's privileging of law rather than individual sovereignty is anything but Hobbesian even if both shared a profound distrust of private interests. As Harrington noted, any government that privileged one man or a few was more likely to produce "an empire of men, and not of laws." Although this is not to say that Harrington, an acquaintance of John Wildman, adopted Leveller ideology through and through (given his personal antagonism to public discussions of legislation), his awareness of general welfare and equity was nonetheless uncommon among other writers from the gentry. More interestingly, Harrington would propose a return to the description of agrarian law under the Israelites as found in the Bible, touting it as one "first introduc'd by God himself, who divided the Land of Canaan."[53] The principle of agrarian law, commonly understood as the division of public lands (as opposed to private land and common pastures) in ancient Rome, was now to be applied to all land. Although he was less concerned with social welfare than Winstanley, stopping short of promoting any form of Digger communitarianism, it is significant that Harrington did not share Machiavelli's vision of republicanism. If agrarian law preserved "the balance of dominion" whereby aristocrats could "overpower the whole people by their possessions in lands," the strife between the Roman people and their senators could be avoided. Here, his assertions on the avarice of the wealthy and powerful corroborate Nedham's characterization of the grandees: only by capping land income at £2,000 a year could the struggle for political dominance be prevented.[54] Such would ensure that the elites would not be able to "oppress the people" or dampen their aspirations. At the same time, like Winstanley, Harrington would criticize primogeniture, stating that it was wrong to "use our Children as we do our Puppies" by feeding one and "drown[ing] five." All large properties should thus be broken up and distributed equally amongst children. It is therefore hardly surprising that Harrington supported Winstanley's and Nedham's arguments against monarchy with another reference to Samuel's antagonism to monarchy while also pointing out that it was better to be governed by many rather than be "number'd as the Herd and Inheritance of One." Moreover, the idea of a "mixed monarchy" was ridiculous and "little other than a wrestling match" between a king and aristocracy. Harrington's conviction in the powers of a republican government was such that he did not believe a monarchy could be established for more than seven years if it were to return to England.[55]

This is not to say that Harrington was not without certain prejudices in favor of a government presided by the elite. Whatever his doubts concerning the viability of hereditary government, he did not share the same level of antipathy as voiced by the Levellers and Diggers: instead, he willingly acknowledged that "The wisdom of the few may be the light of mankind" just as "a nobility of gentry, in a popular government, not overbalancing it, is the very life and soul of it." Yet, perhaps not surprisingly, even if the truth of the matter was that "exorbitant riches overthrow the balance of a Commonwealth" just as "extreme Poverty cannot ... be trusted with it," Harrington was not altogether opposed to the idea of a meritocracy either. It is certainly noteworthy that he advocated a system of public education for all boys since "the health of a government" relies on "the education of the youth." Similarly, he sanctioned a society that would allow the most impoverished man to advance and earn "preferments and honors" in the government.[56]

It was Sidney, however, who would deliver the strongest criticisms of monarchy. Not unlike Nedham, Sidney challenged the fitness of monarchs for the office in *Discourses on Government*; if

Buchanan distinguished the king from the tyrant more than a century earlier, Sidney was more apt to posit them as one and the same by assuming that the "absolute monarch" seeks to "place himself above the law" (286) and thus create disorder by turning reason and nature upside down. It is here that the idea of a meritocracy emerges. There is something wrong when those who must "perform civil functions are inferior to others"; "miseries" can only result from the inversion of "the laws of nature and reason" by "placing children" or "fools" in the government when there were others more qualified (89, 94). It was partly why Sidney, as did Walwyn before him and Paine afterwards, professed scant little respect for Magna Charta; if Walwyn considered it a "messe of Potage ... wrestled out of the Pawes of kings," Sidney complained that it "could give nothing to the people, who in themselves had all; and only reduced into a small volume the rights which the nation was resolved to maintain" (493). In short, there was little in the way of law or liberty that could be expected in monarchies since governments were not to be created for the pleasure of any one man, but for the good of a nation (119).

To a greater extent than Harrington, Sidney highlighted consent.[57] After all, the "end of all government" was the "publick Good" (357) where the free are governed by laws and magistrates of their choice (440). Applying a Harrington-like herding analogy in his statement that kings were guilty of regarding the people as "their herds and flocks," Sidney lamented the unpredictable will and understanding of a king: "He is sometimes a child, and sometimes overburden'd with years." Some were "weak, negligent," or "vicious" (440). Delving into Samuel's antipathy for monarchies, he elaborated on the more arbitrary aspects of monarchy, pointing out that kings were more likely to "err in the choice of men" (190). Absolute monarchies were mired in "corruption and decay" as the worst kings seek toadies (257) or are unduly swayed by wives or servants who join with enemies to "pervert him" (188). More significantly, unlike other writers, Sidney questioned the presumed merits of lineage, denying that rational merit proceeded from "blood or extraction ... but consisted solely in the virtues of the persons" (84). Virtues were not necessarily "transmitted to their successors" (211); indeed, it was too often the case that "children seldom prove like to their fathers" (257). Nor were elective monarchs much better; they, too, had their "defects" (257).

On the other hand, republics were better equipped, and more successful at war because commanders in hereditary monarchies were chosen from personal reasons rather than talent (213). This was chiefly by virtue of the fact that republics and popular governments were more likely to have excellent men at their disposal while their willing armies were also more naturally inclined to fight for "the publick interest as of their own" (213): an idea that may have been handed down from the Levellers who declared that they were not "a meer mercinary Army but one defending Oure own and the people's just rights, and liberties" (Houston, 172). Such explained why "a free people" had never been conquered by an "absolute monarch" whereas "many great kings have been overthrown by small republics": if virtue was absolutely necessary for the preservation of liberty, according to Machiavelli, monarchies were conspicuously deficient in this respect (134–5). At the same time, far from being peculiarly disposed to political turmoil as commonly presumed, republics were just the opposite, for malicious "seditions" are "hurtful to the people" (218). Indeed, more often than not, disturbances were fanned by disaffected nobles. Here, too, Sidney also resurrected the idea of resistance as articulated by Ponet, Buchanan, and such regicidal pamphlets of the 1650s and '60s as *Naphtali* and *Killing no murder*, demanding why should kings "not be deposed, if they become enemies to their people" particularly when "they were created by the publick consent, for the publick good" (226).

Although the popularity of republicanism had all but entirely receded by the 1760s, particularly as George III ascended the throne, a distrust of the monarch and the aristocracy soon surfaced. If John Wilkes had already stirred up discontent with his publication of *The North Briton*, he would again challenge authority during his election at Middlesex for a seat in the Commons in 1768 as Parliament attempted to deny his clear victories by replacing him with their favored candidate: Colonel Luttrell, the son of an earl. When standing for alderman at Farringdon, Wilkes avowed that he did not wish to become so by mandate, but rather by the free choice of voters because such a man "is not likely to desert his Constituents," while adding that he "abhors the idea of an aristocracy." In short, by interpreting his conflict with members of Parliament and the ministry as one between a powerful aristocracy and an ordinary English commoner, who stood to lose his English birthright of freedom and liberty, Wilkes generated a highly politicized awareness of social class and power that had not been witnessed since the Civil War. Indeed, with popular prints drawing historical parallels between George III and Charles I, and others linking Wilkes to Sidney and other 17th century Whig heroes,[58] it did not take long for Civil War issues and themes to reappear. It is even possible that this interest fueled Thomas Hollis' bold republication of Nedham, Harrington, and Sidney during the 1760s and '70s. Yet, it is striking that despite emphasis on the disproportionate power of elites in legislation and government, few 18th-century reformers advocated an end to hereditary government.

In fact, one of the few publications in 18th-century England to acknowledge the problems posed by a monarchy was actually drafted by a foreigner—namely, the 31-year-old Swiss-born radical journalist of the French revolution, Jean-Paul Marat. Here, his *Chains of Slavery* (1774)—written when he was visiting England—scrutinized not only the injustices borne by the poor, but also argued that even though "the people at large" were the "real sovereign," the king "has circumscribed the boundaries of national liberties": such signified a capital defect in the constitution. Likewise, in his criticisms on the history of monarchy in England, he had scarcely better words for the House of Lords, remarking that their "fatal privileges" were consequences following from "the plunders, usurpations, and violences of their ancestors."[59] No less was Marat one of the few who pointed out that money was preferred over virtue and service as wealth "without merit" opens the door of the senate to "fools and knaves" (205). He would also criticize irregular elections, subject to the whims of Parliament: if representatives were privileged to prolong the frequency of elections from three to seven years, they could as easily render their Parliaments perpetual, and thereby "overturn the constitution" and "reduce the nation to slavery" (note on p. 180). But overall, perhaps the worst problem was the servility of the British people, who were "inclined to" regard princely authority as "sacred," never believing themselves authorized to forcefully oppose "arbitrary mandates" (185) despite their supposed awareness of public good.

III REPRESENTATION AND ENFRANCHISEMENT

As the awareness of rights and class privilege arose, the idea of popular representation and the concept of populism also took hold, slowly inching its way up through *Rights of Man* and beyond to the 20th century. Certainly, in Walsingham's account of Jack Straw's supposed confession during the Revolt of 1381, a desire for a more democratic system of representation can be gleaned alongside of the desire for the eradication of aristocracy, and for some, an end to the monarchy: in their view, there was no reason to believe anyone to be "senior, stronger, or more knowledgeable than ourselves." These demands may help explain why Paine defended the rioters in *Rights of Man*. Similarly, as if echoing the rebels of 1381, Thomas More not only lamented a condition where a few men possessed everything while others had next to nothing but also envisioned a state that was governed through a representative democracy: the latter, he believed, would provide a voice to the poor, allowing their needs to be met.

To an even greater extent than the rebels of 1381 and 1549, Levellers and Diggers accentuated the idea of commonalty—touting "common good," "common right," and "Common-wealth" while mocking the idea of three branches of government. Some began to propose universal suffrage regardless of property since "the poorest he that is in England has a life to live, as the greatest he" (*The Putney debates*).[60] They were certainly ready to inform Parliament that the principal ends of elections and parliamentary sessions were to heed the "cries and groans of the people" and to "redress and ease their grievances." Here, too, the notion of government by consent was introduced. It was "unjust, devilish and tyrannical" for any man to govern others "without their free consent" because all men should be "absolutely free" from all "exorbitances, molestations or arbitrary power."[61] In May 1652, William Walwyn, a merchant and Lilburne's assistant,[62] deemed free trade "a common right conducive to the common good" and that legislation should be directed for a "common good."[63] Although the Diggers disapproved of trade, they nonetheless agreed with the Levellers on the concept of a representative government for the people, one where representatives would be handily selected from any number of mature and experienced men. After all, a Commonwealth government "implies a Government by our equalls" ("A Letter to Lord Fairfax," 163). Perhaps not surprisingly, criticism of outdated laws and legislation—which would resurface in *Rights of Man*—would also accompany the desire for a more consensual government. As if anticipating Paine, William Walwyn gave short shrift to Magna Charta, telling Lilburne that it "hath been more precious in your esteeme then it deserveth" because people still remain under "intolerable oppressions." People were foolish to "call bondage libertie, and the grants of conquerours their Birth-rights"; rather than create a "newer and better Charter," people prefer to "patch the old" ("England's Lamentable Service," *WWW*, 148).

Given Marchamont Nedham's friendship with John Lilburne and other Levellers, it is not fortuitous that he championed representative democracies. Although Nedham was probably less democratically inclined than the Levellers in his qualified definition of "the people" when he explained that he did "not mean the confused promiscuous body of the people" or those who had "forfeited their rights by delinquency, neutrality, or apostacy," he nonetheless agreed with the Levellers on the necessity of annual elections, while also declaring that "common sense" and "reason" were sufficient for the people's assembly in a bicameral legislature. For Nedham, it was evident that in nations where liberty was enjoyed, the "Best share" of power "hath been retained in the people's hands." Much like Harrington, who was working on *Oceana* around the same time, he asserted the importance of "Equability of condition" so that no one "shall be permitted to grow over-great in Power" nor be allowed to assume "the State and Title of Nobility." Conversely, Harrington recommended a scheme of rotation by thirds not unlike Nedham's for the purpose of circumventing warring factions amongst representatives and magistrates as well as deterring the passing of unjust laws: after all, brief terms would ensure that legislators deal personally with the consequences of any flawed laws after the completion of their terms.

It is not until Sidney's *Discourses on Government*, however, that an emphasis on individual reason and sense begins to emerge. Here, he questioned the complacent trust demanded from the powers-that-be and their advocates: "Who will wear a shoe that hurts him, because the shoe-maker tells him 'tis well made?" Those endowed with "reason" and "common sense" will "see with their own eyes" rather than trust deceivers (13). It was crucial for the legislative power as exercised by Parliament to be "radically in the People" (564) and for people to live with laws "made by his own consent" (440). Nonetheless, if Sidney, like Harrington, expressed more confidence in leadership from the ranks of the propertied elites while shirking from what he believed to be the excesses of democracy, he was also somewhat less hesitant about accepting a monarchy and democracy under ideal circumstances:

> If a few men, tho equal and alike among themselves, have the same advantages above the rest of the people, nature for the same reason seems to establish an aristocracy in that place; and the power is more safely committed to them, than left in the hands of the multitude. (453)

Overall, the histories of Athens and Rome still proved that "the best and wisest men" generally preferred aristocratic government and there was little doubt that a "pure democracy" was only appropriate for a small town if only because ordinary citizens were too likely to "err" in the choice of men "or the means of preserving that purity of manners."

But even if populist ideas on representative democracy and consensual government had been percolating for at least three centuries, the concept of populist writing had not yet materialized. With John Wilkes' *North Briton* and his subsequent speeches, a new plebeian style not witnessed since Lilburne's pamphlets. For instance, by weaving his invective on George III and his administration into humorous burlesque dialogues and strategically pointed histories of the English monarchy, Wilkes excited his readers like no other contemporary writer; here, Bute was alternately satirized as a lowly servant attempting to overthrow the mistress of the house or demonized as a monster. Just as Wilkes cannily construed parliamentary interference in his

1768 election as an elitist infringement on the political rights of the people, he introduced the relatively novel view that M.P.s should be guided by the wishes of their constituencies rather than by Parliament or members of the ministry. As such, even though Wilkes—unlike Lilburne—ultimately came to be regarded by his contemporaries as more of a political opportunist than a reformer,[64] his subsequent success at protecting the freedom of the press, opposition to the prohibition imposed on the publication of parliamentary debates, support of the American colonies, and efforts to procure suffrage for "every free agent" would enable others to envision reform on a much wider scale.

Certainly, other writers of the 1760s would reaffirm many of Wilkes' ideas. In addition to censuring the limited rights granted to Protestant Dissenters, Joseph Priestley deplored the inadequate state of political representation for vast swathes of the population, embracing the notion that government must pay "an attention to what is most conducive to the happiness of mankind" (10). The very debarment of men by "either birth or fortune"—and, of course, religion—meant that they had "no share in the government" and therefore "no political liberty at all" (13). In turn, James Murray, a lapsed Presbyterian minister and activist in Newcastle politics, became one of the first to confront disproportionate political influence from the elites and to encourage political participation on the part of non-elites. The preface to his first publication, *Sermons to Asses* (1768)—a work that went through multiple publications in Britain and the American colonies—quickly set the pace by quipping daringly in Wilkesian fashion, "We read of the asskind preaching to mankind: and why may not men preach to asses?"[65] before proceeding to complain of the burdens placed on the backs of ordinary Britons by church and state alike: namely, the burdens of taxation, tithes, corrupt electioneering, as well as disabilities faced by Protestant Dissenters. Just as Wilkes had solicited concern for the "middling and inferior class of the people, which stands most in need of protection," Murray deprecated a system of taxation by which lower and middling Britons paid the most relative to their incomes. Reminding his readers that "the poor cannot well live without necessary food than the rich: neither can they go naked" (14), he argued that necessary expenses should be reduced. There is palpable, populist anger as he points out in a fiery, italicized passage the challenges faced by ordinary workers who face high taxes on necessities but suffer low wages for their work. Adding, "*If they complain, they are not heard; if they resist, they are belaboured like ASSES,*" he mentions the possibility of rebellion, reminding readers that "pinching hunger" is the true cause (15). But all things considered, according to Murray, this lamentable state of affairs is quite predictable given the very nature of representation in Parliament: one almost entirely grounded upon property.

He explains that for too long, the power of determining elections has been lodged in the hands of a few wealthy and powerful men (27): a belief that can be said to echo the resentments of earlier rebels at their lack of political representation. Yet, it was no less unremarkable that ordinary voters were apt to blindly accept "every burden" imposed on by "any overgrown duke or knight" rather than carefully evaluate "the qualifications and merit of the candidate," to determine whether he is "a friend to his country or a tool of the state" (27). The tragedy was that unthinking voters enabled the election of a man by thoughtlessly heeding the beck and call of his wealthy friends and supporters. Murray urged voters to weigh more carefully the candidacy of M.P.s for re-election by recalling the various measures and policies supported by the candidate and to be more aware of "their natural rights and privileges" (42). More importantly, to think independently was no sign of "disloyalty to your King"; nor was it wrong to issue instructions to one's favored candidate (26). In all, a failure to exercise "resistance" argues the want of "sense of the rights of human nature" (42)—especially with the arbitrary state of domestic affairs.[66] Even if Murray did not think or dare to propose an end to hereditary government, his stinging criticism of haughty and hypocritical Anglican prelates and corrupt ministers, along with his mockery of aristocratic avarice and sexual incontinence in subsequent writings such as *New Sermons to Asses, Sermons to Ministers*, and *Sermons to Lord Spiritual* (much like the anti-aristocratic allegations made by the rebels of 1381), form a collected call for change.

These populist sentiments would be echoed in James Burgh's hefty three-volume *Political Disquisitions* (1769–1774). With a preface that quoted Locke's definition of politics as "common sense applied to national, instead of private concerns,"[67] *Disquisitions* quickly came to serve as a treasury for other reformers and radicals of the period on both sides of the Atlantic, including Paine himself, while finding occasional vindication from Nedham, Harrington, and Sidney on the viability of annual parliaments, "enormous emoluments" affixed to "offices of state," ministerial influence, press freedom, abuses of parliamentary privilege and prosecutions, and the evils of standing armies. Not unlike Rousseau who declared less than a decade earlier that sovereignty is "not a convention between a superior and inferior" but rather a compact "between the body and each of its members" steered towards "the general good" (*Social Contract*, Book II, Chap. 4),[68] Burgh decided that "all lawful authority ... originates from the people." He would also reinforce Murray's observations regarding disproportionate taxation on the poor; but unlike Murray, he ventured further by recommending suffrage to the poor, blaming their sufferings on their disfranchisement *(PD*, I, 37). However, it was not just the poor and middling orders who were denied a voice; equally, if no less justifiable, was the near-exclusion of the "mercantile and manufactural" interest from matters of legislation. For instance, had there been more M.P.s engaged in commerce, the unpopular bill for restraining paper credit in America would not have been introduced (*PD*, I, 51); nor would there be any restrictive Corn Laws contributing to the increased living expenses of manufacturers (*PD*, I, 11). Instead, far too much political weight rested in the hands of the propertied elites who occupied Parliament and other lucrative public offices by dint of birth and familial connections. Not least was aristocratic heft further exacerbated by courtly influence. Even if outright "regal encroachments" no longer posed as grave a danger as in the days of Charles I, influence wielded by "the power of the court over the parliament" (*PD*, I, 226) was potentially more insidious—making it all the more necessary to establish annual Parliaments (*PD*, I, 110) according to Burgh.

In turn, with the brewing conflict between Britain and the American colonies, the slogan of "no taxation without representation" led Britons to reflect upon their own inadequate representation, particularly amongst the middling and lower classes. Major John Cartwright, an early supporter of the American colonies and a vigorous proponent of universal male suffrage throughout his life, was amongst the first to address these issues. In *Take Your Choice* (1777), he quoted Nedham in his complaint about aristocrats who sought to exclude less well-off Britons from political power.[69] For Cartwright, it was plain that the poor actually had a more pressing right to enfranchisement than the rich[70] since "the lower orders" form "the very basis and strength of the constitutional pyramid." It was an exclusion which denied them "the common rights of humanity" while teaching "the strong to oppress the weak, the rich to despise the poor, and the poor to have no feelings of the public weal ...."[71] Moreover, while praising the idea of a "republican prince and commonwealth" (*People's Barrier*, v–vi), he noted, like Nedham and Sidney, that kings were more often than not as mentally and personally frail as their subjects, perhaps even "more liable to errors than most others" since they were surrounded by selfish courtiers (38). Indeed, many of Cartwright's ideas can be compared to those of Abbe Sièyes in the latter's revolutionary pamphlet, *What is the Third Estate?* with its emphasis on popular sovereignty and representation. In *The People's Barrier*, for instance, Cartwright claims that "the third estate of the realm" has "no part of the government" since its share "is swallowed by the aristocratical and monarchical powers"—an idea he would reiterate in *Give us our rights* (1780).

Given the collected impact of Wilkes' triumphs, the combined distrust of the governing elites, and renewed concern with natural rights, it would not be long before reformers contested the traditional assumption that non-elites, particularly those deprived of formal schooling, were incapable of understanding government or politics. Even though Priestley did not deny that propertied elites were better suited than others to occupy the highest government offices on account of their "best education," he would nonetheless qualify his remarks by adding that those "born to a moderate fortune" were "generally better educated" with "more enlarged minds"; they were more likely to be "truly *independent*, than those who are born to great opulence" (*Essay*, 15). Other writers would encourage greater confidence and participation to all other Britons. Just as Murray had urged his readers to ignore advice offered by any "duke or lord, knight or squire" who "come with their drunken rabble of attendants" (*Asses*, 23), he would exhort the high and mighty to view themselves as no more than "creatures of the public."[72] Elites were to bear in mind that their "present distinction" was merely derived from "blind fortune"; indeed, "no uncommon application, or distinguishing abilities, will justify their superiority" (*Freemen's*, 124). Having instructed his readers not to vote for anyone failing to repeal oppressive laws (23), he avowed a bold confidence in ordinary voters in his undated *Sermons to Ministers of State*. To assume that ordinary men "are not competent judges" was most certainly "the highest insult to their understanding."[73] It was time for politicians to relinquish "that foolish threadbare maxim of minor politicians"—particularly that the "vulgar are not qualified to judge of matters of state" (*Ministers*, 57). Perhaps not all commoners understood "financiering" but it was nonetheless possible that even those in the lowest class can "understand the theory of financiering as well as the First Lord of the Treasury" for his wisdom can barely be "much admired" (*Ministers*, 57).

Nor is it accidental that this championing of the common man and woman was increasingly aligned with increased references to "common sense"—a term that was already in use as discerned during the Civil War. If Sidney declared in *Discourses on Government* that "Common sense teaches ... that governments are not set up for the advantage, profit, pleasure of glory of one or a few, but for the good of the society" (91), this seemingly ubiquitous phrase would also gain much currency in Scotland, Holland, and France through the course of the 18th century, as recently detailed by Sophia Rosenfeld in *Common Sense*; it continued to flourish in England throughout much of the 1760s and '70s with uniquely populist and anti-establishment connotations, arguably much more so than in Scotland. In *Crito* (1766), for instance, James Burgh wondered "whether common sense, common honesty, and a moderate knowledge of history" were not sufficient in themselves for political administration.[74] Similarly, supporters of the American cause opined that the violation of the colonists' rights by the British government was evident to all, with Granville Sharp observing in *Declaration of the People's Natural Right*, that everyone can draw "plain conclusions of reason and common-sense:"[75] a sentiment shared by Cartwright when he advocated a confederation between the colonies and Britain with separate domestic legislatures. While lambasting Parliament for opposing "the invincible powers of ... common sense,"[76] Cartwright deprecated its members as "our political popes" who would "have us distrust our common sense" and "believe implicitly in their infallibility" (7); any man who concurred with their interpretation was in essence "unlearn[ing] his common-sense, and even his ABC" (9). Finally, the anonymous author of *An argument in defence of the colonies* (1774) would mock the idea of virtual representation, remarking that the "very sound of it does such violence to common sense."[77]

IV ECONOMIC JUSTICE

Not least important was the idea of economic justice: that everyone, as according to William of Ockham, had the right to "live well": an idea that would be strongly emphasized in the final chapter of Paine's *Rights of Man*. Given his admiration for the rebels of 1381, is it possible that Paine recalled John Balle's words that everything be held "in common?" Certainly, in *Utopia*, Thomas More longed for a world where everyone would work and the products of labor would be stocked in storehouses from which householders could fetch what was needed without payment.

But perhaps the strongest and most comprehensive proposal prior to Paine was disseminated in the writings of the Diggers, particularly Gerrard Winstanley. What stands at front and center of his texts is an exceptional awareness of poverty and a discussion of the means for its alleviation. His denunciation of "buying and selling" and criticisms of employers who compelled younger siblings or "the plain-hearted poor" to work for "meager wages" in order to make large profits ("Declaration to the Powers of England", *CW* II, 11) can easily be said to echo the angst of the 1381 rebels at their stagnant wages while anticipating Marx's criticisms of capitalism by two centuries. Diggers declared that the poor had every right to make productive use of the commons and wastelands in order to render England "the richest, the strongest, and most flourishing land in the world." Gross inequality where the few enriched themselves at the expense of the many was wrong; if a man is helped by others, "then those Riches are his Neighbors, as well as his" for everyone has labored together (*Free Commonwealth*, 289). Here, too, Winstanley emphasized the centrality of law while reiterating the importance of commonalty, with legislation to be placed in the hands of an annually elected government by which "common preservation moves the people to frame a law": a populist plan diametrically opposed to that advanced by Hobbes in *Leviathan*, published only a few years later in 1651. In short, the Diggers' world was one where reason, popular democracy, and social justice would prevail with peaceful agrarian activity replacing perpetual militarism. Only when a people abandon "single interest"—which divides people, causing "Wars and Bloud-shed"—by forming a "Common Community of livelihood" can their nation "become the strongest Land in the World" (Winstanley, *CW*, I, 15). But just as the Diggers incurred the contempt of Lilburne and other Levellers despite the considerable support and sympathy they enjoyed in their various locales, it is less astonishing that they aroused even greater consternation on the part of the landowning gentry when they called in Fairfax's armies to destroy the Diggers' settlements.

With Lilburne, Winstanley, and other Levellers and Diggers becoming Quakers, one might wonder to what extent the Quakers were influenced by the earlier groups. Is it possible that Paine "inherited" Leveller and Digger ideology by attending Quaker churches? After all, many continued to praise the Quakers for their attention to poverty and inequality as did John Scott, who noted in *Observations on the Present state of the Parochial and Vagrant Poor* (1773) that "they maintain the indigent members of their society at their own expence in a decent and reputable manner." Quakers commonly made inquiries to ensure that the poor were "well-provided for" and their children educated.[78] As Paine himself asserted years later, "[The Quakers] are remarkable for their care of the poor of their society ... I am a descendent of a family of that profession; my father was a Quaker; and I presume I may be admitted an evidence of what I assert."[79]

Although comprehensive schemes for the provision of the poor were rare in the earlier half of the 18th century, writers increasingly began to turn their attention to poverty in the 1760s and '70s.

In a lecture delivered to the Philosophical Society of Newcastle in 1775, Thomas Spence—a former pupil of James Murray—advocated a land plan by which individual ownership of land would be replaced by parish ownership: a speech that got Spence expelled from the society. Every parish would become incorporated with all men residing within the parish serving as members; in turn, each man would be entitled to an individual plot of land for lifetime use only. It was as such that "mankind" would "reap all the advantages from their natural and equal rights of property in land and liberty."[80] According to Spence, natural rights and privileges should be maintained against foreign and domestic oppressors. It was therefore only just for all men to lay claim to soil without being impeded by game laws. Here, he provided a sketch of the history of property not unlike Winstanley's, censuring the practice of private landholding and inheritance laws which excluded others from making full use of land. At the same time, like the rebels of 1549, Spence emphasized a self-sufficient local government, complete with militia. Other writers, such as William Ogilvie, would reintroduce the idea of agrarian law in *An Essay on the Right of Property in Land* (1781), for alleviating the struggles of the poor and increasing the population of Britain. There is another near-echo of Winstanley as Ogilvie asserts that everyone has by nature "a right to possess and cultivate an equal share" of the earth since it was granted to mankind "in common occupancy" as a "birthright."[81] For Ogilvie, landowning power was arguably "the bane of Europe" (195) as "established government" protected the rights of propertied elites while ignoring those of their workers (205). It was time to "encrease the number of independent cultivators" (30) in order to ensure comfort for "the lower classes of men" by putting an end to the enclosures or allowing the poor to cultivate the waste lands (an idea similar to that of the Diggers). So long as "cultivable lands remain locked up … under the present monopoly," any rise in population would inevitably diminish wages, thereby depriving the poor of their "necessary subsistence" (42).

By the early 1770s—right before Paine's departure for American shores—the state of England was posited as a precarious one. Priestley fretted that liberty was quickly fading away (*Essay*, 125) while Burgh painted an even bleaker picture: "Liberty seems indeed to be bidding mankind farewell ... Now all Europe is enslaved, excepting what shadow of liberty is left in England, Holland, Switzerland, and a few republics in Italy" (*PD*, III, 416). It was as such that Burgh called for a "Grand Association for Restoring the Constitution," a call that was echoed by Cartwright in 1776 with his first pamphlet in support of universal male suffrage and annual elections. Yet, despite the broad appeal for electoral reform in the 1760s and '70s, a growing awareness of economic and social injustice, greater confidence in the intellectual capacities of the poor and middling orders, as well as a new sense of activism, a tacit, inherent satisfaction with the British constitution and government is equally salient. After all, reformers of the 1760s–'80s were not so much the direct heirs of the Diggers, or Nedham, Harrington, and Sidney, but rather of the Levellers and ultimately, Locke; many shared the latter's overall acceptance of a monarch, House of Lords and Commons—not to mention his estimation of individual rights and liberties.

For one thing, many of Paine's and Priestley's contemporaries probably believed, as did the latter, that the highest political offices in the nation should be hereditary since elective monarchies were full of "cabal, confusion, and misery" (Priestley, *Essay*, 15); perhaps not unlike Priestley, they shuddered at the "horrid excesses" of the Levellers. Even the more outspoken Murray reminded readers that a "dependence upon the minister"—as opposed to one on the monarch—was "infinitely more *dangerous*" (*Freemen's Magazine*, 157). It is also telling that although Burgh was willing to contemplate a republic, he would advance such a notion with evident trepidation:

> Why may we not say at once, that without any urgency of distress ... and though the safety of the whole should not appear to be any immediate danger, if the people of a country think they should be, in any respect, happier under republican government, than monarchical ... and find, that they can bring about a change in government, without greater inconveniences than the future advantages are likely to balance; why may we not say, that they have a sovereign, absolute, and uncontrollable right to change or new model their government as they please? (*PD*, II, 277)

No less significant is the fact that despite his sympathy for the poor, he accepted the view that the wealthy deserved greater political weight since "property ought in all states to have its proportional weight and consequence" (I, 49). Even Cartwright who believed that kings were "the scourges, instead of the defenders and protectors, of their people" did not call for the end of hereditary government.[82] It is also worth noting that many reformist Dissenters such as Burgh and Priestley did not care for the militaristic values of conquest espoused by Harrington and Sidney; as it was, by the latter half of the 18th century, militarism had come to be more associated with hereditary governments and feudalism.

Not least to be discerned in these English reformist texts is an emphasis on the return to earlier, simpler times—namely, the days of a supposed Saxon egalitarianism. Despite a consensus on the necessity of change and reform, Burgh, Cartwright, Sharp and their immediate followers sought vindication much like the Levellers, Diggers, Harrington, and Sidney by expressing admiration for the classical past or the days of Saxon England in order to convince their audience that their ideas were not new-fangled, but rooted in tradition. Indeed, the subsequent struggle for wider suffrage from 1776 through 1830 was firmly anchored around the idea of Saxon rights: reformers such as John Jebb, Christopher Wyvill, and Sir Francis Burdett all relied on the notion of "Saxon birthrights" rather than, say, Gratian's or William of Ockham's more essentialist vision of natural rights. No less prominent was their strong sense of Christianity, regardless of their individual beliefs: much like the populist Levellers and Diggers, the Dissenting Burgh and Murray as well as the Anglican Sharp shared the belief that contemporary Britain was dogged by anti-Christian men. All had ready recourse to the Bible to vindicate the rights of slaves, colonists, and Britons which explains why so few British reformers chose to discuss or cite radical French writers such as d'Holbach and Rousseau: many of whom were regarded as atheists, even if reformers on both sides of the Atlantic shared a fundamental cynicism towards ecclesiastical hierarchies and courtly corruption. Only with the arrival of the French revolution and the publication of Paine's *Rights of Man*, Part 1 would both sides begin to see eye to eye on these topics.

V. "'TIS THE INEQUALITY OF RIGHTS THAT KEEPS UP CONTENTION": THE UNCOMMON SENSE OF THOMAS PAINE

By any stretch of the 18th-century imagination, it would have been inconceivable for a man of Paine's circumstances to embark on a career in political writing—much less to produce three bestsellers of the century. Compared to his close contemporaries, Cartwright, Murray, Priestley, and Sharp, Paine began life with far fewer resources. Unlike Cartwright and Sharp, both of whom belonged to prosperous, well-connected families, or the more middling Burgh, Murray, and Priestley, all of whom were university-trained clergymen, Paine belonged to the artisan classes. Born to a Quaker corsetmaker, Joseph Pain and his Anglican wife, Frances Cocke, on January 29, 1737 (O.S.) in Thetford, Paine—or rather, Pain, as his name was originally spelled—was pulled out of school at the age of 13 and apprenticed to his father's trade: that Paine did not relish the prospects of pursuing a lifetime of corset-making was already evident when he secretly attempted to board a privateer—only to be deterred minutes later by his father. From 1750 to 1767, Paine would fill a number of capacities: as corsetmaker in London, worker on a privateer, excise official at Alford, teacher in London, and perhaps Methodist preacher at Sandwich. It was not until 1768 that Paine's life would assume any semblance of stability with his reinstatement by the Excise, this time at Lewes. But this stability would end in 1774, two years after he took a leave of absence in London without permission in order to appeal for a raise on behalf of the excise officers. Nor were Paine's marital affairs much better: his first marriage ended in less than two years with the death of his wife and stillborn infant while his second marriage was terminated with his wife's demand for a separation upon the failure of their grocery and his dismissal from the Excise. Having sold off his effects and declared bankruptcy, Paine sailed across the Atlantic with a letter of recommendation from a recent acquaintance, Benjamin Franklin. On the face of things, much of the first 37 years of Paine's life would have appeared just short of painfully disastrous.

Even though Paine claimed that "it was the cause of America that made me an author" (*American Crisis*, April 1783), his apprenticeship can be traced back much earlier: one might make a case for 1760, when he attended the lectures of mathematician Benjamin Martin and Scottish astronomer James Ferguson in London, or perhaps 1762, when he may have preached at a Methodist chapel in Sandwich. One might also consider his teaching experience at a London school where he probably acquired skills for explication. There is little doubt, however, that his experience at Lewes from 1768 to 1774 proved the most transformative, despite his apparent failure in the short run. As John Keane has demonstrated, Paine was already attuned to current events—especially during a highly charged period of political drama.[83] In addition to serving on the town council and the vestry linked to St. Michael's church, the future radical was to engage in nightly political debates at the White Hart Inn, winning its Headstrong awards on several occasions; his abilities were such that he eventually earned a mock eulogy that predicted "Immortal Paine, thy fame can never die" before being tapped by other excise officers to appeal for a raise. Although we can only guess how Paine felt about the turbulence brewing about Wilkes and whether or not he met him in 1770—or indeed, how he parsed the issues surrounding religious toleration, the abolition of slavery, and the rising turmoil in America, there is little doubt that they must have played a part in shaping his political thought. His reputed habit of devouring newspapers and magazines would have allowed him insight into those topical concerns—and perhaps more than a passing acquaintance with the writings of Cartwright, Murray, and Sharp since newspaper editorial practices condoned lengthy excerpts from new publications. To what extent did Paine engage with these very ideas in the texts he published prior to *Rights of Man*, whether or not he was entirely cognizant of evolving trends in reform? Here, it is instructive to examine not only the parallels between Paine's early writings and those of his contemporaries, but also the ways in which he honed his radical thought and rhetoric.

Not unlike the publications of Murray and Burgh, one of Paine's earliest pieces of political writing, "The Case of the Officers of the Excise,"[84] reveals a marked sensitivity towards financial hardship on poor and middling Britons, even if written for a different audience with a different purpose: certainly, not long after the publication of Part 2 of *Rights of Man*, Paine would acknowledge that his experience as an excise officer allowed him to witness the distresses which resulted from high taxes (cited in Keane, 330). He would not only argue that the excise officer's annual income of £50 was insufficient to support a single man, especially those residing in large cities (to say nothing for those with families), but also that such a pittance was likely to encourage dishonest behavior, compelling officers to accept bribes and thereby shortchange government revenue. In anticipation of *Rights of Man*, he identified poverty as a significant cause of crime, observing that conscience was all "too often overmatched by the Sharpness of Want" because "No Argument can satisfy the feelings of Hunger:[85] an argument that may have been supported by his recollections of hangings for theft and other crimes at Gallows Hill of Thetford, a site within view of the Pain family's cottage. His observation that if the wealthy could only experience "Polar Poverty," their minds would change (9) is equally telling, with the assumption here being, of course, is that the affluent simply don't understand neediness. Although *Excise* won Paine a few admirers—among them, possibly Benjamin Franklin and Oliver Goldsmith—the measure was defeated, with his extended leave of absence from the Excise culminating in his dismissal. Even if his sacking did not necessarily turn him into an enemy of the state as construed by the radical reformer William Cobbett, it may have served to convince Paine that the English government—one largely presided by propertied elites—was deaf to the plight of ordinary people. Such an experience may even have convinced him of the truth of contemporary reformist writings if he was in any way skeptical; he may have nodded in agreement with Burgh's and Murray's remarks on selfish aristocratic interests in Parliament and beyond. As such, it would not have required exceptional effort for the former excise officer to cross the aisle, so to speak, by defending the colonists and their resistance to taxation without representation while criticizing a Parliament oblivious to the wants and needs of the people.

One can only guess that this sense of frustration with the powers-that-be would eventually lead Paine to go beyond contemporary reformers in his criticism of hereditary government and the veneration of property and status when selecting articles for *The Pennsylvania Magazine* and writing *Common Sense* and the *American Crisis* papers. If such works as *New Sermons to Asses* and *Political Disquisitions* intimated that the titled and propertied were barely capable of governing themselves, much less others, Paine went further by challenging the very premises of hereditary privilege and questioning the excessive veneration of wealth by either injecting such ideas into his own writings or by inserting essays with similar themes into *The Pennsylvania Magazine*, a monthly periodical under his editorship from January through July 1775. For instance, even though the authorship of "Reflections on Titles" has recently been questioned, it is nonetheless significant that Paine approved of an essay that linked aristocratic government with criminality while treating the title "Right Honourable" with a dose of irony.[86] It is even more striking to find him brushing aside hereditary government altogether in his "Dialogue between the ghost of General Montgomery and an American delegate" with Montgomery summarily positing "monarchy and aristocracy" as "vehicles of slavery" throughout history:[87] he feels no need to explain why because it is just "common sense." Broadly speaking, then, even if Paine did not write either essay, he seems to have equated the greed that leads people to seek spouses for mercenary or other extrinsic reasons with that exhibited by nations which practice what we regard today as colonialism.

Indeed, the conjoined ideas of empire and slavery—the oppression of "others" beyond Britain would occupy a larger part of Paine's own writings in America—along with a condemnation of military glory. If both issues rarely take up more than a few short paragraphs or lines, Paine was nonetheless one of the few writers on either side of the Atlantic to integrate these issues into his writings on American independence. Two other early articles for *The Pennsylvania Magazine*, "Alexander the Great" and "Reflections on Lord Clive," the first of which is verified as a work by Paine and the other somewhat more doubtful both question the premises and abuses of empire: a topic rarely addressed by other reformers of the period except once by Burgh in *Political Disquisitions* and a decade later by Paine's future antagonist—Edmund Burke.[88] Like the Diggers who spurned "Government by the sword" and Cartwright who opined more recently that the time for empires had long passed, Paine challenges the glorification of military conquest in "Alexander," by presenting the reincarnated conqueror as a horse and putrid pimple-eating bug that "exhibit[s] ... the downfall of tyrant greatness" prior to being devoured by a tom tit "with as little ceremony as he put whole kingdoms to the sword."[89] Elsewhere, Paine would view Britain as nothing short of a "military government"—a charge that becomes even more apparent in *Rights of Man*: in *Four Letters on Interesting Subjects* (1776), for instance, he scolds the British for establishing "military governments throughout the provinces," so that the "savage and hellish oppressions and cruelties" committed on the "wretched inhabitants of the East-Indies" will be repeated elsewhere.[90] Here, too, Paine displays a greater sense of justice towards native Americans than the vast majority of his contemporaries. Had the kings signed a treaty with the Indians for their lands, they would have a fair right to dispose of them as they pleased. However, the claims of the Crown were founded on "poor pretence" because some "adventurous navigator was invited on shore." What would happen if a few Indian chiefs had decided to dispose of England in the same manner? "We should have moved heaven and earth to have chastised their imposition: Yet the right of the one was equally as good as the other." It is obvious that Paine had little reluctance in placing whites and natives on equal footing in these circumstances, which is further reinforced when he adds that "an Indian may settle in England, or elsewhere, purchase and occupy lands, and an European may settle in America for the same purposes, without injustice in either case" for "Any individual has a natural privilege to settle in any part of the world that suits him"; yet, there is no excuse for a king "to assume a right to give away the lands in another, which they never were in possession of, either by treaty or purchase." Such would be "no better than qualified robbery, and downright arbitrary power."

Many of Paine's sentiments on the natural rights and the equality of men would be intensified over the following years in his *American Crisis* papers as he cast his eyes over the globe,

scanning a wider geographical range than any of his contemporaries. Britain, as he observes in *Crisis 2*, had "the means of
civilizing" the East and West, but did nothing more than "rip up
the bowels of whole countries for what she could get"; moreover,
"like Alexander," Britain "has made war her sport, and inflicted
misery for prodigality's sake" for spilling the blood of India and
creating wretchedness in Africa, not to mention enacting more
"national cruelties by her butcherly destruction of the Caribbs of
St. Vincent's."[91] The issue of slavery returns in *Crisis* 3, where
Paine comments caustically on Britain for "fill[ing] India with
carnage and famine, Africa with *slavery*, and tamper[ing] with
Indians and negroes to cut the throats of the freemen of America."[92] Paine also zeroes in on Clive in *Crisis* 5, as he presents his
actions in India "not so properly a conquest as an extermination
of mankind," especially given "the prodigal barbarity of tying
men to mouths of loaded cannon and blowing them away."[93] Nor
is it surprising to find Paine persisting in his claims of British
brutality and savagery in *Crisis* 7 where he expostulates that
"instead of civilizing others," Britain has "brutalized herself";
that the civilizer is in need of civilization is again implied when he
blames his native country for being no better than the Indians;[94]
how ironic then, he muses, that the goods of the latter "trans-
ported to America, should there kindle up a war to punish the
destroyer." In the same essay, deploying much more pointed language than the Diggers, Nedham, or Sidney, Paine not only
implies the lack of an English constitution but also questions the
value of the monarchy, demanding "Whether the prerogative does
not belong to the people? Whether it is not a shame for a man to
spend a million a year and do no good for it, and whether the
money might not be better applied?" (152)

It is *Common Sense*, however, that most fully exhibits the
extent of Paine's radicalism in his earlier works while helping us
understand how and why his writings gained as much popularity
as they did.[95] Given his advocacy of independence from Britain,
republicanism, as well as his crisp yet passionate rhetoric, it is
instructive to juxtapose the arguments and style of *Common
Sense* directly with other contemporary writings on the widening
rift between Britain and the American colonies: particularly John

Cartwright's *Letters on American Independence*, a compilation of public letters that was published in the pages of the *Public Advertiser* between March 20, 1774 and April 14, 1774. Although Cartwright may not necessarily have been the first to contest the idea of complete British sovereignty, the *Letters* was one of the most thorough texts on both sides of the Atlantic to promote an independent legislature for the colonies. Whether Paine actually read it at Lewes or after his arrival in America remains unknown; but a brief examination of *Letters* can help us better determine and appreciate the nature and originality of Paine's contributions to the subject of independence.

Arguing from the stance that the American colonies were largely British—an assumption shared by Americans and Britons alike—Cartwright defended American rights to pass their own laws and tax themselves. Even as he asserted the king's sovereignty in the first and final letters, stating that it is "consistent with the spirit of the English laws," Cartwright trusted that as a "free people," Americans had "every right to choose their own governors." Cartwright also denied the necessity of having to prove "the liberty of mankind" by means of "mouldy parchments" or even "the most ancient inheritance." Anticipating the Declaration of Independence with its claim that men "are endowed by their Creator with certain unalienable Rights," Cartwright valued liberty as "the universal gift of God," as well as "inherent and unalienable," which he would reiterate in Letters 4 and 5, mentioning the "inherent and unalienable rights" (25) repeatedly and their "rights of independency." More interestingly, he would also underscore the necessity for breaking up empires which were "too large," separated by "immense oceans" or did not operate by "principles essentially belonging to all free governments" (41); furthermore, whenever the people find themselves subject to such a tyrannical power, it was "an indispensible duty" to "shake off such an unjust yoke, and to erect a free government" (15)—ideas which also resurfaced in The Declaration of Independence:

> That whenever any Form of Government becomes destructive of these ends, it is the Right of the People to alter or to abolish it, and to institute new Government, by laying its foundation on such principles

> and organizing its powers in such form, as to them shall seem most likely to effect their Safety and Happiness ... But when a long train of abuses and usurpations ... it is their right, it is their duty, to throw off such Government, and to provide new Guards for their future security.

He would proceed to excoriate "those degenerate Englishmen, who are now seeking to enslave the Americans," imagining that they would hardly tolerate the Emperor of Germany to reclaim England (15). Equally problematic was the issue of legislative practicality: it was no more possible for representatives from America to "visit their respective counties" during the parliamentary recesses than it was to receive a reply from England in two days or to meet with their constituents at "short notice" (19).

Cartwright was equally quick to cast doubt on a few assumptions shared by Britons and Americans alike. First and foremost, he debunked the notion that military assistance provided to the Americans was initiated out of "pure *affection* and *generosity*". Was it not for "her *own* safety, her *own* interest, her *own* honour?" It was clear to him that had any other nation occupied the place of the American colonies, she would have been "as lavish of her blood and treasure in their support" (21). At the same time, he denied the usefulness of the parent–child metaphor for the relationship between Britain and America, claiming that the latter was mature enough to govern herself. Not least, as we have already observed in the preceding sections, did Cartwright repeatedly refer to "common sense," pointing out that it required no more than "common sense and common honesty" to know that no one had a right to take anything from another "without his consent" (3–4). Those who attempted to justify Parliament would "have us distrust our common sense" (7) and "unlearn his common sense, even his ABC" (9). Indeed, the universality of "the inherent rights of mankind," meant that pleading the permanent sovereignty of Parliament was "mockery to our common-sense." At the same time, having no "freedom to resist taxation from another legislature" indicated a lack of "common sense." With two editions published in London during 1774 and 1775 in addition to an American edition in 1776, it is a testament to Cartwright's powers of persuasion that he was requested to join the American navy which he refused out of loyalty to Britain.[96]

But if Cartwright ventured farther than most Britons or the colonists themselves with his proposal for American legislative independence, Paine would take many of these ideas further to their logical fruition in *Common Sense* while rendering them in what might be referred today as a "user-friendly" style. The difference in this first American best-seller is already apparent from the very opening where Paine surveys the beginnings of society in a manner that is nearly reminiscent of Locke in Chapters 2 and 8 of the *Second Treatise*. [97] However, even as Paine promulgated the broadly accepted liberal belief that government was intended to provide security with "the least expence and greatest benefit," it is telling that he departs from Locke not only by grounding his sketch of early society on America itself but also by imagining its national history of elective governments. According to Paine, the growth in population will demand a representative government by which "The legislative part" will be managed by those who share "the same concerns at stake which those have who appointed them." Not unlike Harrington, he highlights the need for frequent elections, pointing out that since the elected will soon return to the ranks of the electorate, they will prudently refrain from "making a rod for themselves."[98]

It is here, however, that Paine takes a more radical turn, weighing in on the disadvantages of a monarchy. Unlike the vast majority of other defenders of the American colonies—both British and American—he refrained from rehearsing the familiar argument that Americans were more or less British and deserved to be treated as such. Instead, he pointed out the problems he associated with the "sickly constitution" of Britain. Why were Americans and Britons so blinded by the so-called superiority of British government? Such beliefs, in Paine's view, derived from "national pride and prejudice" (9). If anything, he contended, the constructs of British government were unnecessarily complicated. Not unlike Harrington, Paine suggested that "it is the republican and not the monarchical part of the constitution of England which Englishmen glory in" (16) so that there was little need for either a monarchy or aristocratic branch of government. Moreover, not unlike William Walwyn, Paine scorned the three branches of government checking each other as "farcical" (17)—an explanation not unlike Harrington's, who compared it to a "wrestling match" between a king and his aristocracy: the power enjoyed by the king was something which people are "always obliged to check" (8). And not unlike those engaged in the uprising of 1381 and Kett's rebellion, Paine would tout the God-given equality of man, noting that since all men were "originally equal," no one had the "right to set up his own family in perpetual preference to all others for ever"(13); similarly, just as Winstanley referred mockingly to "the Norman bastard William," Paine would refer to the latter as a "French bastard." (No doubt Paine was aware that many colonists already harbored a number of British prejudices.) And not unlike Sidney, he drew attention to the uncertain talents or suitability of the king's lineal successors, while relating the accounts of Gideon and Samuel. At the same time, Paine had recourse to Burgh's criticisms of aristocratic weight in Parliament, applying them to the monarchy as he warned that "Men who look upon themselves born to reign, and others to obey, soon grow insolent" (15) in addition to the fact that their world "differs so materially from the world at large." Not least did Paine highlight the instability caused by wars over succession, as well as the sheer expense involved in maintaining such useless personages—particularly where kings do nothing but "declare war and give away places" (19).

But if section 2 on the monarchy unexpectedly resurrects republicanism, sections 3 and 4 are even bolder as Paine delivers his *coup de grace*. His proposal for American independence opens unassumingly enough as he promises to "offer nothing more than simple facts, plain arguments, and common sense" (17), laying out the facts in simple, yet compelling language. If one examined the relationship between Britain and the American colonies with "common sense," one might realize that there were only ill-conceived excuses. Like Cartwright, Paine criticizes the parent–child analogy, observing that America had already outgrown childhood; more bitingly, however, Paine denies that Britain has ever behaved like a parent. If Britain were indeed a parent, "then the more shame on her conduct" for "even brutes do not devour their young" (19). Equally provocatively, Paine dismisses the idea that America was predominantly British. After all, since no more than a third of inhabitants "are of English descent," the term "of parent or mother country applied to Britain only" was "false" and "selfish." Instead, "Europe, and not England, is the parent country of America" (19).

No consideration of *Common Sense*, however, is complete without some examination of Paine's rhetoric. Again, the forcefulness of Paine's rhetoric contrasts all the more with Cartwright's. While Cartwright shrewdly contests the usefulness of the parent–child metaphor for Britain and maturing America, Paine does so more concretely, stating "We may as well assert, that because a child has thrived upon milk, that it is never to have meat" (18). It is also worth contrasting Cartwright's words on Britain's military assistance to Paine's:

> When the colonies were in a danger of falling a prey to France, was it pure *affection* and *generosity* towards *them*, or *jealousy of that ambitious power*, which caused Great Britain to take up arms? Did not her own existence depend on the preservation of her American colonies? ... it will be admitted that her *own* safety, her *own* interest, her *own* honour, were the only motives that could have engaged her to proceed such lengths at that juncture ... she saw the protection of her colonies, literally in the light of *self*-defence, and the more heartily undertook it accordingly.

Paine argues similarly, but more succinctly:

> But she has protected us, say some. That she hath engrossed us is true, and defended the continent at our expence as well as her own is admitted, and she would have defended Turkey from the same motive, viz., the sake of trade and dominion. (18)

The same may be said for Paine's defense of religious toleration where he seemingly condenses so many pages of Dissenting arguments on toleration to a pithy paragraph. Here, it is no longer an issue of doctrinal difference, but more importantly, of broader humanity. It is as such that he offers the following aphoristic statements: "Suspicion is the companion of mean souls, and the bane of all good society" and that "there should be diversity of religious opinions among us." Also remarkable is the canniness of his observations. The distance between England and

America was "strong and natural proof" that one should not govern the other (21) since there was "something very absurd" in a continent "perpetually governed by an island" and it was patently absurd for a "satellite" to be "larger than its primary planet" (24). The references to God and planetary science not only help Paine appeal to his various audiences, including regular readers of the Bible and science enthusiasts alike, but reinforce the prevailing impression of a common sense that is shared by all.

Paine's recourse to the passions is also more strategic in comparison with other political writers. It is not difficult to view Paine as a populist heir to Wilkes with his dramatic and energetic prose—particularly in his demonization of the villains: the British and George III. Rather than recite the acts passed by Parliament that outraged many—the Stamp Act, the Townshend Acts, and the Intolerable Acts—Paine zeroes in on the physical violence unleashed by the British with a series of questions. There is no room for forgiveness:

> But if you say, you can still pass the violations over, then I ask, hath your house been burnt? Hath your property been destroyed before your face? Are your wife and children destitute of a bed to lie on, or bread to live on? Have you lost a parent or a child by their hands, and yourself the ruined and wretched survivor? If you have not, then are you not a judge of those who have. (22–3)

Anyone who can pardon the British is "unworthy the name of husband, father, friend, or lover" and a "coward." Moreover, Paine not only likens Britain to a "ravisher," but also vindicates feelings of rage because "The Almighty hath implanted in us these unextinguishable feelings for good and wise purposes"; such outrage "distinguishes us from the herd of common animals" (30). To take necessary action against the British is only proper because "The robber and the murderer would often escape unpunished" (30). As Vikki Vickers has pointed out, "Destroying the colonists' emotional ties to Britain was a key component" of Paine's argument for independence (Vickers, 46). In the midst of this discussion of justice, Paine also raises the subject of Indians and slaves, pointing out the necessity of expelling "that barbarous and hellish power" responsible for stirring up the "Indians and the Negroes to destroy us"; the cruelty was double since it is "dealing brutally by us, and treacherously by them" (30). Note that unlike Jefferson in the Declaration of Independence, Paine implies that the "Indians" and "Negroes" are victims of Britain too. Paine's effectiveness becomes even more salient when the dramatic conclusion of the third section, with its call for immediate action, is juxtaposed against a similar passage in Burgh's *Disquisitions*:

Liberty seems indeed to be bidding mankind farewell... All Europe was once free. Now all Europe is enslaved, excepting what shadow of liberty is left in England, Holland, Switzerland, and a few republics in Italy .... (*PD*, III, 415)

O! ye that love mankind! Ye that dare oppose not only the tyranny but the tyrant, stand forth! Every spot of the old world is overrun with oppression. Freedom hath been hunted round the Globe. Asia and Africa have long expelled her. Europe regards her like a stranger, and England hath given her warning to depart. O! receive the fugitive, and prepare in time an asylum for mankind. (*CS*, 30)

Paine's plea is not only impassioned in his personification of freedom as a fugitive, but like Wilkes' pleas to his jury and readers, serves as an empowering call to all readers for action. Hence, in the appendix, he proclaims that should independence transpire, Americans have the chance to "form the noblest, purest constitution on the face of the earth" and to "have the power to begin the world over again" (45). Taken as a whole, these statements replicate Paine's overall participatory strategy, one that pushes his readers to "infer the conclusions to be drawn from his arguments" as rightly noted by Edward Larkin.[99]

No less striking is Paine's mastery of colloquial speech and rhythms. Unlike the lengthy sentences preferred by his contemporaries, whether Cartwright, Jefferson, or Burgh, Paine's are relatively comprehensible as if to be read aloud to a diverse audience. It is clear that Paine shared Murray's and Cartwright's ostensible trust in the judgment possessed by "the vulgar"; Paine's own life was, in fact, a testament to this notion, regardless of his detractors—among them, Gouverneur Morris, who dismissed him as a "mere adventurer from England, without fortune, without family, or connexions, ignorant even of grammar." Consider, for instance, the simple clarity of the following passage, one of Paine's most famous:

> The Sun never shined on a cause of greater worth. 'Tis not the affair of a City, a County, a Province, or a Kingdom; but of a Continent—of at least one eighth part of the habitable Globe. 'Tis not the concern of a day, a year, or an age; posterity are virtually involved in the contest, and will be more or less affected even to the end of time, by the proceedings now. Now is the seed-time of Continental union, faith and honour. (17)

Together, both of the two near-parallel sentences beginning with "'Tis" lend a sense of expansiveness that creates an impression of a grand new nation in the making rather than a mere assortment of random colonies as "city" stretches out to "continent" and "day" to "age." Indeed, that Paine may have been attempting to make his text easily accessible to both readers and listeners comes across in paragraphs replete with italics and capitals:

> And in order to show that reconciliation now is a dangerous doctrine, I affirm, *that it would be policy in the King at this time to repeal the acts, for the sake of reinstating himself in the government of the provinces;* In order that HE MAY ACCOMPLISH BY CRAFT AND SUBTLETY, IN THE LONG RUN, WHAT HE CANNOT DO BY FORCE AND VIOLENCE IN THE SHORT ONE. (26)

Certainly, too, there is an unmistakable air of finality when he proclaims in capitals, "'TIS TIME TO PART" (21). It is a definitive conclusion that cannot be confused with either Cartwright's desire for a confederacy or Jefferson's reluctant threat as expressed in *A Summary View of the Rights of British America*: "It is neither our wish, nor our interest, to separate from her [Britain]. We are willing, on our part, to sacrifice every thing which reason can ask to the restoration of that tranquillity for which all must wish."

Not least, Paine's accessibility is also enhanced by his use of humor. To an even greater extent than Murray, Paine feels little compulsion to mince words. If Murray, like Burgh, was apt to compare the ministry to highwaymen, Paine readily applies the metaphor to the monarchy: no doubt, the intervening distance between America and Britain removed whatever reluctance he may have harbored. Kings, as Paine points out, are anything but elevated beings, especially when their origins are carefully scrutinized: the first ones were generally "nothing better than the principal ruffian of some restless gang" (13). The brief sentence which follows lends greater emphasis to his point: "It certainly hath no divinity in it." Here, too, Paine saves himself a belabored explanation of the irrationality behind hereditary succession by reiterating his earlier comparison to the monarchy as an "ass for a lion," quipping that those weak enough to believe it can "promiscuously worship the ass and the lion, and welcome" (14).

Thus far, Paine's life and writings can be viewed as a microcosm of the radical and revolutionary currents which swept over Britain in the 17th and 18th centuries. If the likes of Burgh, Cartwright, and Murray berated a government that was bloated at the top, with an aristocracy occupying the most lucrative public offices and both houses of Parliament, it is striking, yet not surprising that Paine would return to the intensified radicalism of the Civil War. Indeed, his own position on suffrage and democracy in *A Serious Address to the People of Pennsylvania on the Present state of Affairs* (1778) shares at least a few affinities with those of the Levellers. Like the Levellers, Paine defended the freedom of religion as a "right" rather than a "favor," explaining that "'Tis the inequality of rights that keeps up contention." He clearly desired a democracy comprised of "numerous electors … of men of all conditions, from rich to poor," noting that "Property alone cannot defend a country against invading enemies" and defence "must be personal"; there must be "an equal share of freedom … which wealth, [n]or the want of it, can neither give or take away." Nonetheless, he would exclude not only those in state offices and employments "to which there are profits annexed," but also servants; like the Levellers, he believed that the latter's votes would be unduly determined by their masters. More strikingly, a personal anecdote from a Boston novelist, Royall Tyler, reported Paine to have asserted that "the minority, in all deliberative bodies, ought, in all cases, to govern the majority" since "the majority of mankind are consequently most prone to error."[100] Here, we might be tempted to wonder, how, then, did *Rights of Man* become so notoriously radical? How did Paine acquire new conceptualizations of democracies and constitutional republics? How do we assess his vision of political, social, economic rights?

NOTES

1 Harvey Kaye, *Thomas Paine and the Promise of America* (New York: Hill and Wang, 2005) p. 259.

2 Robert Lamb, *Thomas Paine and the Idea of Human Rights* (Cambridge: Cambridge University Press, 2015) p. 4.

3 Although J.C.D. Clark does not state this concept in so crude a manner, he writes: "[Paine] was so influential in his day precisely because he was not original, but because he brilliantly mobilized anglophone political languages already widely familiar." See *Thomas Paine: Britain, America, and France in the Age of Enlightenment and Revolution* (Oxford: Clarendon Press, 2018) p. 1.

4 Cited in Gregory Claeys, *The Social and Political Thought of Thomas Paine* (London: Routledge, 1989) p. 85.

5 Thomas Paine, *The Life and Major Writings of Thomas Paine*, Vols. 1–2, ed. Philip Foner (New York: The Citadel Press, 1948) 1, p. 805.

6 From a petition by Robert Kett and his followers at Mousehold Heath, outside Norwich, in 1549.

7 Brian Tierney, *The Idea of Natural Rights* (Grand Rapids, MI: William B. Eerdman's Publishing Co., 2001) pp. 60–9. All subsequent references to Tierney are drawn from this edition.

8 Clair Valente, *The Theory and Practice of Revolt in Medieval England* (London: Routledge, 2003, 2016) p. 14. She notes that medieval political texts such as Aquila's 13th-century *Summa Theologica* and *De Regimine principium* as well as Bartolus of Sassferrato's *Tractatus de Tyrannia* determined that a tyrannical king was no king and could be justifiably overthrown.

9 http://www.constitution.org/cmt/ponet/polpower.htm

10 Alan Houston, *Algernon Sidney and the Republican Heritage in England and America* (Princeton, NJ: Princeton University Press, 1991, 2014) p. 128.

11 http://www.constitution.org/cmt/buchanan/powers_crown.htm

12 "The Causes of the Revolt according to Froissart in *Peasants' Revolt*" in R.B. Dobson, *The Peasants' Revolt of 1381* (London: Palgrave Macmillan, 1970) p. 371.

13 The lords raised rents and dues while attempting to increase profits on their own lands and make use of commons. For further details on their attempts to reintroduce serfdom and to exert greater control over their communities, see

Chapter 1 of Wood's *1549 Rebellion and the Making of Early Modern England* (Cambridge: Cambridge University Press, 2007).

14 Christopher Hill, *The World Turned Upside Down: Radical Ideas during the English Revolution* (London: Penguin, 1972) p. 14.

15 See Derek Heater, *Citizenship in Britain: A History* (Edinburgh: Edinburgh University Press, 2006) p. 24; he notes on p. 30 that although there were no newspapers in 1640, there were 722 only five years later. Others have made wider claims; Paul A. Rahe claims that the surviving English pamphlet literature from 1628 to 1660 is "greater than that of the American and French revolutions put together." See *Against Throne and Altar: Machiavelli and Political Theory under the English Republic* (Cambridge: Cambridge University Press, 2008) p. 181. See also Jonathan Scott, *England's Troubles: Seventeenth-century English Political Instability in European Context* (Cambridge: Cambridge University Press, 2006) p. 231.

16 Cited in Jonathan Scott, *England's Troubles*, p. 235.

17 Some have attributed the "Leveller" moniker to Commissary General Henry Ireton, Cromwell's son-in-law. See the introduction by Andrew Sharp to his edition of *The English Levellers* (Cambridge: Cambridge University Press, 1988), p. xxi.

18 John Lilburne, "Postscript to *The Freeman's Freedom Vindicated*" in Sharp, pp. 31–2, p. 31.

19 Richard Overton, *An Arrow against all Tyrants* in Sharp, pp. 54–72, p. 55.

20 Cited in Scott, p. 255.

21 "A Watchword to the City of London" in *Winstanley: The Law of Freedom and other writings*, ed. Christopher Hill (Cambridge: Cambridge University Press, 2006) p. 128.

22 Cited in Scott, p. 122.

23 Christopher Hill, "Introduction," *Winstanley*, p. 30.

24 Gerrard Winstanley, *Complete Works of Gerrard Winstanley*, Vols. 1–2, ed. Thomas N. Corns, Ann Hughes, and David Loewenstein (Oxford: Oxford University Press, 2009) 2, p. 116.

25 Christopher Hill, *Puritanism and Revolution: Studies in Interpretation of English Revolution of the 17th century* (London: Pimlico, Random House, 1958, 2001) p. 62.

26 It is worth noting that Winstanley sought to distance the Diggers from the Ranters when he complained that some "through the same unreasonable beastly ignorance, think there must be a Community of all men and women for Copulation" (Winstanley, *Complete Works*, Vol. 2, 302).

27 Adrian Davies, *The Quakers in English Society* (Oxford: Oxford University Press, 2000) pp. 68–9. Quakers became less vocal after the Restoration.

28 In Essex, a significant number of Quakers made some bequest to the poor in their wills in addition to various donations and contributions made to the parish poor rates.

29 It is worth noting that Quakers believed in an inner light, privileging the workings of the Spirit, while also giving less weight to Biblical authority (Davies, *The Quakers in English Society*, 15, 17). In *The Age of Reason*, Paine would write: "My own mind is my own Church." Paine's views on religion can

be said to be as uncompromising as those of the Quakers (see Davies, 173). Not least, Davies mentions that many Quakers opted for private burials (81). Paine himself was buried in his own garden since the Quaker cemetery turned down his request.

30 Catharine Macaulay, *History of England*, Vols. 1–8 (London, 1763–83) 5, p. 383.

31 See Rachel Hammersley, *French Revolutionaries and English Republicans: The Cordeliers Club, 1790–1794* (Woodbridge: Boydell Press, 2005).

32 Nedham may have contributed to Wildman's *Lawes Subversion*. See Blair Worden, *Literature and Politics in Cromwellian England: John Milton, Andrew Marvell, and Marchamont Nedham* (Oxford: Oxford University Press, 2007) p. 147n.24.

33 Nedham penned a preface to Lilburne's *An Answer to Nine Arguments* (1645). Lilburne appeared to have returned the compliment when he praised the "notable preambles published in Nedham's *Mercurius*." See Rahe, *Against Throne and Altar*, 213n.75, 234. For a text of *Free State*, see: http://www.con stitution.org/cmt/nedham/free-state.htm

34 See Alan Craig Houston, *Algernon Sidney and the Republican Heritage in England and America* (Princeton, NJ: Princeton University Press, 2014) p. 29. Houston adds that in later years, "Sidney waxed nostalgically on the wealth, power, and independence of the Commonwealth."

35 Algernon Sidney, *Discourses on Government*, ed. Thomas G. West (Indianapolis: Liberty Fund, 1990, 1996) p. 358. All subsequent quotations from Sidney are drawn from this edition.

36 The Whigs opposed James II while the Tories supported him as the successor to Charles II.

37 *Two Treatises on Government* in *Political Writings*, ed. Peter Laslett (Cambridge: Cambridge University Press, 1970, 1988) p. 129.

38 Jeremy Waldron, *Nonsense upon Stilts: Bentham, Burke, and Marx on the Rights of Man* (London: Routledge Revivals, 1987, 2015) p. 7.

39 Locke, *Letter concerning Toleration*. See: http://oll.libertyfund.org/titles/locke-a -letter-concerning-toleration-and-other-writings

40 These include Grenville, Rockingham, Chatham, Grafton, Shelburne, and Portland.

41 See Edward Vallance, "Reborn John? The eighteenth-century afterlife of John Lilburne," *History Journal Workshop*, 2012, http://hwj.oxfordjournals.org/content/ early/2012/08/17/hwj.dbs012.full#content-block. Derek Heater's description of Lilburne could easily apply to Wilkes: "he presented his arguments not as a personal case but as a case that affected all the people of the country" (33).

42 John Brewer, *Party Ideology and Popular Politics at the Accession of George III* (Cambridge: Cambridge University Press, 1981) pp. 139, 142, 158, 160.

43 Wilkes fled to France after being charged with obscene libel in 1764. He returned to England when his French creditors began to pursue him.

44 In Joseph Priestley, *Political Writings*, ed. Peter Miller (Cambridge: Cambridge University Press, 1993) p. 69.

45 See Carla Hay, "The Making of a Radical: The Case of James Burgh," *Journal of British Studies* 18:2 (Spring, 1979) pp. 90–117, p. 108.

46 Despite Sharp's sympathy for the colonists, he deplored their reliance upon slavery. He corresponded with the Quaker abolitionist, Anthony Benezet, as well as Benjamin Rush—a friend of Paine in the 1770s.

47 Granville Sharp, *A Declaration of the People's Natural Right to a Share in the Legislature* (London, 1774) p. 2.

48 *The Peasants' Revolt of 1381*, ed. R.B. Dobson (London: Macmillan, 1970) p. 368.

49 Marchamont Nedham, *Case of the Commonwealth*. See: http://www.constitution.org/cmt/nedham/com_eng.htm

50 Marchamont Nedham, *Excellencie of a Free State*. See: http://oll.libertyfund.org/titles/nedham-excellencie-of-a-free-state

51 Harrington's friendship with one of Cromwell's daughters, Lady Claypole, saved him on this occasion as she interceded on his behalf.

52 J.C. Davis, *Utopia and the Ideal Society: A Study of English Utopian Writing 1516–1700* (Cambridge: Cambridge University Press, 1981) p. 231.

53 See: http://www.constitution.org/jh/oceana.htm

54 William Sprigge would recommend agrarian law in his *Modest Plea for an equal commonwealth* (1659) but for reasons closer to Winstanley's than Harrington's.

55 See note 28 in Rachel Hammersley, "Rethinking the Political Thought of James Harrington: Royalism, Republicanism and Democracy," *History of European Ideas* 39:3 (2013) pp. 354–70.

56 James Harrington, *The Art of Lawgiving*. See: https://oll.libertyfund.org/titles/harrington-the-oceana-and-other-works

57 See Houston, p. 140n.173.

58 Kathleen Wilson, *The Sense of the People: Politics, Culture, and Imperialism in England, 1715–1785* (Cambridge: Cambridge University Press, 1995, 1998) p. 214.

59 Jean-Paul Marat, *The Chains of Slavery* (London, 1774), pp. 197–9. See also Rachel Hammersley's "Jean-Paul Marat's *The Chains of Slavery* in Britain and France, 1774–1833," *The Historical Journal* 48:3 (2005) pp. 641–660.

60 *The Petition of Divers Well-affected Women* (1649) is most likely the first pamphlet to propose female suffrage. "Extract from the debates at Putney" in Sharp, (Cambridge: Cambridge University Press, 1998) pp. 102–130, p. 103.

61 Lilburne, "Postscript," p. 31; "A Remonstrance of many thousand citizens" in Sharp, pp. 33–53, 35.

62 Walwyn was instrumental in mobilizing Lilburne's supporters; he also held meetings, appointed committees, drafted and printed petitions. In short, his role was not unlike that of a modern campaign manager. See Heater, p. 34.

63 William Walwyn, "The Bloody Project" in *The Writings of William Walwyn*, ed. Jack R. McMichael and Barbara Taft (Athens, GA: University of Georgia Press, 1989) pp. 296–307, p. 305. All quotations from Walwyn are drawn from this edition unless otherwise noted. Interestingly, one of Walwyn's publishers included a Thomas Paine. Whether this Paine was related to our subject is unknown.

64 As Lord Mayor of London, Wilkes' harsh quelling of those who participated in the Gordon riots angered many.

65 James Murray, *Sermons to Asses to Doctors in Divinity to Lords Spiritual and Ministers of State* (London: William Hone, 1819). All subsequent quotations to *Asses* are drawn from this edition.

66 [James Murray], *The Freemen's Magazine, or The Constitutional Repository* (Newcastle-upon-Tyne, 1774) p. 31. All subsequent quotations from *Freemen's* will be drawn from this edition.

67 James Burgh, Preface to *Political Disquisitions* (London, 1774), p. x. All subsequent quotations from *Disquisitions* will be drawn from this edition.

68 Jean-Jacques Rousseau, *The Social Contract*, Book II, Chap. 4. See: https://www.marxists.org/reference/subject/economics/rousseau/social-contract/

69 The Society for Constitutional Information, a political club organized by Cartwright and John Jebb frequently reprinted extracts from Nedham's *Excellencie of a Free-state*. See Blair Worden's introduction to *Excellencie* in the Online Library of Liberty.

70 John Cartwright, *Letter to the Deputies* (London, 1781) p. 33n.2.

71 John Cartwright, *The People's Barrier* (London, 1782) p. iii.

72 James Murray, *Freemen's Magazine*, p. 124

73 James Murray, *Sermons to Ministers of State* (London: William Hone, 1819) p. 33.

74 James Burgh, *Crito*, Vols. I–II (London: 1766–7) I, p. 1.

75 Granville Sharp, *A Declaration of the People's Rights* (London, 1774) pp. 1–2.

76 John Cartwright, *Letters on American Independence* (London, 1774) p. x.

77 Anon. *An Argument in Defence of the Colonies* (London, 1774) p. 83.

78 John Scott, *Observations on the Present State of the Parochial and Vagrant Poor* (London, 1773) p. 53.

79 Thomas Paine, "Worship and Church Bells: A Letter to Camille Jordan," 1797, *Complete Writings of Thomas Paine*, ed. Philip Foner (New York: Citadel Press, 1945) 2, p. 759.

80 All quotations from Spence are drawn from https://www.marxists.org/archive/hyndman/1882/03/spence.htm

81 Note the use of "common" here. William Ogilvie, *An Essay on the Right of Property in Land* (London, 1781) pp. 11–12.

82 John Cartwright, *The People's Barrier against Undue Influence and Corruption* (London, 1780) p. 48.

83 See chapter 2 in Keane, *Tom Paine: A Political Life* (New York: Little, Brown, and Co., 1995).

84 According to Gary Berton in a private conversation, there is some belief that Paine may have contributed to the *Sussex Advertiser* upon his arrival in Lewes.

85 "The Case of the Officers of Excise" in *Complete Writings of Thomas Paine*, ed. Philip Foner, Vol. 2, p. 8.

86 See the list of questionable works at: http://thomaspaine.org/pages/writings.html#questionable-authorship. It is worth noting, however, that much work is still being done on them according to a recent private email from Gary Berton dated July 17, 2018.

87 Thomas Paine, "Dialogue Between the Ghost of General Montgomery and an American Delegate" in *Complete Writings of Thomas Paine*, ed. Philip Foner, 2, pp. 88–93, p. 92.

88 See Burgh, *Political Disquisitions*, III, p. 159 where he notes that English newspapers in April 1771 were filled with accounts of the most infernal cruelties committed by them [the English] in East India.

89 Thomas Paine, "Alexander the Great," in *Complete Writings of Thomas Paine*, ed. Philip Foner, 2, p. 1115.

90 See: http://thomaspaine.org/recently-discovered/four-letters-on-interesting-subjects.html

91 Thomas Paine, "The American Crisis," #2 in *Complete Writings*, 1, pp. 58–72, p. 66.

92 Thomas Paine, "The American Crisis," #3 in *Complete Writings*, 1, pp. 73–102, p. 93.

93 Thomas Paine, "The American Crisis," #5 in *Complete Writings*, 1, pp. 106–29, p. 119

94 Thomas Paine, "The American Crisis," #7 in *Complete Writings*, 1, pp. 140–57, p. 142.

95 *Common Sense* also exhibits a completely different style from his *Case of the Excise Officers*. See pp. 53–7 in Vikki J. Vickers, *My Pen and My Soul Have Always Gone Together: Thomas Paine and the American Revolution* (London: Routledge, 2008).

96 Equally noteworthy was Cartwright's earlier refusal of Lord Howe's offer of a lieutenancy in the British navy. See John W. Osborne, *John Cartwright* (Cambridge: Cambridge University Press, 1972) pp. 11–12.

97 Nearly half a million copies of *Common Sense* were sold during the course of the revolution.

98 Thomas Paine, *Common Sense* in *Complete Writings of Thomas Paine*, ed. Philip Foner, 1, p. 6.

99 Edward Larkin, *Thomas Paine and the Language of Revolution* (Cambridge: Cambridge University Press, 2005) p. 36.

100 Cited in Keane, p. 302.

1

THOMAS PAINE'S *RIGHTS OF MAN* PART 1, SECTIONS I–VIII

These two famous performances revived, as it were, the royal and republican parties that had divided this nation in the last century, and that had lain dormant since the Revolution in 1688. They now returned to the charge with a rage and an animosity equal to that which characterized our ancestors during the civil wars in the reign of Charles I.

—Annual Register for 1794

As the newly independent American republic began drafting a constitution while Britain debated the expansion of suffrage and the repeal of the Test and Corporation Acts, France found herself steeped in debt to the tune of 4.5 billion livres. There were new fears of yet another imminent bankruptcy, not long after the one of 1770 even though the American revolution resulted in a victory for the French rather than a loss as in the disastrous Seven Years' War. The fact that national accounting suffered from an absence of clear and regular periodic checks, a large number of motley accounts, and no consistent system of accountancy complicated things further.[1] Desperate to avoid another cataclysm, Louis XVI appointed and fired his finance ministers in rapid succession: the dismissal of the Swiss-born Jacques Necker in 1771 was followed by those of Charles Alexandre de Calonne in 1783 and Lomenie de Brienne in 1787, before Necker himself was ushered back into office in 1788.

At the advent of the revolution, the Third Estate (commoners) comprised nearly 98% of the population of 28 million people while the First and Second Estates (ecclesiastics and nobles, respectively) comprised another 0.5% and 1.5% respectively (approximately 470,000 people). The Third Estate included a vast range of the population from financiers and affluent attorneys at the top to the peasantry (nearly 23 million) at the base, all of whom who were variously subject to a number of taxes and payments including the *taille* to the state, Church tithes, and dues to their locally presiding lord. On the other hand, regardless of their income, clergy and nobles paid far fewer taxes proportionately speaking—whether they were high ranking ecclesiastics (predominantly from titled families), socially prominent nobles who congregated around the king, or considerably less well-off provincial nobles and parish clergy. The little they paid—namely in the form of the *vingtième* (direct tax on property) and the *capitation* (poll tax)—was poorly allocated and haphazardly collected.[2] As it grew increasingly evident that taxes could not be raised any more on the Third Estate, Calonne proposed a tax in August 1786 on land that would be more proportionately levied, with those who earned more paying higher taxes. Since the *parlements*—appellate courts which served to register new edicts and taxes—were largely comprised of nobles who had either purchased or inherited their offices, it was hardly surprising that they balked at this plan. Six months later, Calonne was no more successful when he attempted to circumvent the *parlements* by handpicking an assembly of 144 notables to approve a similar plan. The royal court's sense of urgency was heightened when Calonne's successor, Brienne, again unsuccessfully attempted to force the *parlements* to register new loans in order to avert a national default on payments. By July 16, 1787, the Parisian *parlement* had already proposed a meeting of the Estates-General which had not convened since 1614, claiming that it was the only body which could raise taxes legitimately. Further conflicts between Louis XVI and the *parlements* ensued as the former held at least two *lit de justices* to force a tax and loan in August and November.[3] In 1788, after Louis attempted to reduce the judicial powers of the *parlements* by creating 47 "Grand bailiwicks," the *parlements* would demand once more the return of the Estates General to which Brienne acceded shortly before his resignation on August 24, 1788. With a meeting of the Estates General scheduled for May 1, 1789, preparations began to take place, as discussions were held at the Parisian residences of Marquis de Lafayette and Thomas Jefferson, who had just been appointed the first U.S. minister to France in 1784.

As if a looming financial crisis were not enough, the period between the conclusion of the American revolution and the dawn of the French revolution was rife with rural and urban public disorders. The poor harvest of 1788, resulting from a drought and hail, caused prices to rise—thereby triggering food riots. At the same time, the free trade treaty of 1786 with England came to cripple the French textile industry, which was not as advanced in mechanization, while the poor silk harvest of 1787 halved employment in the silk industry. The panic caused by the combination of food shortage, high prices, increased rents and unemployment soon led to a major riot in Paris after the wallpaper manufacturer, Réveillon, was alleged to have insulted workers in addition to calling for a reduction of wages in order to lower prices and stimulate the economy: a plan that was echoed by an owner of saltpetre works, Henriot. The rampant sense of discontent can be easily gleaned from the *cahiers doléances*: notebooks submitted by members of the First, Second, and Third Estates in response to the king's demand for commentary on the state of the nation.[4] In short, as Alexis de Tocqueville explained in *The Ancien Régime and the French Revolution* some 67 years later, people demanded "the wholesale and systematic abolition" of all laws and current practices: a potential issue "of the most extensive and dangerous revolutions ever observed in the world."[5]

In the meantime, not unlike his landing on American shores thirteen years earlier, Thomas Paine did not immediately indicate any willingness to engage in politics upon his arrival in France in May 1787. Having partly relinquished this interest since the mid-1780s, he had become absorbed in erecting a single-span iron bridge that he had worked on for a few years. As his attempts to seek financial backing in America and France stalled, Paine quickly turned to England, filing patents for his bridge design. It was during this search for sponsorship that he met and quickly befriended Edmund Burke. Having informed Burke that he'd rather "erect the largest arch in the world than be the greatest Emperor within it," Burke himself would mention in a letter of September 3, 1788, to Sir Gilbert Elliot that "He is not without some attention to Politics" but is "much more deeply concern'd about various mechanical projects."[6] Nonetheless, Paine kept an eye on current events, publishing a pamphlet, *Prospects on the Rubicon* (1787) that was critical of William Pitt's attempts to drum up a war with Holland. In fact, it was only a matter of time before the conflicts between Louis XVI and his *parlements* escalated, thereby fully capturing Paine's attention. In a letter to Thomas Jefferson of December 16, 1788, Paine marveled at the "good things from France"; some ten months later, he would express satisfaction in the progress of the French revolution to Benjamin Rush, observing that in spite of minor inconveniences, natural consequences of "pulling down and building up," there was relatively little trouble.[7] His excitement was no less palpable in another letter to Burke where he exulted in the prospects of the revolution spreading to other nations (qtd. in Keane, 287). But little did either man anticipate that their writings on revolutionary France would not only resurrect the seemingly long forgotten conflicts between commoners, lords, and monarchy from the Civil War as suggested by the epigraph from *The Annual Register*, [8] but also establish the fault lines for modern conservative and liberal thought.

I. PROLOGUE: RICHARD PRICE'S *DISCOURSE ON THE LOVE OF OUR COUNTRY* AND EDMUND BURKE'S *REFLECTIONS ON THE REVOLUTION IN FRANCE*

In many respects, the debate over the French revolution was anything but unpredictable given the number of shared concerns on both sides of the Channel regarding the limited state of political representation and overweighted aristocratic influence in politics. Not fortuitously, British reformers were initially elated by the election of a more egalitarian National Assembly, the storming of the Bastille, the abolition of feudal privileges and the disestablishment of the church; it was an enthusiasm shared by journalists as well as by dramatists and producers who staged the triumphant destruction of the Bastille numerous times. Amongst the many admirers was Richard Price, a founding member of the Society for Constitutional Information whose friends and acquaintances included such men as James Burgh, Major John Cartwright, John Adams, Benjamin Franklin, and Thomas Jefferson. Although Price did not intend his *Discourse on the Love of Our Country* (1789) to be anything more than a brief celebratory sermon on the centenary of the Glorious Revolution, his text would nonetheless define some of the central issues of the French revolution debate: political inequities, religious toleration, and above all, the rights of men.

According to Price, Britain remained insufficiently enlightened—particularly in the wake of the French revolution. By overturning conventional ideas of patriotism, he lamented that people were "too apt" to view their nation as the sole repository of "wisdom and virtue" simply because people were prone to overvalue "everything related to us."[9] Continuing the contemporary critique of military conquest, he identified, a "thirst for grandeur and glory" and the desire to attack other countries "in order to extend dominion, or to gratify avarice": if offensive wars were undeniably "wicked and detestable," he also deplored the ways in which men act perversely against their own "common rights and liberties." Exhorting Britons to love their nation "ardently," but not "exclusively," he urged them to regard themselves more broadly as "citizens of the world" and to pay "a just regard to the rights of other countries." Britons were also urged to "defend their rights" and prevent situations where the "few" could oppress "the many"; it was certainly ironic that Britons were all too apt to exhibit "adulation and servility" to authority figures as were the more purportedly passive subjects of Turkey, Russia, Spain, and Germany. Here, too, it was far more often the case that men tended to be "too passive than too unruly" while "the rebellion of Kings against their people" proved far more common than the opposite. For Price, the addresses proffered to George III during his illness betrayed this dangerously demeaning tendency: many were apt to forget that a king was "no more than the first servant of the public" for his authority was actually "the majesty of the people."

Not least, Price would reflect upon the contemporary relevance of the Glorious Revolution. Amongst the most important lessons to be drawn from the revolution were:

First, the right to liberty of conscience in religious matters.

Secondly, the right to resist power when abused. And

Thirdly, the right to chuse our own governors, to cashier them for misconduct, and to frame a government for ourselves.

Placing particular emphasis on the third, he observed that the aims of the revolution were imperfectly realized so long as the Test laws remained intact and the state of political representation woefully inadequate. Finally, Price concluded his sermon with a stern warning to tyrants, proclaiming that "the ardor for liberty" was "catching and spreading," whereby kingly and ecclesiastical authority were respectively yielding to the "the dominion of laws" and "the dominion of reason and conscience." No longer could the "oppressors of the world … hold the world in darkness," struggling against "increasing light and liberality." In short, Britain remained unenlightened and Gothic when compared to France and America.

Although numerous reformers and Dissenters shared Price's elation, there were some who did not. Among them was Edmund Burke: a man long involved in liberal causes, who had previously sided with the American colonies and supported the Dissenters prior to launching an investigation and prosecution of Warren Hastings for abuse and misconduct as Governor-General of Bengal. To the astonishment of many—including Paine himself—Burke decried the revolution. But whatever we make of Paine's assumption that Burke was presumed to be "a friend to mankind" from his part in the American Revolution, Burke had long harbored an intrinsic distrust of popular movements, one that only strengthened over the years, particularly after his defeat at Bristol in the election of 1780; if anything, his self-acknowledged abhorrence for what he deemed the "metaphysical" issue of rights had already been apparent in his defense of the American colonists (*Speech on American Taxation*, April 19, 1774). When understood in this context, his animosity towards the French revolution was anything but unpredictable; it would only be a matter of time before he publicly averred his sentiments in a parliamentary speech of January 1790. Although it is difficult to determine whether his writing of *Reflections on the Revolution* in France was directly prompted by popular enthusiasm, Price's *Discourse*, or even Paine's ecstatic letters, an inquiry from a young French nobleman, Charles-Jean- François Depont served as a convenient spur. Having mulled over a response to Price—a man he had long disliked—since the publication of the latter's sermon in November 1789, Burke decided to censure him in a public letter to Depont: namely, what was soon to be his *Reflections.* That it was Britain rather than France itself which occupied Burke's thought was openly admitted in his statement that it was "better to be despised for too anxious apprehensions, than ruined by too confident a security." Claiming in a letter of February 20, 1790 that his intention was not to engage in controversy with "Dr. Price, Lord Shelburne, or any other of that set," he nonetheless planned to expose their "wicked principles" while reinstating "the true principles of the constitution."[10] *Reflections* would therefore serve not only as a commentary on English politics, society, and government but also as a refutation of the liberal Whiggism embraced by reformers and Dissenters.

With little ado, Burke opens his response with cool derision aimed at Price and other members of the Revolution Society. Questioning Price's assessment of the Glorious Revolution, Burke dismisses his construction as an "unheard-of bill of rights": a concept that the English would "utterly disclaim," if not wholeheartedly resist "with their lives and fortunes."[11] Parliament's choice of inviting William to reign in place of James II, moreover, did not imply change so much as a retention of custom and tradition: their chief concern was to do "as their *ancestors in like cases*,"—namely, "vindicate their *ancient* rights and liberties" (83). Far from seeking change or any newfangled solutions, Burke argued, proper reformations proceeded from a "reverence to antiquity" (81); after all, Britons now and then had been satisfied with political principles inherited "from our forefathers," rejecting the very idea of forming a new government with "disgust and horror" (81). By stipulating that "the idea of inheritance furnishes a sure principle of conservation" yet not without "excluding a principle of improvement" (83), Burke would also excoriate the French for relinquishing their ancient constitution with an "upstart insolence" (85). In other words, Price had badly misinterpreted the Glorious Revolution and the Bill of Rights (1689) as a sanctioning of natural rights rather than of long held British laws and tradition.

Not surprisingly, Burke found little need for the enlightenment so touted by Price and his fellow reformers. Scorning the concept of enlightenment, while protesting that the last century appeared to him to be "as much as enlightened" (116), Burke took pride in the "sullen resistance to innovation" and "cold sluggishness" that had long distinguished Britons. He was thankful that, unlike the French, few were "converts of Rousseau" or "disciples of Voltaire" (137); after all, wise men found it more expedient to reject "naked reason" for prejudice (138). Burke voiced disgust at the events of October 5–6, 1789, during which a group of women marched to Versailles to complain about the price of bread and angry rioters burst into Marie Antoinette's bedroom. Burke's assumption that "ten thousand swords must have leaped from their scabbards to avenge even a look that threatened her with insult" (126) would yield his much ridiculed regret that "the age of chivalry" had been replaced with that of "sophisters, economists, and calculators"; "never more," he opined, would there be a "generous loyalty to rank and sex" (127).[12] Chivalry was to be valued not only because it distinguished European civilization from others but also because it enhanced social and cultural morale. If few could dispute that "To make us love our country, our country ought to be lovely" (129), it was beneficial to retain "a system of manners" (129) and heed the prejudices of the wider public for the sake of national security and stability. For Burke, then, the sheer pragmatics of government were at least as important as any purported idealism.

No less did Burke deplore the French for rebelling against a "mild and lawful monarch" (89). Warning his readers that "Kings would be tyrants from policy, when subjects are rebels from principle" (129), he censured the overall eradication of various customary monarchical rights, including the power to declare war and peace. To make things worse, the shift in power from top to bottom also propelled the election of unqualified men to the National Constituent Assembly, many of whom were barely more than "country attornies" and "country clowns" (94)—a judgment that in turn elicited howls of indignation from his critics. Indeed, as if making a dig at Paine's former occupation in the Excise, Burke would mention in passing that the legislators of ancient republics were well aware that their business could not be left up to those with "the metaphysics of an undergraduate, and the mathematics and arithmetic of an exciseman" (231). Men with a "sordid, mercenary occupation" were likely to have a "low education," not to mention a "mean and contracted view of things" (101). Having scarcely ventured "beyond the bounds of an obscure village" (97), they were liable to be ignorant and naïve (98). Finally, not the least of their problems was an accompanying envy of the wealthy. This attempt to "level," according to Burke, was a misguided one, for "levellers ... only change and pervert the natural order of things" (100); such a pedestrian mix in the National Constituent Assembly formed a sordid contrast to the British Parliament, comprised chiefly of elite and propertied men.

Although Burke was far from wishing to "confine power, authority, and distinction to blood, and names, and titles" (101), he nonetheless stipulated "some preference" to birth (103). As far as the French nobility was concerned, Burke found little cause for complaint. There was scant reason to believe that the nobility was unusually oppressive (186) particularly since they—along with the church—paid their share of taxes: an erroneous assumption on his part since peasants paid a far greater burden of taxes in addition to a share of tithes and seigneurial dues to the clergy and nobility. Instead, noblemen and women served as a "Corinthian capital of polished society" (187–8). Moreover, unlike France, which had just dissolved its church, Britain wisely retained hers. If "church and state" were inseparable (149), Britons were comfortable with 14th-century ecclesiastical practices; such establishments were crucial to national stability since "The consecration of the state by a state religious establishment" operated with "wholesome awe upon free citizens" (143). Because religion was not to be exclusively relegated to the poor, but to be "blended" with all classes, Britons did not resent those bishops earning a highly substantial sum of "ten thousand pounds a year" (153).

But if Burke shocked many with his defense of the Church and aristocracy and hostility towards reform, it was arguably his summary dismissal of rights that infuriated them. Having already brushed aside "natural rights" in his defense of the American colonists, he would reiterate the same contempt as he scorned the "rights of men" and "rights of man" no less than 34 times. Quick to claim that all men have equal rights, he also qualified his statement by adding "not to equal things"; for instance, even though "a man with five shillings in a partnership has as much right to it as a man with five hundred pounds to his own respective portion," the former had no right to an "equal dividend in the product of the joint stock"; in other words, he should not have the same rights in the "management of the state"(110).[13] Wealth and property therefore merited full consideration in the allocation of political power. Indeed, however inadequate the state of political representation appeared, Britons were in fact better off than the French, who were beginning to undergo an ostensibly impractical and arbitrary redistricting by the National Constituent Assembly; at least, Britons could claim the "king and lords" as "several and joint securities for the equality of each district, each province, each city" (235). No less did Burke deny "man's abstract right to food and medicine" (111), refuting the notion that the overall purpose of government extended beyond the provisions for human wants in the form of "sufficient restraint" upon "the passions." It was time to discount the weight accorded to "the rights of men" by metaphysical theorists (112).[14] In short, Burke all but rejected the notions of individual, social, and economic rights which had been gradually strengthening through the centuries. Since the true rights of men in government ultimately stood somewhere in the middle, "in compromises sometimes between good and evil, and sometimes between evil and evil" (112), there was no need for "the paltry blurred shreds of paper about the rights of man" when "we fear God, we look up with awe to kings ... with reverence to priests; and with respect to nobility" (137). Nor was there any need to investigate, much less, subvert the present form of government (146). Altogether, to foment a revolution was to "subvert the ancient state of country; and no common reasons are called for to justify so violent a proceeding" (214).

Even though *Reflections* was neither the first to comment on the revolution or Price's *Discourse*, its criticism of both quickly unleashed an avalanche of antagonistic replies, with several appearing only weeks after its publication in November 1790: namely, Mary Wollstonecraft's *Vindication of the Rights of Men*, John Butler's *Brief Reflections upon the Liberty of the Subject*, and Major Scott's *Letter to the Right Hon. Edmund Burke*. By the time that Paine completed Part 1 of *Rights of Man* in February 1791, additional replies had surfaced, including Catharine Macaulay's *Observations on the Reflections of the Right Hon. Edmund Burke on the Revolution in France* (1790) and Joseph Priestley's *Letters to the Right Honourable Edmund Burke* (1791); there were still others that followed the publication of Part 1, including James MacIntosh's *Vindiciae Gallicae* (1791) and those which compared and contrasted Burke and Paine. With varying emphases, nearly all took Burke to task for his attack on the National Assembly, disputing his interpretation of the Glorious Revolution even if they disagreed over the extent to which reform was required in Britain: some would argue that Britain stood in no danger of contamination, while others would assert that reform was long overdue. But few, if any, came to overturn Burke's ideas so thoroughly or attract as much notice as Paine's *Rights of Man.*

II "THE MANUSCRIPT ASSUMED AUTHORITY OF THE DEAD"

Not unlike other respondents to Burke, Paine begins by voicing astonishment and indignation at Burke's criticism of the National Assembly before moving swiftly to address his erstwhile friend's attack on Price; no doubt Paine probably gleaned that Burke's true intention was to derail reform in Britain, just as the latter had indeed promised in a letter to Philip Francis. If Burke disclaimed Price's lessons from the revolution—namely, the right to "choose our own governors, to cashier them for misconduct, and to frame a government for themselves," Paine would open his text by disarming Burke's somewhat disingenuous statements before proceeding to ridicule his claims.

But in order to understand—if not appreciate—Paine's interpretation of the Glorious Revolution and his overall refutation of Burke's emphasis on tradition, let us step back and examine the English Bill of Rights (1689) briefly. To what extent was Burke accurate in claiming that there was little in the document to indicate "a general right 'to choose our own governors, to cashier them for misconduct, and to form a government for ourselves?'" (67) Although Burke was not entirely wrong when questioning the notion of choosing "our own governors" or affirming the idea of conservation given the reference to "auntient rights and liberties" in the Declaration of Rights, a closer look reveals that the document not only highlights the protection of rights but also implicitly criticizes the abuse of monarchical power:

> That it is the right of the Subjects to petition the King and all Commitments and prosecutions for such petitioning are illegall ... And they doe claim demand and insist upon all and singular the premisses as their undoubted Rights and Liberties And that noe Declarations Judgments Doings or Proceedings to the prejudice of the People in any of the said premisses ought in any wise to be drawn hereafter into Consequence or Example To which Demand of their Rights they are particularly encouraged by the Declaration of his Highnesse the Prince of Orange as being the only meanes for obteyning a full Redress and Remedy therein Having therefore an entire Confidence that his said highnesse the Prince of Orange will perfect the Deliverance soe farr advanced by him and will still preserve them from the violation of their Rights which they have here asserted and from all other Attempts upon their Religion Rights and Liberties.[15]

Even though the text does not issue an explicit call for a new government, it nevertheless establishes and inscribes certain duties, conditions, and rights for monarch, Parliament, and subjects alike. If anything, what is remarkable here is not the weight conferred on tradition as maintained by Burke but rather the frequent repetitions of the word "rights" in the brief text of the Declaration: no fewer than five times.

Nonetheless, it is noteworthy that Paine bypasses Burke's misreading, refusing to sift through and dissect the Declaration word for word. Perhaps seeking to avoid what he despised as Burke's obsession with "mouldy documents," Paine points to the obvious facts, not the least of which is the sheer energy involved in a revolution. Scoffing at Burke's belief "That men should take up arms, and spend their lives and fortunes ... to maintain they have not rights,"[16] Paine proceeds to tackle his claims for the binding authority of the Parliament of 1688. Where Burke attempts to controvert Price by accusing the latter of presenting William as an elective monarch, Paine challenges the conjoined notions of tradition. Just how feasible is it for "The Lords Spiritual and Temporal, and Commons" to decree that the English should "most humbly and faithfully submit themselves, their heirs and posterities, for EVER?" Although the lines from the Declaration were more likely intended as a rhetorical flourish than a statement of material significance, Paine would appear to devote a seemingly unwarranted number of paragraphs for the perusal of this idea.

The idea of altering or amending laws had begun to enjoy increasing currency throughout the 1780s as Whiggish reformers sought to repeal anachronistic legislation even as they equally acknowledged the possibilities that their own laws might become subject to future repeal. In 1781, Cartwright had implied as much when proposing broader suffrage, warning against laws that would "deprive posterity of the rights essential to freedom" (*Letter to the Deputies*, 36). Five years later, Paine himself adopted a comparable argument in *Dissertations on Government* (1786) when discrediting the assumption that the national bank (as was planned in America) would necessarily exist forever:

> As we are not to live for ever ourselves, and other generations are to follow us, we have neither the power nor the right to govern them, or to say how they shall govern themselves. It is the summit of human vanity, and shows a covetousness of power beyond the grave, to be dictating to the world to come. It is sufficient that we do that ... which is right in our own day, and leave them with the advantage of good examples.

It would be preferable, Paine proposed, if constitutions incorporated a proviso stipulating the termination of all laws and acts in thirty years in order to "prevent their becoming too numerous and voluminous." In turn, Jefferson adopted nearly identical rhetoric, in a letter to James Madison of September 6, 1789, when arguing against the idea of heirs and debtors being forced to pay the debts of the deceased:

> The question Whether one generation of men has a right to bind another, seems never to have been started either on this or our side of the water. Yet it is a question of such consequences ... set out on this ground which I suppose to be self evident, "that the earth belongs in usufruct to the living;" that the dead have neither powers nor rights over it. The portion occupied by an individual ceases to be his when himself ceases to be, and reverts to the society.[17]

Brooke Boothby, Capel Lofft, and Catharine Macaulay would rely upon similar logic in their replies to Burke, with Lofft detecting "little difference" between an "unalterable monarchy" and an equally unalterable parliamentary government[18] and Macaulay declaring the notion of "bind[ing] their posterity to all successive generations" by an "unalterable law" to be very "incompatible with the conditions of humanity."[19] Like Macaulay, Boothby agreed that such overwhelming power "presents a complication of injustice and absurdity."[20] These sentiments were no less common in France as Condorcet refuted the notion that political liberty had anything to do with precedent and much more with popular will.[21]

In comparison with these explanations—including his own earlier version from 1786—Paine's commentary in *Rights of Man* is less verbose, yet more extenuated as if he were attempting to communicate with those unaccustomed to reading political texts. Take, for instance, the passage below which echoes the passage from *Dissertations on Government* as he underscores the necessity of progress and enlightenment:

> There never did, there never will, and there never can, exist a Parliament, or any description of men, or any generation of men, in any country, possessed of the right or the power of binding and controlling posterity to the "end of time" ... Every age and generation must be as free to act for itself ... The vanity and presumption of governing beyond the grave is the most ridiculous and insolent of all tyrannies.

> Man has no property in man; neither has any generation a property in the generations which are to follow ... It is the living, and not the dead, that are to be accommodated. When man ceases to be, his power and his wants cease with him ... he has no longer any authority in directing who shall be its governors, or how its government shall be organised .... (74)

Whereas Lofft and Macaulay take it for granted that their audience can readily grasp how changing circumstances necessitate changes in law and legislation, Paine does otherwise. Drawing from a number of accessible tropes, he cleverly manages to project Burke as a man out of step with other Britons, if not downright un-British. Here, Paine conflates this arbitrary, temporal binding with such topical issues as slavery ("Man has no property in man") and far-reaching patriarchal power ("In England, no parent and master ... can bind or control the personal freedom even of an individual beyond the age of twenty-one years"). Similarly, he has recourse to the long familiar government-as-highwayman metaphor by demanding "who authorised, or who could authorise, the Parliament of 1688 to control and take away the freedom of posterity" to run their own government; after all, "In England it is said that money cannot be taken out of the pockets of the people without their consent" (75). As he professes a near-skepticism redolent of a Diderot or d'Holbach in his mockery of the "divine right to govern" which is "imposed on the credulity of mankind," Paine does not hesitate to draw upon popular anti-Catholic prejudices and the many jocular allegations of Burke as a closet Catholic when joking that the latter "has shortened his journey to Rome, by appealing to the power of this infallible parliament of former days" (75). All of these comparisons—particularly as Paine emphasizes what is done "in England" several times—are designed to highlight not only the unnatural premises of Burke's assumptions, but also to undermine the latter's appeals to Englishness and Protestantism. The implied question that resounds throughout *Rights of Man*, Part 1 is how can a man as fundamentally un-English and un-Protestant as Burke determine policy for Britain at large?

But Paine does not stop there. Having likened Burke's pre-occupation with precedents and antecedents to slavery and exorbitant paternal authority, he equates the eternal powers assumed by the Parliament of 1688 with the religious tyranny practiced by James II—one positively perceived, the other much less so; for Paine, James' assumption of power barely differs from that of the parliament that "expelled him" (75). Rather, if James II was an "usurper over the living," Parliament was "an usurper over future generations." In other words, the two forms of tyranny are affinitive, with neither being more inherently justifiable than the other in the larger scheme of things. Here, Paine has recourse to nature, reminding his reader that the "right of any human power to bind posterity for ever" is an impossibility since "it is the nature of man to die" (76). As such, no law should outlive its usefulness. Similarly, the retention of a law should not be assumed to indicate its continuing viability even if many are willing to uncritically accept Rousseau's belief in *The Social Contract*, that "the precedent of antiquity makes them daily more venerable" (Book 3, Chap. 11)—regardless of the fact that laws in existence are not always scrutinized for relevance. Here, one might think back to the Witchcraft Act of 1735—passed only two years prior to Paine's birth—which marked a dramatic reversal in attitude when many began to regard witchcraft as fraud rather than an actual crime as accepted in the 16th and 17th centuries. Indeed, Paine may also have been cognizant of the ongoing repeal of centuries-old anti-Catholic laws in Burke's native Ireland. The reality was that despite the reverence for centuries-old laws, many stood in need of re-evaluation for retention, revision, or nullification. Not least does Paine deprecate the idea of an immortal-seeming Parliament, clinging onto power well past its prime. Again, he implies that such an idea is anything but English, verging on an "oriental style of antiquity" with its declaration, "O Parliament, live forever" (77); for the 18th-century reader, this allusion to the East would have immediately triggered the stereotype of oriental despotism. In short, not unlike William Walwyn or Gerrard Winstanley, Paine tries to persuade his audience that there is little use in clinging to the way of one's ancestors: such a notion, while seemingly overplayed here, may have served as yet another nail in the coffin of Burke's argument for tradition and the sanctity of the "establishments."

More remarkable still is the rhetoric deployed by Paine as he builds his case against anachronistic laws and customs. If he had already introduced the idea of the living dead in his *Dissertations on Government* by alluding to "a covetousness of power beyond the grave", he zeroes in on this idea in *Rights of Man* by comparing the prospect of future generations governed by the decisions of a Parliament of 1688 to a world controlled by the living dead: an idea that may have contributed to the flourishing of the Gothic novel and drama in the 1790s, with their legions of ghosts, animated corpses, and vampires, whether real or pretended. Indeed, the trope of the "living dead" is repeated multiple times as Paine observes that "The vanity and presumption of governing beyond the grave is the most ridiculous and insolent of all tyrannies," prior to asserting that "It is the living, and not the dead, that are to be accommodated" (74). That Paine has not yet tired of his metaphor is evident in the following paragraph where he "contend[s] for the rights of the living, and against their being willed away … by the manuscript assumed authority of the dead" (74). Here, Burke is all but consciously posited as a preternatural villain, "contending for the authority of the dead over the rights and freedoms of the living" as Paine circles back to the metaphor near the close of the section, maintaining that the opinions of men shift with "continually changing" circumstances so that laws which are proper in one age, "may be thought wrong and inconvenient in another" (77). Quite simply, since "government is for the living and not for the dead, it is the living only that has any right in it" (77). Although Paine's emphasis on the necessity of change expressed in these fourteen paragraphs might arguably be said to overstate the obvious, his discussion serves to lay an unequivocal foundation for the prevailing idea that laws, legislation, and customs should not persist beyond utility. By underscoring the naturalness of changing circumstances, governments and laws while reifying the familiar assumptions of Englishness, rights, and liberty, Paine prepares to defend the French revolution while defying Burke's veneration for the past.

III THE FALL OF THE BASTILLE AND EVENTS OF OCTOBER 5–6, 1789

No less radical is Paine's presentation of the Fall of the Bastille. Directing his attention to the revolution itself, he begins by introducing the Marquis de Lafayette, a recent hero of the American revolution, establishing him as a foil to Burke. Presented in a manner that harks back to the centuries-old conflation of republican virtue and manliness, as seen from Machiavelli through Sidney, the unquestionably masculine Lafayette is praised for having relinquished effeminate luxury during his "flowery years of youth" for the more masculine "woods and wildernesses of America" (78). Paine further reinforces the links between liberty and manliness in his approbation of the "clear, concise, and soul-animating" sentiments of the Declaration: a work posited as one so gloriously at odds with Burke's *Reflections*, replete with undue deference to "musty records and mouldy parchments" (78). Not unlike Mary Wollstonecraft or Brooke Boothby, both of whom had already taken Burke to task for his "flowers of rhetoric" and a "wild and flowery field," Paine draws attention to the latter's "ineffectual" declamation and arguments, "gay with flowers." Here, too, when addressing Burke's claim that the French rebelled against a mild-mannered king, Paine pursues a familiar line of argument followed by earlier critics of *Reflections*: namely, that the revolution was only displaying an ineluctable reaction to a long corrupted French monarchy rather than personal animosity for Louis XVI. Boothby, for instance, had already defended the revolution by deploring the loss of liberty under the "omnipotence of the Crown" for a century and a half (16–7) while Benjamin Bousfield placed the blame more squarely on Louis XVI, observing that "he is suffering for his follies, and the vices of his administration."[22]

Interestingly, however, Paine manages to deliver a more incisive argument while carefully absolving Louis XVI of any incapacity or errors of judgment.[23] Unlike the Civil War, the Glorious Revolution, or other uprisings in Europe, the French revolution did not arise from the "person or principles" of Louis himself, but rather from a larger animus against the "established despotism" of an absolutist monarchy. It is here that Paine resurrects some of his anti-monarchical arguments from *Common Sense*, raising the possibility that a successor to Louis XVI may easily abuse his powers like his great-great-grandfather, Louis XIV. Since the personal dispositions of kings can vary widely, the "despotic principles" inherent in monarchies have the potential of surfacing with little warning (79). At this point, however, we can't help but reflect that if the French revolution represented a much needed means for vanquishing the source of evil rather than the mere symptom—such as in the case of the overvalued Glorious Revolution—why not do away with monarchy altogether? What could explain Paine's guarded criticism of monarchical despotism both here and in much of Part 1 of *Rights of Man*, particularly when compared to such earlier writings as *Common Sense* (1776), *Crisis* papers (1776–82), and *Four Letters on Interesting Subjects* (1776)? Especially when it was growing increasingly evident after August 1789 that Louis XVI was losing the enthusiasm and will to adopt the desired reforms initiated by the National Constituent Assembly? Modern historians still wonder why Louis did "not receive the same harsh treatment as George III."[24] Perhaps Louis' assistance to the American colonies and his initial sympathy to the revolution factored in as Paine mentioned in a letter to George Washington that the king appeared to "pride himself on being at the head of a revolution."[25] It may also be possible that Paine believed—not unlike Richard Price and Joseph Priestley—that monarchies were more tenable in Europe given "The distance of America from all the other parts of the globe" (*Address to the People of France*).[26] After all, Lafayette and a majority of the deputies in the Third Estate, not unlike the American Federalists, approved of a British-styled constitutional monarchy even if they eventually ditched plans for a bicameral legislature.[27]

More interestingly, unlike other writers, Paine identifies a general diffusion of despotism, observing that monarchical power is not its only source even if it is a predominant one:

> When despotism has established itself for ages in a country, as in France, it is not in the person of the king only that it resides ... Every office and department has its despotism, founded upon custom and usage. Every place has its Bastille, and every Bastille its despot. The

original hereditary despotism resident in the person of the king, divides and sub-divides itself into a thousand shapes and forms ... It strengthens itself by assuming the appearance of duty, and tyrannies under the pretence of obeying. (81)

Even if revolutions and rebellions tend to be lumped together indiscriminately as disorderly, chaotic events by the likes of Burke and other detractors, they are not necessarily so. Indeed, this Burkean assumption is overturned with little ado as he claims counterintuitively that the French revolution is anything but frenzied and irrational because its origin was "generated in the rational contemplation of the Rights of Man" with its supporters proving capable of distinguishing "between persons and principles" (81).

This reference to the Bastille, however, makes Paine's relatively scant discussion of the prison itself appear all the more striking—even as he complains of Burke that "not one glance, not one commiserating reflection" has been "bestowed on those" locked in "the most miserable of prisons" (91); this relative silence is conspicuous when compared to Dufresnoy's response to Burke and Helen Maria Williams' accounts of unwarranted imprisonments in *Letters from France*. The reader is also left clueless as to the extent of oppression in other aspects of French life since Paine also curiously bypasses the fact of poor wages, disproportionately heavy tax burdens, tithes, seigneurial dues, and rapidly rising costs of food, while overlooking the uprisings and acts of defiance on the part of French peasants and commoners during the spring and summer of 1789. Just who and what ills comprised that which he referred to as "the augean stable of parasites and plunderers too abominably filthy to be cleansed, by anything short of a complete and universal revolution?"[28]

If Paine stops short of identifying the injustices suffered by French commoners, he moves to surer ground when describing the fall of the Bastille, providing one of the most stirring and comprehensive descriptions of the three weeks leading up to the climax even though he was not physically present in Paris. A sensationalized tale of an active, virtuous citizenry, Paine's narrative can be said to retread the general course of the *American Crisis* papers as he highlights a conflict between a committed citizenry pressing successfully against much larger, better-trained mercenary forces. Indeed, what follows over the next few pages forms a diametric counterpoint to Burke's tale of revolutionary brutality. Here, Paine spins the destruction of the Bastille into a tale of heroism against the "treacherous and hostile aggravations of the enemies of the Revolution" (85) beginning with the Count d'Artois' dismissal of the recently re-appointed minister of finance, Jacques Necker, and the summoning of the king's foreign mercenary troops to Paris: a subterfuge that was implemented in order to derail the reforms launched by the Estates General through much of May and especially June 1789 when the separate orders of clergy, nobility, and commons, began to reorganize into the unicameral National Assembly. Although it is not entirely clear whether the Parisians who stormed the Bastille did so in order to protect themselves or members of the Assembly itself, their actions are delineated by Paine in highly charged terms. The approaching melée between the people and their presumed enemies—the newly implanted ministers and mercenary troops—is rendered as nothing less than a "crisis" and "a cause at stake, on which depended their freedom or slavery" (87) while the members of the National Assembly are dramatized as "the devoted victims" who had "the hearts and wishes of their country" but no "military authority" (86). As if endeavoring to make the actors involved less foreign, less French, and perhaps more English, Paine invokes the Giant Despair and his Doubting Castle from Bunyan's Protestant allegory, *The Pilgrim's Progress*, pitching the Bastille as "either the prize or the prison of the assailants" (85) and an edifice that symbolized "the high altar and idea of the downfall of despotism" (89). Finally, the outcome of the fateful day is recounted in heightened language: the would-be oppressors are astounded since they were "accustomed" to slavery and therefore had "no idea that ... a body of unarmed citizens would dare to face the military force of thirty thousand men" in the name of liberty (88).

Even more significantly, Paine takes a triple-pronged approach when exonerating the citizens and the National Assembly from Burke's imputations of cruelty, doing so more vigorously than other respondents. In order to apprehend the scale of Paine's radical vision more fully, however, let us turn briefly to Macaulay's discussion, where she reflects upon a people who had been used to the "barbarous spectacles" of cruel punishments (25), confessing that she does not know "how many individuals have fallen a sacrifice in the public commotions," but only that it must pale in comparison with the "history of monarchies." Another reply to Burke would register a similar incredulity, evincing astonishment "at the moderation of the poor whip-galled slaves"; the writer would have "pardoned—though not approved—much greater excesses had they been committed in the moment of emancipation, when the *lex talionis*, the law of retribution must operate very powerfully on vulgar minds" (8–9).[29]

In contrast, Paine goes to greater lengths to justify the actions of the crowd, noting that the citizens and National Assembly were anything but violent in light of the insidious purposes of their antagonists: if anything, many more citizens than aggressors were injured and killed. The distasteful manner in which the heads of the mayor of Paris, the intendant of Paris, the governor of the Bastille, and a new member of the ministry were displayed was hardly unexpected given the frequent enactments of violent punishments which had only been abolished a few years earlier in 1787. Indeed, Paine reminds his readers that far from being perpetrators of violence, members of the National Assembly exhibited an exceptional degree of forbearance and forgiveness despite being the intended victims.

> Whom has the National Assembly brought to the scaffold? None. They were themselves the devoted victims of this plot, and they have not retaliated; why, then, are they charged with revenge they have not acted? ... When men are sore with the sense of oppressions, and menaced with the prospects of new ones, is the calmness of philosophy or the palsy of insensibility to be looked for?

In short, far from being the savages portrayed by Burke, the Assembly has demonstrated remarkable grace under pressure.

But Paine does not stop there. More significantly, he elaborates on the use of "terror" by French and British governments alike. It's not just the implementation of cruel punishments that stands out. Rather, what is more disturbing is the use of terror by governments as a means of intimidating the lower classes. This is not to say that other writers did not criticize the inefficacy of such practices; in *Observations on the present state of the parochial and vagrant poor* (1773), John Scott declared that executions "certainly harden the human heart" because "those who see life taken and resigned in so careless a manner, will not have a proper value for their own lives or the lives of others."[30] Paine, however, goes further to say that such grotesque and cruel punishments only encourage further brutality. History, after all, has long demonstrated how "dreadfully vindictive and cruel" governments can be when they quell a revolt (86) such as in the aftermath of populist uprisings stirred up by Wat Tyler, Jack Cade, the Kett rebellion, and Masaniello. Conversely, the "vulgar"

> learn it from the governments they live under; and retaliate the punishments they have been accustomed to behold. The heads stuck upon spikes, which remained for years upon Temple Bar, differed nothing in the horror of the scene from those carried about upon spikes at Paris; yet this was done by the English Government. It may perhaps be said that it signifies nothing to a man what is done to him after he is dead; but it signifies much to the living; it either tortures their feelings or hardens their hearts, and in either case it instructs them how to punish when power falls into their hands. (90)

Interestingly, long before 20th-century psychologists and sociologists discovered the link between corporal punishment and brutality, whether in schools or jails, and their role in fostering rather than deterring violence, Paine was already aware of the causality between punishment and future crime:

> Lay then the axe to the root, and teach governments humanity ... The effect of those cruel spectacles exhibited to the populace is to destroy tenderness or excite revenge; and by the base and false idea of governing men by terror, instead of reason, they become precedents. It is over the lowest class of mankind that government by terror is intended to operate, and it is on them that it operates to the worst effect. They have sense enough to feel they are the objects aimed at; and they inflict in their turn the examples of terror they have been instructed to practise. (91)

That Paine was largely correct in his interpretation is attested to not only by the emulation of official punishments by the rebels of 1381 but also by the words of the authorities themselves: including Henry VIII in 1536 when he instructed the Earls of Shrewsbury, Rutland, and Huntingdon to carry out executions "to the example and terror of all others" (cited in Wood, 76) and by Neville and Woods in their detailed description of punishments to be enacted for the purposes of "terror" (cited in Wood, 238).

Indeed, there's more to the fact that the violence was carried out by "mobs" when he denies that such people are hardly any more representative of France than those involved in the Gordon riots of 1780 are of England. Rather, the truth is that the very type of authoritarian governments which are lauded by Burke are in fact responsible for inculcating the thuggish behavior of the lower classes:

> But everything we see or hear offensive to our feelings and derogatory to the human character should lead to other reflections than those of reproach. Even the beings who commit them have some claim to our consideration. How then is it that such vast classes of mankind as are distinguished by the appellation of the vulgar, or the ignorant mob, are so numerous in all old countries? ... They rise, as an unavoidable consequence, out of the ill construction of all old governments in Europe ... It is by distortedly exalting some men, that others are distortedly debased, till the whole is out of nature. (92)

At the same time, Paine's comment on the distorted exaltation of certain members of society forms a consistent thread of criticism aimed at what he perceived as Burkean superficiality and theatricality. Having lashed out earlier at Burke's lack of concern for prisoners of the Bastille by accusing him of "pity[ing] the plumage, but forget[ting] the dying bird" since "his hero or his heroine must be a tragedy victim expiring in show, and not the real prisoner of misery" (84), Paine returns to this theme with his penetrating observation that "A vast mass of mankind are degradedly thrown into the back-ground of the human picture, to bring forward, with greater glare, the puppet-show of state and aristocracy" (92). It is an awareness that may be said to reach back to the Leveller, Digger, and early republican awareness of the few overruling the many. Note, however, that Paine does not explain the means by which the "vulgar" came to be so: the explanation does not actually arrive until Part 2 where he addresses the problems stemming from a lack of education and familial resources.

Equally prescient is his analysis of such behavior in revolutions. Even if Burke's "theatrical exaggerations" have some foundation in truth, Paine argues, they in fact affirm the very "necessity of the French revolution." Far from being an "effect of the principles of the Revolution," the outrages attest to the "degraded mind that existed before the Revolution, and which the Revolution is calculated to reform" (92) especially when "that vast mass of mankind" are usually "the followers of the camp than of the standard of liberty, and have yet to be instructed how to reverence it" (92). The revolution is therefore more than simply a manifestation of vulgarity, but ironically one of the few means of extricating the populace from economic and social degradation: quite simply, a reformation of the people can only begin with a reformation of the government. Not surprisingly, Paine has a different interpretation of the women's march and the other momentous events of October 5–6, 1789, endeavoring to straighten out Burke's biased and incomplete account. That the latter has failed to factor in the "plots against the revolution," the true source of "all the mischiefs," by conveniently omitting details on the disrespectful handling of the revolutionary cockade by the Garde du Corps and the journey of Louis XVI's family from Versailles to Paris, provides additional evidence of Burke's habit of displaying "consequences without their causes," which is "one of the arts of the drama to do so" (93). Burke's account is thus a misleading one that can be said to form a parallel of sorts to the act of "exalting some men in order to bring forward the puppet-show of state and aristocracy." These references to drama, of course, serve to amplify the sense of Burkean artifice, distortion, and unnaturalness all the more.

When Paine reflects on the events of October 6, he again subverts Burke's narrative by replacing the focus on the forced entry into the private quarters of the royal family with a narrative of the events prompted by the actions of Louis XVI and his guards; nor does he fail to mention the anxiety caused by Louis' delay in ratifying the declaration of August 4 in addition to rumors that members of the king's Garde du Corps had torn off the revolutionary cockades from their hats and trampled on them during a lavish feast: a gesture that would have naturally added a sense of insult to injury during a period of high food prices. Paine is also quick to note the poor judgment displayed by a guard who shot and killed a member of the Paris militia, instead of retiring prudently (96). In other words, much of the disorder criticized by Burke could have been easily averted with a dose of rational judgment on the part of the authorities. Nonetheless, it is also difficult to explain Paine's general oversight of the rationale behind the women's march to Versailles—namely, to protest the price of bread. Again, could Paine—not unlike Burke—have felt uncomfortable with populist disturbances, regardless of his sympathies? Or did he imagine that the idea of marching over bread prices would be incomprehensible to the British: and thereby unlikely to garner much sympathy?[31]

IV WRITING ABOUT RIGHTS

So what can be said about the basis of the much-celebrated French Declaration of the Rights of Man then? Or as Paine puts it, "What are those rights, and how came man by them originally?" (98) Rather than delving into the Declaration itself, which he addresses more directly towards the conclusion of Part 1, he begins with basic questions on the historical development of natural rights: an approach that constitutes yet another challenge to Burke's subordination of rights. For just as the accounts describing the storming of the Bastille and the events of October 5 and 6 must be traced back to their original causes, rights should also be traced back to their very origins. The trouble, according to Paine, is that Burke's privileging of antecedents, precedents, and "mouldy documents" fails to go back all the way to creation. Such an interpretation, of course, was hardly unprecedented, as we have noticed in the writings of Gratian, William of Ockham, John Ball, the Diggers, and Locke, all of whom variously spoke of the divine origins of natural rights. These ideas also resurfaced in the wake of the Wilkes crisis when Obadiah Hulme observed that those who arrived at the idea of representative governments were guided by "the natural rights of mankind" when "they considered every man alike, as he came from the hands of his maker" so that every man was "preserved in his natural, and equal rights" regardless of personal wealth.[32] Similarly, some twenty years later, Capel Lofft would reiterate this idea when he explained in his response to Burke that "whatever privileges, whatever glory, are inheritable from civil institution, the rights of men" is "of date far higher, and of origin transcendently more venerable" because it is "an inheritance coeval with the commencement of humanity" (30).

Paine adopts a similar approach, but replaces Locke's (see p. 14), Hulme's and Lofft's long-winded approaches with a terseness that verges on the sublime when he follows up his own observation with a simple question and an even simpler answer, "What was he then? Man" (99). The very spareness of the five words can be said to enhance the idea of a simple, unencumbered divine origin of man. Paine likewise also beats his allies—Saxon-right reformers such as Cartwright and Sharp—at their own game when he upholds the rights of man as much more than a mere man-made invention. Explaining that the misperception is a consequence of "upstart governments" attempting to "thrust themselves between and presumptuously working to *un-make* man" (99), he insists on a return to the very creation of man for the recovery of natural rights and original humanity: it is for this reason that political philosophers have claimed Paine's ideas to be "normatively secular but foundationally theological" (Lamb, 6) while certain historians have attempted to claim that the theological basis for Paine's beliefs on rights make him anything but modern.[33] Yet, despite this grounding, as we will see, what is remarkable is how it serves as a basis for aims that we identify as modern:[34] namely, the eradication of hereditary government, a more democratic orientation of government, and a scheme of welfare that protects the poor and elderly. In other words, these seemingly traditional underpinnings—no different from the statement that "All bonde men may be made ffre for god made all ffre"—can be said to introduce the modern concept of rights possessed by all human beings, just as the earlier statement helped put an end to feudalism. Similarly, when weighing once more on the stranglehold of niggling precedents through the ages just as he had done earlier in his commentary on the Parliament of

1688, Paine contends that the only generation of men that "ever possessed the right of dictating the mode by which the world should be governed for ever" was "the first generation that existed." But in the case of all other generations, each "is equal in rights to the generations which preceded it" and none beholden to another (99). Indeed, Paine's principle here may be read as a variation on his statement in *Common Sense* about having it "in our power to begin the world over again."

Perhaps taking a cue from Diderot who upheld natural law as "man's most sacred natural right to everything," one which could be easily discerned from "the principles of written law of all the organized nations,"[35] Paine claims that "every history of the creation … whether from the lettered or unlettered world … all agree in establishing one point, the unity of man": namely, that all men "are all of one degree," and "all born equal, with equal natural right." Not unlike John Ball, who observed "We be all come from one father and one mother, Adam and Eve: whereby can they say or shew that they be greater lords than we be," Paine insists that "MANKIND" were "originally equals in the order of creation," while pointing out that "male and female are the distinctions of nature, good and bad the distinctions of Heaven." It is here that Paine returns to his anti-monarchical argument from *Common Sense*—yet sidesteps any detailed criticisms of monarchy or Louis XVI (perhaps in hopes that the latter would somehow adhere to revolutionary ideals) while leaning more heavily on the idea of equality with his repetition of "all" and "equal." Like Diderot, Paine does not supply examples of cultures which gave credence to the idea of "natural rights"; it may be that Paine presumed that a simple reference to the Bible would suffice for a British audience when contending that "divine authority" decreed "no other distinction" than the "distinction of sexes" (100). By declaring that the "equality of man, so far from being a modern doctrine, is the oldest upon record" (100), he not only upends potential allegations of "innovation" but also any sense of national privilege—particularly as Britons still largely believed themselves to be more egalitarian than other cultures. As presented here, the original idea of equality is far more ubiquitous than anyone can guess, belonging to numerous cultures. Why then should they be denied to mankind?

Likewise, after chiding Burke for being "accustomed to kiss the aristocratical hand that has purloined him from himself" (84), Paine briefly begins to deflate any notion of aristocratic lineage, declaring that "it is only when he forgets his origin, or, to use a more fashionable phrase, his birth and family, that he becomes dissolute" (100)—even though it is not until some pages later that he expounds upon the ills associated with hereditary privileges and government. The problem with so many European governments, Paine suggests, is the manner in which "man is thrown back from his Maker" (100). What he desires here is a new foundation for government and society as a whole. Why not judge people for intrinsic rather than extrinsic, artificial distinctions imposed by society? Here, Paine's mode of expression is direct and immediate, as if reinforcing his message of naturalness. What matters more, Paine insists, is one's "duty to God, which every man must feel; and with respect to his neighbour, to do as he would be done by" (101). No wonder, then, that Paine deemed a Declaration of Duties superfluous in his section on the French Declaration of Rights, explaining that it is also a "Declaration of Duties also" because "Whatever is my right as a man is also the right of another." The fact that the truth of such an equation is not immediately apparent betrays the curtailment of natural rights through the centuries: moreover, so long as extraneous matters enter into consideration—distinctions based upon birth or any other arbitrary, extrinsic privileges, the rights and duties of humanity will never be properly understood.

Not least, just as Paine had ridiculed the farcical prospect of men taking up arms to maintain they have no rights, he dismisses the equally ludicrous probability of men "enter[ing] into society to become worse than he was before" or "to have fewer rights" (101): again, it's just common sense. Here, too, he attempts to clarify the relationship between natural and civil rights, observing that while the former comprise those which man has the power to execute individually—for instance, intellectual thought—the latter involve those which pertain to man "in right of his being a member of society," relating to "security and protection" (101). In contrast to Burke who expected natural rights to be surrendered in civil society, Paine is careful to remind readers à la Rousseau that civil power should not be "applied to invade the natural rights which are retained in the individual" (102) even though man must occasionally sacrifice some of his natural rights for civil rights: for instance, by settling a dispute over property through a jury of peers rather than by enacting private vengeance. Nonetheless, governments continue to fail miserably at guaranteeing any security of natural or civil rights beyond this evident truth by refusing to grant liberty of thought especially where religious worship is concerned.

V THE CONQUEST AND ITS CONSEQUENCES

For Paine, the harsh intrusion of civil power that inevitably curtailed the exercise of natural rights in Britain was none other than the Conquest, even if Britain was still widely viewed as the most democratic and egalitarian nation in Europe: Dissenters and Catholics, after all, were permitted to worship freely at their own chapels while the existence of a representative government indicated a rare degree of political independence. Although Paine was far from unique in making use of the Norman Yoke theory, he was nonetheless arguably the first to apply it on so comprehensive a scale since the Diggers when they blamed William the Conqueror for introducing a militarized government to England. For Paine, the Norman Yoke was responsible for instituting government from without, rather than within.

Here, he begins by attributing the makings of arbitrary government to the church and military conquests. Despite the difficulty in determining the sources, if any, which may have informed Paine's distrust of church–state alliances or ideas on military conquests, it is worth outlining some of the parallels to d'Holbach's *Christianity Unveiled* (1761) and Obadiah Hulme's *Essay on the English Constitution* (1771) as well as to Paine's own *Serious Address To The People Of Pennsylvania* (1778). In *Christianity Unveiled*, an underground favorite that inveighed against Christian dogma and clerical influence, d'Holbach maintained that religion was "invented to relieve governments from the care of being just, and reigning by equitable laws." Similarly, in *English Constitution*, a tract which received great attention from English reformers during the 1770s and '80s, Hulme execrated the "baneful influence" of "every religious hierarchy," with their "artful, designing set of men" (*Essay*, 35). As if combining their ideas, Paine posited two ways of governing mankind, equating ecclesiastical and monarchical tyranny.

First, By keeping them ignorant.

Secondly, By making them wise.

The former was and is the custom of the old world. The latter of the new. All the forms of government now in being in the old world bring forward into present view the ignorance and superstition of the times in which they were erected; but the sufferers under them, by constantly looking at them, grow familiar to their absurdities, then reconciled to them, and impose a silence upon themselves which is often construed into consent. It is a decided point with me that ... were governments to be now established in Europe, the form of them would not be monarchical. (*CW*, 289–90)

In other words, both forms of tyranny are outdated, rooted as they are in superstition. Note, too, Paine's emphatic criticism of monarchy in a text written for an American audience. It is thus particularly interesting to see how Paine retains the message in *Rights of Man* while shifting his focus to the ways in which political government harnessed the powers of the ecclesiastical authorities:

... it will be proper to take a review of the several sources from which governments have arisen and on which they have been founded. They may be all comprehended under three heads.

First, Superstition.

Secondly, Power.

Thirdly, The common interest of society and the common rights of man.

The first was a government of priestcraft, the second of conquerors, and the third of reason. When a set of artful men pretended, through the medium of oracles, to hold intercourse with the Deity, as familiarly as they now march up the back-stairs in European courts, the world was completely under the government of superstition. The oracles were consulted, and whatever they were made to say became the law; and this sort of government lasted as long as this sort of superstition lasted.

After these a race of conquerors arose, whose government, like that of William the Conqueror, was founded in power, and the sword assumed the name of a sceptre. Governments thus established last as long as the power to support them lasts ... they united fraud to force, and set up an idol which they called Divine Right, and which, in imitation of the Pope, who affects to be spiritual and temporal, and in contradiction to the Founder of the Christian religion, twisted itself afterwards into an idol of another shape, called Church and State. (102–3)

Like Hulme, Paine similarly blames "a set of artful men" pretending to "hold intercourse with the Deity," along with "a race of conquerors," both of whom collude by means of "force and fraud" (103). Paine detects scant differences between a priesthood feigning exclusive knowledge of the divine and a monarchy governing by virtue of "Divine Right," especially when the latter not only follows directly in the footsteps of the Pope but leans on a church and state alliance to buttress their joint powers. At the same time, it is notable that while the earlier passage boldly attacks monarchy, equating it with outmoded ecclesiastical superstition and arbitrariness, the passage from *Rights of Man* skirts a direct attack on monarchy, preferring to dwell on the co-opting of the Church: a move that is not surprising given Paine's reluctance to demonize monarchy as we have seen thus far in Part 1. Instead, Paine decides to zero in, as it were, on the contrast between the new and old governments that he broached in *A Serious Address*. Whether considered separately or combined, both Church and State hierarchies can be blamed for oppression, presenting a diametric opposite to a more beneficent form of government arising directly out of society—one in which "the *individuals themselves ... entered into a compact with each other* to produce a government."[36] In contrast to the British government, Paine asserts, the new government of France has emerged directly from the people, who are beginning to enjoy an unprecedented political leverage. A government created by a majority of its society is the only one "in which governments have a right to arise" and "to exist" (103): an idea that may have inspired Abraham Lincoln's notion of "government of the people, by the people, for the people" in the Gettysburg Address. Here, Paine's idea manifests a more idealistic, if optimistic, view of man when compared to Burlamaqui in his *Principles of Natural and Political Law* (1747) and Rousseau in *A Discourse on Inequality* (1751), both of which imagined governments largely to be byproducts of ambition and conquest—especially when the former attributed the origins of political societies to the subjection of the "simplest and weakest" by "the most dexterous, the strongest, and the most ambitious."

Even more troublesome for Paine is the fact that England never acquired a true constitution since it "never regenerated itself": an issue that continues to be debated through the 21st century. He deplores the lack of a document detailing the principles, organization, powers, elections, and duration of Parliaments, to which one could refer and quote "article by article." As such, there is little regularity in the proceedings of English government. Although a mixed government with its supposed checks and balances would appear to presuppose a certain element of logic and moderation, Paine counters this argument by implying that the potential for arbitrariness on the part of the king and both houses of Parliament is actually far worse.

But in order to grasp the source of Paine's criticisms and the extent of his radical analysis, however, it is worthwhile to glance over a few historical and contemporary views of the English constitution. As early as 1600, legal historians and antiquarians generally believed that the constitution prevented the king from assuming the utmost powers over other branches of government from the days of the Saxon witenagamot, but particularly after the signing of Magna Charta. The veneration of the ancient constitution existed side by side with one for the Common Law, also widely believed to have been dated from the heyday of the Saxons. Given such, many of Paine's contemporaries expressed generous and unequivocal praise on the present state of the constitution. Richard Price, for instance, expressed little interest in a purely republican government, regarding "our own constitution of government, as better adapted than any other to this country, and, in THEORY, excellent."[37] In their separate replies to Burke,

Belsham, and Boothby pooh-poohed the possible contagion of the French revolution, with Boothby approving wholeheartedly of the ways in which "nothing of pure democracy or pure monarchy, or pure aristocracy, in a distinct or separate state, is to be found in our Constitution" but are instead "blended and tempered together into one common mass." So while not altogether a perfect entity in practice, the ideal form of an ancient British constitution and a set of unwritten common laws were still to be treasured as one worthy of emulation.[38] Such ideas were in keeping with the ideas of Sir John Davies, who preferred Common Law to written laws which were "imposed on the Subject before any Triall or Probation made, whether the same be fit and agreeable to the nature and disposition of the people" (Burgess, 52).

On the other hand, there was also a range of opinions from those who harbored a few doubts about the positives of the English Constitution to those who denied its existence altogether. For the Genevan theorist, Jean Louis De Lolme, the English constitution was not only "fully established," but one enshrined in written and unwritten sources alike: an idea that lingered from the early 17th century with the likes of Edward Coke, John Selden and others who venerated the idea of an evolving Common Law and Constitution. Eighteenth-century English reformers, on the other hand, were more likely to insist that as admirable as it was, the constitution remained yet unfulfilled or incomplete. Cartwright, for instance, marveled at the way in which "our constitution of government" aligns with the "law of nature" (*Take your choice*, 10–11). He relished the "uncertainty of our common law," which was "glorious" in its flexibility, maintaining that this "uncertainty" proved more advantageous than not by permitting men to "depart from former precedents and decisions which are in any way defective" or to "vary" and "refine, as experience and wisdom dictate" (11); only when "the perfection of reason, on any point, is once attained" could a law become finalized or "*unalterable*" (11). Still others, including David Williams and Obadiah Hulme, both of whom largely concurred with Cartwright's goals for restoring annual parliaments and expanding enfranchisement, regretted how the promise of the Saxon constitution remained largely unfulfilled; Williams, indeed, went from claiming that the constitution had been "left unfinished and incomplete"[39] to denying it altogether in his reply to Burke—"FOR ENGLAND HAS NO POLITICAL CONSTITUTION."[40]

It was left to Jean-Paul Marat, however, to address the problem in his *Chains of Slavery*, which received only minimal distribution in 1774. In a lengthy footnote spanning two pages, Marat feared that unless the power of the sovereign's deputies was "limited by the fundamental laws of the state," a single attempt to infringe upon the rights of the people was "often times sufficient to ruin liberty." Since few boundaries constrained the authority of the people's representatives, "the guardians of our rights," there was no doubt that "the English constitution is extremely defective." Likewise, representatives should not be authorized to amend the constitution without consulting the people or "the advice of the nation." The extension from a triennial to a septennial Parliament, after all, could be easily extended or even "made perpetual" (*Chains of Slavery*, 180–1). It was no less deplorable that while national liberties were all too often circumscribed by the Prince, it was the royal prerogative which should have been restrained; this "defect in the constitution" was all too glaring in the history of relationships between kings and their parliaments dating from James I (197). All told, if the English constitution could be reckoned superior to others, it was hardly perfect because when "traced to its first principle," it would be found to be only suitable for uncivilized men or those "who subsisted by pillaging" (195).

Let us now return to Paine and look more closely at his assessment. At first glance, his call for a more permanent scheme of government would appear to fly in the face of his criticism of "unalterable," eternally binding acts. However, this apparent contradiction vanishes when he raises the possibility of "alterations, amendments, or additions" with instructions to be spelled out by the constitution: an idea that he explores in more depth in Part 2, Chapter 4. Unlike those who took pride in Britain's ancient constitution and Common Law, Paine voiced a strong preference for a written constitution. Perhaps his reasoning was similar to Cartwright's who posited a hypothetical subversion of the constitution by legislators in a passage from *Take your Choice*:

> would it not be time to act a little for ourselves, instead of continuing wholly to confide in such treacherous agents? We ought at least to act the part of a distrustful master; by requiring them, on the points in question, to make the written law speak the true language of the constitution .... (12)

In *Four Letters on Interesting Subjects* (1776), Paine had already broached the problem of the English Constitution, claiming that few countries had viable constitutions, including England herself, which had "no fixed constitution." Even though monarchical prerogative is laid under "several restrictions," the overall legislative power, distributed among king, lords and commons, wound up being "ever so oppressive or arbitrary." Moreover, the constitution was "defective" in three other respects since the monarch was able to increase the number of lords or incorporate any town or village, thereby allowing it to send representatives to the House of Commons. Conversely, it also had the capability of disenfranchising any county, city, or town.

> ... it is the particular business of a constitution to mark out how much they shall give up. In this sense it is easy to see that the English have no constitution, because they have given up everything, their legislative power being unlimited without either condition or controul, except in the single instance of trial by Juries. No country can be called free which is governed by an absolute power; and it matters not whether it be an absolute royal power or an absolute legislative power, as the consequences will be the same to the people. That England is governed by the latter, no man can deny, there being, as is said before, no constitution in that country which says to the legislative powers, "Thus far shalt thou go, and no farther." There is nothing to prevent them passing a law which shall exempt themselves from the payment of taxes, or which shall give the house of commons power to sit for life ....[41]

Whereas defenders of the ancient constitution argued that it served its purpose by guarding against incursions of monarchical power, Paine construed it differently: the very dearth of a definitive guard against these incursions betrayed the very lack of a viable constitution, making an apparent mockery of the much vaunted "checks." As such, the English constitution fell short of its purpose by failing to curb legislative or executive power in any meaningful way

It is telling that not unlike Marat, Paine took exception to what he refers to as the "arbitrary" empowerment of Parliament to sit for seven years as proposed in the Septennial Bill of 1716; indeed, the irregular timing of elections and terms of office were issues which had also irked the American colonies into crafting their own constitutions with greater specificity well before the signing of the Declaration of Independence. In *Rights of Man*, the retention of tradition connotes not so much a preservation of British culture as intimated by thinkers from Edward Coke to Edmund Burke, but rather a perverse unnaturalness and un-Englishness at work as Paine charges the present government with a mode of governance that is "out of nature." Even today, we might add that Paine's observations—particularly those concerning the arbitrary length of a sitting parliament and the overall lack of codification—remain relevant to current debates on the British constitution.[42] Anthony King, for instance, can be said to concur with Paine in principle, despite his lack of reference to the latter, when explaining that what Britain lacks is not a written constitution but rather a codified one that "has been formally adopted in accordance with some legal process generally acknowledged as appropriate to the purpose";[43] not unlike Paine, King evinces reservations on account of its absence of a legal mechanism for changes or amendments, by which the British constitution is "remarkably easy to change" such that "politicians and others do not even notice that constitutional change—as distinct from other kinds of change—is taking place" (*The British Constitution*, 8). More significantly, others—most notably, Vernon Bogdanor—have contended that however real the existence of a British constitution may be, present arrangements do not conform to the principles of constitutionalism, particularly with the unspecified concentration of power wielded by the Prime Minister and his/her Cabinet. As he observes in *The Monarchy and the Constitution*, this specification may have been even more vague and amorphous during the 18th century, given the monarch's still considerable influence on policy—in spite of being unable to govern without parliamentary approval:[44] an argument that partly affirms Paine's allegations of parliamentary arbitrariness as we will see in his conclusion to Part 1.

Yet, even as Paine rejects the safe Whiggism of a Cartwright, Hulme, David Williams or any of Burke's critics, his failure to embrace universal male suffrage is especially puzzling, in light of his agreement with their criticisms on the glaring lack of representation in larger cities. Although Paine points out that the French, unlike the English, have standardized qualifications for suffrage, granting a vote to all men who pay a tax of sixty sous a year, he does not quibble with the prerequisites for voters: a satisfaction that may have derived from his mistaken assumption that barely more than one out of a hundred men in Britain were enfranchised. Unlike Capel Lofft who deemed the qualification of three days' labor an inappropriate guarantor of independence, especially one that infringed upon "the Principle which justly regards the Choice of a Representative as a Right attached to the person of the citizen, not to his property" (*Remarks*, 65), Paine's acceptance of the conditions attached to suffrage in France implies a reluctance comparable to that of conservative-leaning English and French reformers such as Christopher Wyvill or the Abbe Sièyes, both of whom were loathe to extend the vote to propertyless men; indeed, it was a position that he himself had advocated in *A Serious Address to the People of Pennsylvania* (1778), as noted earlier, when he denied servants the right to vote. Not surprisingly either, Paine fails to question either the additional precondition for greater wealth amongst those entitled to vote for members of the National Assembly— or those seeking to become electors who were required to have paid a tax amounting to a sum of ten days' worth of work. Paine's acceptance of restrictions on suffrage and representation also places him to the right of the Society of Constitutional Information and French radicals such as Desmoulins and Robespierre, who vehemently protested the restrictions in a speech of October 22, 1789:

All citizens, whoever they are, have the right to aspire to all levels of officeholding. Each individual therefore has the right to participate in making the law which governs him and in the administration of the public good which is his own.[45]

In fact, the proportion of active citizens who enjoyed suffrage—a pool from which foreigners, the poor, the propertyless, and servants were excluded—was one-sixth of the population:[46] that is, nearly the same as it was in Britain. Moreover, Robespierre went so far as to advocate that voters with little or no property should be paid an indemnity from public funds to compensate for the loss of time and money during the voting process: a plan that was set in place in September 1793.[47] It was not until the following year with Part 2 of *Rights of Man* that Paine was ready to embrace universal suffrage.[48] Nonetheless, he brushes aside Burke's concern, deeming the English constitution "capricious" because

the lowest character that can be supposed to exist, and who has not so much as the visible means of an honest livelihood, is an elector in some places; while in other places, the man who pays very large taxes, and has a known fair character, and the farmer who rents to the amount of three or four hundred pounds a year, with a property on that farm to three or four times that amount, is not admitted to be an elector.

Applying Burke's words elsewhere against him, Paine notes once more in keeping with the theme of unnaturalness that "everything is out of nature" (106). Yet, it is certainly ironic that Paine's disgust at the imbalance—poor men who are enfranchised and rich men who are not—reveals an underlying Burkean assumption that property and political rights should be commensurate.

No less disturbing to Paine was the continued existence of game laws and chartered towns. The latter of which was probably no better exemplified than his native town of Thetford.[49] At first glance, his criticisms of both may not appear particularly novel since Marat and earlier respondents to Burke had already addressed these issues. Wollstonecraft, for instance, found ample cause for complaint in the general state of British law which almost unfailingly privileged the rich at the expense of the poor—with the game laws furnishing some of the most notorious examples:

> The game laws are almost as oppressive to the peasantry as press-warrants to the mechanic. In this land of liberty what is to secure the property of the poor farmer when his noble landlord chooses to plant a decoy field near his little property? Game devour the fruit of his labour; but fines and imprisonment await him if he dare to kill any—or lift up his hand to interrupt the pleasure of his lord. How many families have been plunged, in the sporting countries, into misery and vice for some paltry transgression of these coercive laws. (Wollstonecraft, *Vindication of the Rights of Men*)[50]

What is implicit here is that Britain is anything but a land of liberty for the impoverished, proving more "oppressive" and "coercive": a conclusion that is rendered even more explicit by John Butler in his repeated mockery of Britons retaining a "firm belief in imaginary liberty."[51] If the Abbe Sièyes had already execrated the monopolizing presence of corporations and guilds in his pamphlet on the Third Estate (*Brief Documentary History*, 69), Butler would in turn refer to Britain itself as a "charter'd isle" where "every city, town, borough and cinque port, have their charters also" (30), bemoaning that

> we have customs amongst us, which lead us to a belief, that we are born free, and the next moment we are told that we cannot obtain that freedom without a purchase, compelling us to buy that right which the constitution of our country tells us nature had given us bountifully at our birth, and which no authority on earth can lawfully deprive us .... (*Brief Reflections*, 104–6)

Town corporations and charters, in other words, ultimately deny freedom and the rights of nature commonly assumed to be guaranteed by the British constitution.

What is unique and powerful in Paine's approach to these issues, however, is not so much the substance of his complaints, but rather his analysis and interpretation. Let us first turn to his approach to corporations in *Four Letters on Interesting Subjects* (1776):

As to corporations themselves, they are without exception so many badges of kingly tyranny, and tend, like every other species of useless pomp, to the oppression and impoverishment of the place, without one single advantage arising from them. They keep up a perpetual spirit of distinction and faction, engross emoluments and advantages to themselves ... They diminish the freedom of every place where they exist. The most flourishing towns in England, as, Birmingham, Sheffield, Manchester, have no corporations.

Moreover, whereas Wollstonecraft, Butler, and other respondents to Burke variously hone in on laws that favor the affluent or animadvert more generally on the oppressiveness of local and federal government, Paine magnifies the sense of injustice. There is nothing more ironic than the notion of Britons residing in their native land as estranged foreigners—thanks to the lingering after-effects of the Conquest, whereby "the country is yet disfigured with its marks." William I's "Conquest and tyranny" is therefore to blame not only for the general eradication of suffrage according to the likes of Hulme, Cartwright, Sharp, and other reformers, but for large-scale injustice and inefficiency as well in towns or across localities. Paine delves into the lack of liberty entailed by town charters even more energetically:

In England, game is made the property of those at whose expense it is not fed; and with respect to monopolies, the country is cut up into monopolies. Every chartered town is an aristocratical monopoly in itself, and the qualification of electors proceeds out of those chartered monopolies. Is this freedom? Is this what Mr. Burke means by a constitution? In these chartered monopolies, a man coming from another part of the country is hunted from them as if he were a foreign enemy. An Englishman is not free of his own country; every one of those places presents a barrier in his way, and tells him he is not a freeman—that he has no rights. Within these monopolies are other monopolies. In a city, such for instance as Bath, which contains between twenty and thirty thousand inhabitants, the right of electing representatives to Parliament is monopolised by about thirty-one persons ... A man even of the same town, whose parents were not in circumstances to give

him an occupation, is debarred, in many cases, from the natural right
of acquiring one, be his genius or industry what it may. (107)

If the insistent repetition of "monopolies" and "Chartered"
invokes the very principle of entrapment,[52] it also distinctly
echoes Paine's earlier observations on the combined forces of
monarchical form and the symbolic Bastille where "Every office and
department has its despotism" and "The original hereditary despotism resident in the person of the king, divides and sub-divides
itself into a thousand shapes and forms, till at last the whole of it is
acted by deputation." Here, too, the "badges of kingly tyranny" that
Paine referred to in *Four Letters* are "badges of ancient oppression"—as if the collected weight of the past is at least as burden-
some as monarchical authority itself. In many respects, 18th-century
England, with its chartered towns, might as well be *ancien-régime*
France. A sense of irony is doubly reinforced as Paine insinuates not
only that the Englishman is rendered a foreigner in his own land by
local and national government alike, but also that a French revolution transpiring right in the native land of William I himself can
"regenerate the freedom" (108) that existed prior to his landing on
English shores.

From the wrongs heaped on Englishmen by flawed electoral
representation, charters and corporations, Paine shifts to the
respective powers exercised by Parliament and the King, contrasting them to the decrees of the National Assembly published
in August 1789. Reiterating his conceptualization of a deeply
flawed, irrational government, he claims "Many things in the
English government appear to me the reverse of what they
ought to be, and of what they are said to be" (109): an allegation made by numerous reformers and critics of Burke but
seldom so boldly stated. With his observation that the National
Assembly has wisely excluded placemen and pensioners—a
restriction that would have resonated with the likes of Burgh,
Cartwright, and other reformers, Paine clearly holds these mer-
cenaries responsible for "fleecing their countries by taxes."
Modern historians, however, have estimated that the sums lavished on sinecures and pensions in Britain were not particularly
high by contemporary European standards; in fact, the minimum

figure in France, according to John Brewer, was at least four times higher.[53] Similarly, Paine disapproves of the ease with which Parliament was able to raise taxes: even though the stream of readily available tax revenues provided a sense of security that instilled confidence in creditors, thereby inclining them to grant loans at lower rates than in France.[54] When Parliament is "supposed to hold the national purse in trust for the nation," Paine notes, there is an obvious conflict of interest as "those who vote the supplies are the same persons who receive the supplies" (109).

Nonetheless, the bonds between the king and Parliament—which were largely absent in France—reinforced a sense of trust (*Sinews*, 88–9), illuminating the distinction between a constitutional and personal monarchy. This was a salient distinction, for unlike the British parliament, the thirteen French *parlements* (of which the most important was the Parisian one) were not legislative bodies, but rather local appellate courts. Moreover, the vast majority of the nobles frequently opposed the Crown's measures in order to promote their own class interests, financial and otherwise, all while relying on the language of enlightenment and democracy to protect their privileges. The combination of higher taxes, where annual taxes in Britain were nearly triple that in France per head and loans granted at a lower interest rate may explain why Britain was able to remain solvent despite the fact France enjoyed a gross domestic product that was more than triple the amount, in addition to a near comparable output per capita (within 10%), and an economic growth that exceeded that of population.[55] Indeed, as John Sinclair explained in *The History of Public Revenue*, which was read by Paine himself, it was "hardly possible" for any person who "attentively considers the subject, to deny the beneficial consequences resulting from public credit." Quoting the Bishop of Cloyne, Sinclair noted that not only was credit "the principal advantage which England has over France, and indeed overall all the other States of Europe" but that "it is a mine of gold to this country; and that any measures taken to lessen it, ought to be dreaded."[56] Moreover, he hypothesized that the great military success of Britain "has been entirely owing to the ease with which any sum, however great, could be procured for the public service." It was no less true that according to an unnamed "respectable writer," borrowing allows the "revenue of individuals" to be "necessarily less burdened, than if the supplies were raised within the year" (*History*, 310).

Especially praiseworthy on the part of the National Assembly for Paine was its newfound assumption of the power of war and peace that had long been reserved for the king. That this decision represents the awakening of common sense is implied when he adds "Where else should it reside, but in those who are to pay the expense?" (109). Although Paine may have overestimated the monarch's powers in this respect, given the setbacks encountered by the first two Georges from their respective Parliaments over the choice of wars to be fought,[57] he was nonetheless on target in the case of George III who was later referred to by Lewis Namier as "the first of the borough-mongering, electioneering gentlemen of England."[58] After all, George had notoriously chosen to prolong the war in America after 1780 in the face of increased popular opposition: a fact that proves Paine's point—not to mention Burke's own criticism of George III's apparent influence on the defeat of the Fox–North Coalition to William Pitt the Younger in 1784. Here, too, despite the many criticisms of wars of conquest by Richard Price, Joseph Towers, John Butler, and other reformers, Paine's interpretation of the rationale for war stands out. When claiming that wars are carried out for the convenient purpose of raising taxes (and not vice-versa as widely assumed), Paine observes that mixed governments hold as much potential for despotism as any absolutist monarchy in light of their propensity for war, especially by inciting xenophobia and public frenzy; both forms of despotism ultimately ensure that "revenue is the common object."

Nonetheless, it is equally ironic in the case of Louis XVI that by heeding public opinion and delivering military assistance to America against the advice of Turgot and Necker, both of whom feared that France would be severely crippled by the high costs of the war, France wound up nearly bankrupt. It is also ironic that only a few years after the National Assembly had declared that "the French nation renounces the undertaking of any war with a view to making conquests, and that it will never use its forces against the freedom of any people,"[59] republican France gradually transformed what was initially a defensive war against Austria and Prussia into an increasingly offensive one with its annexation of lands west of the Rhine, Belgium, and south of the Netherlands in 1792. Nor is it any less ironic that the war would not only last far longer than earlier wars of conquest waged by monarchs but also prove much more successful (as if validating Machiavelli and Sidney)—at least until 1812. But all told, it might be argued on a larger scale that the cases of Britain and France vindicate Paine at least partially by illustrating the dangers of capitulation to a monarch's—or that of any leader's—desire for war in the face of significant opposition, whether popular or ministerial.

Not least, Paine's skillful rhetoric and argument in this section deserve attention. If Cartwright identified a strong, self-serving desire amongst ministers and members of Parliament for loaves and fishes in his complaint about "Men who are too ignorant to legislate for a tavern club, or who are voluptuaries and debauchees, or whose whole thoughts are engrossed by the loaves and fishes" (*Take your choice*, xx), Paine further accentuates this very idea when commending the French Constitution for its exclusion of placemen and pensioners. Just as in *Common Sense*, as we have seen, his conversational style, brief sentences, and popular idioms are particularly effective: "What will Mr. Burke place against it? Loaves and fishes. Ah! This government of loaves and fishes has more mischief in it than people have yet reflected on" (108). Likewise, his stream of readily understood similes in his remarks on the arbitrary raising of taxes as seen in the following passage offers a vivid contrast to Cartwright's:

> but in the manner in which an English Parliament is constructed it is like a man being both mortgagor and mortgagee, and in the case of misapplication of trust it is the criminal sitting in judgment upon himself. If those who vote the supplies are the same persons who receive the supplies when voted, and are to account for the expenditure of those supplies to those who voted them, it is themselves accountable to themselves, and the Comedy of Errors concludes with the pantomime of Hush. Neither the Ministerial party nor the Opposition will touch upon this case. The national purse is the common hack which each mounts upon. It is like what the country people call "Ride and tie—you ride a little way, and then I." (109)

The ideas of "a man being both mortgagor and mortgagee" and "criminal sitting in judgment upon himself" are again accessible rather than abstruse, just as references to the "Comedy of Errors" and "pantomime of Hush" and the distinctly plebeian imagery of "ride and tie" create a sense of the burlesque, if not drollery: all are projected as deeply at odds with Burke's image of a magnificent, well-ordered constitution and government.

Likewise, when focusing on British declarations of war, Paine resorts to other clever metaphors as he questions the source of power in declarations of war—whether it rests in the hands of the king or Parliament. Such a right, he notes caustically, might as well literally rest in the crown displayed at the Tower—or with the lions in the menagerie. Here, it is worth glancing back at Paine's words on the monarchy in *A Serious Address*:

> The decline of superstition, the great encrease and general diffusion of knowledge, and the frequent equalities of merit in individuals, would render it impossible to decorate any one man with the idolatrous honors which are expected to be paid to him under the name of a crowned head ... I consider a King in England as something which the military keep to cheat with, in the same manner that wooden gods and conjuror's wands were kept in time of idolatry and superstition; and in proportion as knowledge is circulated through a country ... they will find themselves restless and uneasy under any government so established. This is exactly the case with the people of England. They are not sufficiently ignorant to be governed superstitiously, nor yet wise enough to be governed rationally ... It has been the constant practice of the old world to hold up a government to the people as a mistery, and of consequence to govern them through their ignorance. (*CW*, 290)

In *Rights of Man*, Paine makes the same points—namely, that trust in any kind of monarchy is ridiculous is best and outmoded—but is able to do so more colorfully and concisely by drawing upon the examples of the golden calf and Nebuchadnezzar's golden image.

> In England this right is said to reside in a metaphor shown at the Tower for sixpence or a shilling a piece: so are the lions; and it would be a step nearer to reason to say it resided in them, for any inanimate

> metaphor is no more than a hat or a cap. We can all see the absurdity of worshipping Aaron's molten calf, or Nebuchadnezzar's golden image; but why do men continue to practise themselves the absurdities they despise in others? (110)

These examples immediately convey the backwardness of Britain with the implication that present-day Protestant Britons are just as superstitious as those living in a distant, non-Christian past. He draws upon yet more accessible metaphors in the following paragraphs when comparing war to a harvest for Parliament and the monarch, an act that represents the art of "conquering at home": here, the authorities are reimagined as dangerous domestic invaders, thereby playing up the reformist equation between foreign and domestic threats much more literally. Finally, Paine turns to humor once again when recounting an anecdote related by Benjamin Franklin of a man who claimed his right to become king of America by virtue of his Norman ancestry: this "chivalric character which Mr. Burke so much admires, is certainly much easier to make a bargain with, than a hard-dealing *Dutchman*" (112). Paine's off-handed treatment of the anecdote, already ludicrous in itself, serves to doubly imprint the idea that conquest is neither as grand nor extraordinary as pretended.

It is hardly fortuitous that when Paine arrives at his preliminary consideration of the French Declaration of Rights, he delivers his most stunning indictment of British government, contrasting it with its new French counterpart. The opening lines of the Declaration offer a vision of "the solemn and majestic spectacle of a nation opening its commission ... to establish a Government, a scene so new ... unequalled by anything in the European world" (147). Far from being a destructive force, as implied by Burke, the revolution "rises into a Regeneration of man." In clear reference to the sordid history of conquests, corporations, and corrupt influence, Paine wonders:

> What are the present Governments of Europe but a scene of iniquity and oppression? What is that of England? Do not its own inhabitants say it is a market where every man has his price, and where corruption is common traffic at the expense of a deluded people? No

wonder, then, that the French Revolution is traduced. Had it confined itself merely to the destruction of flagrant despotism perhaps Mr. Burke and some others had been silent. Their cry now is, "It has gone too far"—that is, it has gone too far for them. (147)

Because the revolution "stares corruption in the face," it is anything but astounding that "the venal tribe are all alarmed." Indeed, Paine's assessment proved to be an accurate one as gentry and aristocracy fretted over the influence of *Rights of Man*, leading many to facilitate, if not actively encourage the violent activities of the Church and King mobs and the burning of effigies of Paine across the nation. It is ironic, however, that when denouncing revolutionary brutality in France and articulating concern for the destruction of chateaux and the sale of ecclesiastical property, the hate- and scaremongering driven by hypocritical members of the "establishments" would culminate in the destruction of Dissenting properties across the nation—most notably, Joseph Priestley's house and laboratory—which were barely acknowledged, much less condemned by the authorities.

VI THE ESTABLISHMENTS: ARISTOCRACY, CHURCH, PARLIAMENT, AND THE MONARCHY

A. ARISTOCRACY

With Paine's remarks on aristocracy and hereditary government, we arrive at some of the most radical ideas to be circulated in early 1790s Britain. Although the political heft wielded by the peerage had come increasingly under attack from the collected likes of Wilkes, Murray, Cartwright, and Williams, with social and personal criticism frequently joined to political criticism, Paine was arguably the first writer in Britain since the Interregnum to denounce hereditary titles, privilege, and power so unequivocally. For Paine, the question was no longer merely "Why do such licentious men enjoy disproportionate power"—but rather, why does someone deserve to legislate on the mere basis of birth? Although such a question had already been implied by a certain fictional barber of Seville—Figaro, the brainchild of fellow bridge-designer, supporter of the American revolution, and playwright, Pierre-Augustin Caron de Beaumarchais—it was a relatively new one for political essayists on both sides of the Channel in 1791.[60] The more virulent strain of anti-aristocratic sentiment in *Rights of Man* has led many to wonder how and why Paine's ideas and rhetoric differ so markedly from other contemporary English writings—even if there are no clear answers to such questions as: was Paine aware of the ideas of the Levellers and Diggers via his Quaker upbringing? Was he familiar with Sidney's criticisms of a hereditary monarchy? Or was he inspired by the anti-aristocratic rhetoric and questioning of primogeniture that had materialized simultaneously during the 1770s in America and France?

Although there was no aristocracy *per se* in the American colonies, there was nonetheless a strain of anti-elitist discourse that referred to the wealthiest as "aristocrats," such as when the Marine Anti-Britannic Society of Charleston opposed "aristocratical principles" which they believed would "subvert and destroy every genuine idea of real republicanism."[61] Certainly, just as he defended equal rights for rich and poor in *A Serious Address* and in *Four Letters*, Paine had already remarked that social rank in America was "derived more from qualification than property"—that is, from intrinsic rather than extrinsic qualities in the form of "a sound moral character, amiable manners and firmness in principle"; such an ideology, he believed, would remain intact nationwide until "the origin of families be forgotten, and the proud follies of the old world over-run the simplicity of the new." Then, too, a number of states had already outlawed primogeniture—with Thomas Jefferson being one of the most avid proponents of this eradication. Aware that "an equal division of property is impracticable," Jefferson trusted that legislators could not "invent too many devices for subdividing property" when inequality caused "so much misery to the bulk of mankind"; therefore, a fair distribution of inherited property "is a politic measure and a practicable one."[62] In fact, Jefferson helped pass a law abolishing entails a week after the signing of the Declaration of Independence.[63] Perhaps, too, as Peter Ziesche suggests, Paine may have caught wind of the debate on the proposed order of the Cincinnatus from his friend, Benjamin Franklin, a newly established American veterans organization[64]—even though Paine penned a poem in praise of the Cincinnati.[65] Could he have read a pamphlet written in 1784 by a chief justice of South Carolina, Aedanus Burke (no relation to Edmund Burke), either in America or in England where it was published in 1785? Or Richard Price's *Observations on American Independence* where the latter praised the Articles of Confederation for denying titles of nobility and primogeniture?

> First, granting hereditary honours and titles of nobility. Persons thus distinguished ... are apt to consider themselves as belonging to a higher order of beings, and made for power and government. Their birth and rank necessarily dispose them to be hostile to general liberty ... Let there be honours to encourage merit, but let them die with the men who have earned them. Let them not descend to posterity to foster a spirit of domination ... In a word, let the united states continue for ever what it is now their glory to be—a confederation of states prosperous and happy, without lords, without bishops and without kings.
>
> Secondly, the right of primogeniture. The tendency of this to produce an improper inequality is very obvious. The disposition to raise a name by accumulating property in one branch of a family is a vanity no less unjust and cruel than dangerous to the interest of liberty ....[66]

These observations by Price demonstrate that criticisms of primogeniture were not unheard of in Britain during the early 1780s, even if uncommon.

By contrast, it is helpful to delve into a few assessments of titles and influence found in earlier responses to Burke. If the French, according to Boothby, had long erred by granting "exclusive privileges and oppressive territorial jurisdictions" to the nobility, allowing them to impose "grievances most immediately felt by the people" and effectually preventing any improvement in the condition of the Commons (*Letter*, 27), the opposite was true of Britain; after all, British aristocrats, unlike French nobles, lacked special fiscal immunities and terrestrial rights.[67] Even though Capel Lofft acknowledged that men of landed property were not necessarily wiser or virtuous, he confessed to feeling ill at ease "With the abolition of Titles and armorial Bearings" since they "conveyed no claim to legislative Authority independent of choice." Indeed, he defended titles, finding them useful not only for the inculcation of "domestic sentiments of affection and respect" but also as reminders of "public Virtue, distinguished in Council and in the Field" (*Remarks*, 64). There were some who were still more appreciative of a British aristocracy in comparison to its counterpart in France. John Belsham, for instance, regarded the House of Lords as a requisite balance to "the other branches of the legislature" by "oppos[ing] a firm and permanent barrier to the attacks of regal power" and especially "the encroachments of democratic ambition."[68] In short, for men like Lofft and Belsham, titles and peerages continued to serve a worthy purpose in driving ambition. At the same time, even those who decried the veneration of birth and wealth, such as Wollstonecraft, stopped short of demanding the eradication of titles.

Unlike those writers, however, Paine would call the entire framework into question. Perhaps this is not altogether unexpected on his part since the respect accorded to family lineage and titles, after all, is easily comparable to the veneration of the past for its own sake. If the essay on titles which Paine inserted into *The Pennsylvania Magazine* had already identified a few discrepancies between the perception and reality of the aristocrat, just as the essay on Cincinnatus censures a "body of men" that "decks itself with glory, when it most deserves disgrace,"[69] Part 1 of *Rights of Man* goes substantially further by denying the justice of titles and privileges. Here, Paine can be said to apply a reasoning reminiscent of Nedham and Sidney—not to mention his own in *Common Sense*—as if transferring criticisms on monarchy to the aristocracy. It was an observation that Sidney clearly articulated in his *Discourses on Government*, when he asserted that rarely do the "virtues" required for governing "ever continue in any race of men" (*Discourses*, 94); after all, "where crowns are hereditary, children seldom prove like to their fathers" (*Discourses*, 257). Similarly, when pondering on the absurdity of hereditary judges, mathematicians, and poet-laureates, Paine adds that aristocrats are seldom esteemed for intrinsic merit, but rather for accidents of birth and public perception. Indeed, even with 20th-century research indicating some correlation between genetics and intelligence, there is no certainty that any given generation of a family will inherit the necessary capacities to excel in the family business.

Paine goes further to express impatience with the vagueness of hereditary titles and peerages when observing that the French have abolished titles. What exactly is a duke or a count, anyway? What are their specific duties and how do they contribute to society? In other words, why is it so difficult to assess or describe them in a manner that is analogous to, say, that of a judge or general? As Paine explains, "we think of gravity in the one, and bravery in the other," but there are no distinct ideas that can be associated with the actual title (113). One is thus inclined to wonder "what respect then can be paid to that which describes nothing, and which means nothing?" Ultimately, much of the fuss about titles can be boiled down to public opinion: which he optimistically declares will diminish with increased enlightenment. After all, if knights were held in higher regard during the Middle Ages than dukes at present, isn't it possible for the present worship of titles to vanish with the rise of reason (114)? No less execrable is the practice of primogeniture, a near echo of Mary Wollstonecraft's lament that "hereditary property" and "hereditary honours" impede social progress and domestic stability when younger children are all too frequently "sacrificed to the eldest son," either by being exiled or confined to convents such that "they might not encroach on … the family estate." There is also rich irony in the fact that even as aristocratic government is founded upon the idea of conquest or "the base idea of man having property in man," the principle of exclusivity almost inevitably yields natural degeneration from the practice of inbreeding as nobles frequently married amongst themselves. Not least, it is striking that Sidney and Paine respectively ridicule the worship of monarchy and aristocracy as Quixotic, with Paine taking a dig at Burke's worship of chivalry and the aristocracy.

> I may leave our knight [Filmer], like Don Quixote, fighting against the phantasms as never were …. (*Discourses on Government*, 195)

> As the rhapsody of his imagination, he has discovered a world of windmills, and his sorrows are, that there are no Quixotes to attack them. But

if the age of aristocracy, like that of chivalry, should fall, and they had originally some connection, Mr. Burke, the trumpeter of the Order, may continue his parody to the end, and finish with exclaiming—*Othello's occupation's gone. (Rights of Man)*

Paine not only proceeds to decry its injustice to younger siblings, but its overall impact on legislation given the assumption that little sense of justice can be expected from someone raised with the expectation of inheriting everything by virtue of birth. In short, Paine might be said to provide evidence for Burlamaqui's and Rousseau's criticisms of hereditary aristocracies: Burlamaqui believed that such aristocracies "inspire[d] the nobility with pride," thereby sowing "division, contempt, and jealousy" between the "grandees and the people" (Vol. 2 Part 2 Chap. 1) while Rousseau claimed that hereditary aristocracies were "the worst form of government" (*Social Contract*, Chap. 5) by pointing out the adverse impact of primogeniture on everyone, from the heir's younger siblings to the people at large. If Burke and others applauded the aristocracy for its education and sense of family importance as an advantage for governing, Paine challenges these assumptions. After all, how likely would it be for someone poised to inherit a title and the bulk of the family property to act unselfishly? Most likely, he would treat those he governed like the way he treated his younger siblings.

Not unlike Sieyès who complained about noble "idleness" and claims to "civil and public prerogatives," reminding readers that when any position is assigned to any one person on account of rank, salaries must be paid not only to those who work but to all those of the same caste and "even to entire families who don't work" (Hunt, *Brief Documentary History*, 66), Paine equally criticizes the fact of younger male siblings and relations procuring lucrative positions in government: that is, being "provided for by the public, but at a greater charge" (115). Indeed, in a letter to Thomas Walker dated February 26, 1789, Paine had already reflected on the oddity of two houses of Parliament, neither of which were truly accountable to the people (cited in Keane, 285). It was an assessment shared by a number of Paine's British contemporaries; if the elder Pitt and the Irish MP, Henry Flood, variously referred to the House of Commons as a "parcel of younger

brothers" and a "second rate aristocracy" (Pares, 36, 43), the reformer David Williams rejected its usefulness as a check on the Crown.
The latter believed that since the "aristocratic factions" have
"usurped the government" (*Political Liberty*, 73), it was all but
inevitable that "family influence" would prove as "fatal to liberty as
the influence of the crown" (*Political Liberty*, 44). Such formed a
distinct contrast to the pre-revolutionary Third Estate which was
largely comprised of men with few or no claims to noble ancestry.

Nonetheless, Paine's remarks were probably the most critical
among his contemporaries to undermine the concept of hereditary government so clearly and unequivocally. It is also striking
that unlike Belsham or Boothby who praised the British aristocracy for its apparent lack of special territorial privileges, Paine
bypasses any mention of the disproportionate exemptions from taxes
enjoyed by French nobles or their receipt of feudal tithes from peasants who were already heavily taxed: was Paine, like Burke, simply
ignorant of the extent of these injustices? Or was his antipathy for the
British "body of hereditary legislators" and "a corporation of aristocracy" much stronger, one possibly inflected by the failure of his
petition on behalf of the excise officers? One might even wonder if
this hostility arose from his familiarity with aristocratic political
influence dating from his Thetford days.[70] It is little wonder, then, that
Paine would exult in the first three articles of the Declaration, with its
outright rejection of civil distinctions not grounded on public utility
or national sovereignty, regarding them as "the base of Liberty, as
well individual as national": and that his conclusion, moreover,
would reiterate these articles once more, explaining that "they are
calculated to call forth wisdom and abilities … for the public good,
and not for the emolument or aggrandizement of particular descriptions of men or families" (176).

Many of Paine's arguments in this section are particularly canny
given his choice of images, metaphors, and similes. If Paine was able
to lend the impression that an independent America was natural in
Common Sense, he posits Britain in *Rights of Man* as an unnatural
nation. Just as Burke held that "levellers … only change and pervert
the natural order of things" (100), Paine reverses this idea by presenting the aristocracy and hereditary privilege as unnatural. The
section opens with a paradox as Paine celebrates the abolition of

titles in France for allowing the "peer to be exalted into man" (113). Similarly, he overturns expectations by belittling the lofty title as a "nickname" before proceeding to underscore the theme of aristocratic insignificance in a series of aphoristic paradoxes. At the same time, too, the occasional references to "childish ornaments" and the idea of "ribbands flatter[ing] a childish vanity" in the Cincinnatus essay loom much larger in Paine's paragraphs as he handily subverts the idea of titled dignity altogether.

> It reduces man into the diminutive of man in things which are great, and the counterfeit of women in things which are little. It talks about its fine blue ribbon like a girl, and shows its new garter like a child .... It is, properly, from the elevated mind of France that the folly of titles has fallen. It has outgrown the baby clothes of Count and Duke, and breeched itself in manhood. France has not levelled, it has exalted. It has put down the dwarf, to set up the man. The punyism of a senseless word like Duke, Count or Earl has ceased to please. Even those who possessed them have disowned the gibberish, and as they outgrew the rickets, have despised the rattle.

With his reference to 1 Corinthians 13:11, titled dignity, then, is anything but manly and mature. Just as Sieyès repeatedly refers nobles as "foreign" and "vitiated," branding them as a "malignant tumor that torments and undermines the strength of the body of a sick person" (*Brief Documentary History*, Hunt, 70), Paine similarly classes the aristocracy as deformed, unnatural others. With advances in democracy, "the artificial NOBLE" therefore "shrinks into a dwarf before the NOBLE of nature" (116). Their virtues are purely "imaginary." If titles "are like circles drawn by the magician's wand, to contract the sphere of man's felicity," they also "baffle even the powers of fancy, and are a chimerical nondescript" for "it is common opinion only that makes them anything, or nothing, or worse than nothing" (113–14); a comparison that Bentham would not make until his later, more radical years after 1810. In all, this pervasive sense of the unnatural and supernatural is heightened by connotations of perversion: effeminacy, childishness, dwarfism, disease, and monstrousness. It is a vision that is once more worlds removed from Burke's deferential metaphors for the aristocracy—"a graceful ornament to the civil order" and the "Corinthian capital of polished society." Not surprisingly, the practice of primogeniture is also posited as anything but natural. If Harrington compared the practice to the forced drowning of all but one member of a litter of puppies, Paine would choose a less droll but more grotesque, sensationalized comparison. Not unlike Wollstonecraft who pondered on the "unnatural crimes" traceable to the "desire of perpetuating a name," and chastised the substitution of "natural parental affection" with "overweening, mistaken pride," Paine deprecates primogeniture as downright unnatural, a "law against every other law of nature," which "Nature herself calls for its destruction"; here, he pictures a Goya-esque scene where the "natural parent prepares the unnatural repast" by providing for only one child, with the rest "begotten to be devoured" and "thrown to the cannibal for prey" (114). In sum, it was high time to "exterminate the monster Aristocracy, root and branch."[71]

But if Paine was ready to destroy the monster, contemporary Britons were less so as the populace continued to admire and ogle the titled classes well into the following century—if not beyond. It is telling that while Paine and a mere handful of other radicals were critical of primogeniture and hereditary privilege, regarding this fixation with birth as outmoded, contemporary writers from Gothic novelist Ann Radcliffe to Jane Austen would follow suit not only by demonizing or ridiculing their aristocratic characters (especially those fixated on wealth and lineage) for the faults of pride and prejudice,[72] but also by blaming family friction on the laws of primogeniture: whether in scenarios involving irresponsible heirs, heirs ridding themselves of younger siblings to retain as much property as possible, or conversely, the efforts of envious younger brothers to acquire the titles and estates of the heir. However, it is debatable whether titles and family pedigrees have lost much of their collective allure today, given the popularity of costume dramas centered on landed elites (e.g., *Downton Abbey*) and, ironically enough, endless adaptations of novels by Jane Austen as well as unflagging media coverage in European newspapers and glossies alike of races, balls, and charity events attended by the titled and pedigreed. Even 21st-century America, as we will see in the Conclusion, has not remained immune from this phenomenon. Here, too, regardless of upbringing and education, there is little collective resistance to the idea of political dynasties while universities and the corporate world have adhered more closely to a Burkean veneration for tradition, by displaying few qualms about accepting or hiring the offspring of wealthy alumni or celebrities and other elites—as if forgetting Paine's ridicule of "hereditary judges, mathematicians, and poet laureates."[73] It is similarly ironic that despite the skepticism displayed by the Founding Fathers for hereditary office, (notwithstanding the election of John Quincy Adams), America has witnessed the rise of a Bush, Clinton, and Kennedy dynasties over the last century.[74] All told, the U.S. and Britain seem to have preferred the consensus of John Adams in his *Defence of the Constitutions*:

> The children of illustrious families have generally greater advantages of education, and earlier opportunities to be acquainted with public characters, and informed of public affairs, than those of meaner ones, or even than those in middle life; and what is more than all, an habitual national veneration for their names, and the characters of their ancestors described in history, or coming down by tradition, removes them farther from vulgar jealousy and popular envy, and secures them in some degree the favor, the affection, and respect of the public.[75]

Nonetheless, it is important to remark that despite the prevalence of this idea, it is one that continues to encounter considerable criticism as members of the public occasionally question the justice of legacy admissions and political nepotism today.

B CHURCH

From aristocratic privilege, Paine shifts to the Church, challenging the privileges affixed to the state church. Rather than broaching the broader subject of religious toleration, he begins with the disparities in salary amongst the highest and lowest ranks in the Anglican clergy, as if marking a transition from the subject of the aristocratic might and wealth to unwarranted civic privileges within the church.[76] Not unlike James Murray in *Sermons to Asses*, Paine draws attention to the marked difference in compensation for a parish priest earning 30 or 40 pounds a year and a bishop earning 250 times as much, commending the French for shrinking the salary gap to a multiple of forty since it is immediately apparent to "every man's sense of justice"; it is an inequity that calls "aloud for a constitution" particularly as the bishops desire to "prevent any regulation of income taking place between those of ten thousand pounds a year and the parish priest." Not unexpectedly either, Paine defends the abolition of the tithe as demanded by the church in *ancien-régime* France: yet another boon that served to enrich wealthy ecclesiastics at the expense of ordinary farmers.

If the issue of religious toleration is of much wider scope than that of economic disparity within its ranks, the essential problem of inequity is no less glaring. After all, why should civic or political privileges belong exclusively to any one family lineage or sect? Paine goes well beyond not only those who shared Burke's distaste for the disestablishment of the church in France, but also those who disagreed with Burke. Here, the question is no longer limited to the extent to which religious liberty and civic rights should be granted to Protestants in Catholic France or Catholics and Protestant Dissenters in Anglican Britain but is a much larger one: namely, if the concept of "toleration" is not entirely demeaning in itself. Since any restraint on the liberty of thought constitutes despotism, whether in the shape of active persecution or the more thinly disguised form of civil discrimination, legislation that attempts to prescribe the limits of religious toleration can only be intrinsically flawed. Again, as in his discussion of the rights of man, Paine proposes a clearer, more fundamental approach to the idea of worship—one that easily supersedes even the generous bounds of contemporary English Dissenting writings, not to mention Voltaire's *Treatise on Toleration* (1763), the *Edict of Toleration* (1787), and perhaps even the actual *Declaration of Rights* (1789). The ultimate question boils down to whom and what exactly is man worshipping?

> But Toleration may be viewed in a much stronger light. Man worships not himself, but his Maker ... In this case, therefore, we must necessarily have the associated idea of two things; the mortal who renders the worship, and the IMMORTAL BEING who is worshipped.

> Toleration, therefore, places itself, not between man and man, nor
> between church and church, nor between one denomination of reli-
> gion and another, but between God and man; between the being who
> worships, and the BEING who is worshipped .... (118)

Since God is the sole arbiter of worship, "there is no such thing as a religion that is wrong"; to assume so is both "presumptuous and blasphemous." Indeed, Paine was irked by the article on religion in the French Declaration of Rights (1791) which stipulated that "No man ought to be molested on account of his opinions, not even on account of his religious opinions, provided his avowal of them does not disturb the public order established by the law" (144). Such a qualification detracted "from the divine dignity of religion" (146): a view that was seconded by certain members of the National Assembly, who regarded it as a victory for the conservatives (Tackett, 184). The fact that it took at least two years from the Declaration to grant full liberties to Protestants and Jews in France could be said to vindicate his concerns.

The true motivation behind religious discrimination, according to Paine, is the collected desire of the state church and government to acquire the fullest extent of power and influence: an alliance that Burke fully sanctioned in *Reflections* and for which he was scolded by a number of his respondents. Although Paine overlooks the origins and development of this collusion—perhaps because this subject had remained in the public eye over the course of the 1770s and '80s during the general movement to repeal the Test and Corporation Acts—he nonetheless reminds his readers that "all religions are in their nature kind and benign" (119) until monarchs and their governments variously co-opted the church. In short, all persecutions are alike in spirit, regardless of ideas, punishments, or disabilities: the Spanish Inquisition, the Smithfield burnings, the hounding of Quakers and other Protestant Dissenters collectively exemplify state-supported bigotry. These varying forms of discrimination in Europe, if not the world, can be contrasted to the relative lack thereof in late 18th-century America, where "a catholic priest is a good citizen, a good character, and a good neighbour; an episcopalian minister is of the same description" (120). But the impact of persecution is not limited to the victims alone; nations too can suffer indirectly when their economies are deprived of the skills possessed by the persecuted. Here, Paine mentions the relocation in silk manufacturing from France to England after the revocation of the edict of Nantes, as well as the more recent shift in manufacturing from the chartered towns of England where test laws were more stringently enforced to the free cities of Manchester, Birmingham, and Sheffield; given such, he warns, it is only a matter of time before English Dissenting cotton mill owners depart for France.

Yet even if many of Paine's observations on church establishments and religious toleration were not particularly novel in 1791, his arguments are rendered far more compelling through his choice of analogies and metaphors. One might begin by glancing at Boothby's discussion of income disparity in the Church:

> The ecclesiastical courts are a crying oppression. The miserable and inadequate provision made for the major part of the parochial clergy is also a serious grievance ... the respectable clergyman with a numerous family does the duty of a most extensive parish for sixty pounds a year, while from the same parish the Dean of Lincoln receives a thousand per annum for doing nothing at all. (*Letter to Burke*, 48–9)

Paine's remarks are considerably more pointed as he reinterprets Burke's words, applying the latter's explanation on income parity between nobles and clergymen to income disparity between the highest and lowest ranking clergymen:

> He [Burke] says: "That the people of England can see without pain or grudging, an archbishop precede a duke; they can see a Bishop of Durham, or a Bishop of Winchester in possession of £10,000 a-year; and cannot see why it is in worse hands than estates to a like amount, in the hands of this earl or that squire."
>
> ... Mr. Burke has not put the case right. The comparison is out of order ... It ought to be put between the bishop and the curate, and then it will stand thus—"The people of England can see without pain or grudging, a Bishop of Durham, or a Bishop of Winchester, in possession of ten thousand pounds a-year, and a curate on thirty or forty

pounds a-year, or less." No, sir, they certainly do not see those things without great pain or grudging. It is a case that applies itself to every man's sense of justice, and is one among many that calls aloud for a constitution. (117)

Much like his earlier criticisms of tradition and aristocracy, he deploys imagery that sharply undermines the Burkean notion of stability and security. If the church establishment is anything but holy or natural, his astute acknowledgement that toleration and intolerance are "despotisms" is made all the more effective by his shrewd populist and anti-Catholic analogies to the pope, burnings, and indulgences:

Toleration is not the opposite of Intolerance, but is the counterfeit of it. Both are despotisms. The one assumes to itself the right of with-holding Liberty of Conscience, and the other of granting it. The one is the Pope armed with fire and faggot, and the other is the Pope selling or granting indulgences. The former is church and state, and the latter is church and traffic. (118)

When Protestant Dissenters are "tolerated" in England or Catholics in Ireland, they might be assumed to enjoy the privilege of worship without molestation; yet, the supposed freedom is only partial at best when they lack the full range of civil and political rights enjoyed by those belonging to the established churches in their respective nations. Paine goes so far as to claim that any nation that imposes a state creed is not only bigoted, but "blasphemous" for infringing on God's prerogative.

At least as striking too is Paine's rhetoric when he exhorts governments to abolish religious persecution with a heightened rhetoric that turns the tables on the temporal powers-that-be. Again, this might be compared with Boothby's treatment of man's presumptuousness whereby "No man or body of men under any pretence whatsoever can assume the power of governing or forcing the belief, the thoughts, the reason of others without the most impious and foolish arrogance of God" (*Letter to Burke*, 45). Paine's is much more forceful, as if he were delivering divine judgment:

> Who then art thou, vain dust and ashes! by whatever name thou art
> called, whether a King, a Bishop, a Church, or a State, a Parliament, or
> anything else, that obtrudest thine insignificance between the soul of
> man and its Maker? Mind thine own concerns. If he believes not as
> thou believest, it is a proof that thou believest not as he believes, and
> there is no earthly power can determine between you. (118)

The absurdity of intolerance is equally amplified by Paine's apt
and vivid comparison between the varying modes of worship and
gifts offered at harvest. After all, if a bishop or archbishop will
"not refuse a tithe-sheaf of wheat because it is not a cock of hay,"
why should he deny God the right to "receive the varied tithes of
man's devotion?" (119) Finally, not least remarkable is Paine's
scathing metaphor for the state-sanctioned church—"a sort of
mule-animal, capable only of destroying, and not of breeding
up": a metaphor which recurs in his description of the Spanish
inquisition as the upshot of "this mule-animal," a "heterogeneous
production" and a "strange animal," that is "engendered between
the church and the state" (119). This emphasis on its infertility and
unnaturalness serves—much like his emphasis on the worship of the
dead and a monstrous, deformed aristocracy—as a commentary on
a government that acts "out of nature."

C KING AND COMMONS

If Paine questions the utility of the aristocracy and church alike,
he spares as little adulation for the King and Commons. Circling
back to the Conquest motif, he contrasts the origins of the newly
created National Constituent Assembly in France with those of
the British House of Commons: for Paine, the latter bears an
ignominious history, having arisen as a boon granted by the successors of William I. Such an interpretation was one that stood
dramatically at odds with the idealistic vision created by reformers, many of whom revered Parliament as an acceptable, if
imperfect resurrection of the Saxon witagemots. Continuing his
critique of the Conquest and his theme of unnaturalness, Paine
suggests that it is William I who "turn[ed] everything upside
down" by making the King the head of the nation (122). Given

the monarchical origins of Parliament, it is anything but remarkable that the latter grew subservient to the Crown, evident not
only in the king's ostensibly proprietary reference to Parliament
as "*my* Parliament," but also in the extreme deference proffered
by Parliament to the king: one glaringly obvious in the infamous
parliamentary declaration of 1688 that "we do most humbly and
faithfully submit ourselves, our heir and posterities for ever."
Such an observation was not unlike that of Marat's claim that the
king's person and prerogative almost always precedes "the religion, the laws, and liberty of the kingdom" (*Chains of Slavery*,
197). According to Paine, these expressions of obsequiousness are

> neither of foreign extraction, nor naturally of English production, their
> origin must be sought for elsewhere, and that origin is the Norman
> Conquest. They are evidently of the vassalage class of manners, and
> emphatically mark the prostrate distance that exists in no other con-
> dition of men than between the conqueror and the conquered ...
> Submission is wholly a vassalage term, repugnant to the dignity of
> freedom, and an echo of the language used at the Conquest. (123)

Note again Paine's emphasis on the un-Englishness and the backwardness of English government in his critique. In hopes that it
will not be long before the significance of Revolution of 1688,
"already on the wane," ceases to be so excessively valued, Paine
takes another tentative step towards republicanism. By comparing
Burke's courtiers to actors, Paine links Burke's government to the
theater once more; both types of men rely on little more than
artifice, deriving "their living by a show," milking it for maximum
profit. If Paine refrains from openly avowing the superiority of a
republic, perhaps in deference to the new limited monarchy of
Louis XVI, he nonetheless insinuates it by comparing the differing
grounds for their disrespect towards the monarchy: ultimately, the
courtier makes less of a fuss about monarchy than the republican
in his knowledge that it is "nothing." This simple mockery allows
Paine to condemn monarchy without having to provide a lengthy
explanation and thereby stick out his neck too far—even as Louis
was already balking at the August decrees of August 1789, in his
determination that he would "never allow my clergy and my

nobility to be stripped of their assets."[77] Conversely, the existence of a monarchy necessarily minimizes any differences between ministerial and opposition parties in Parliament since both serve only to unite in "keeping up the common mystery" (124).

If the relationship between Parliament and the King epitomizes a flawed government carved out from an ignominious Conquest, that between the National Constituent Assembly and Louis XVI establishes a new ideal that eschews the flaws and burdens which clog monarchies like Britain. Again, Paine pinpoints the differences in such a way as to pit the new, "natural" French government against an "unnatural" British constitution; the French have elevated the law before the king—"La Loi, Le Roi"—so that the relationship between Parliament and the King appears "upside down" and "unnatural" by comparison. Here, the word "natural" is repeated several times: the very fact that the National Assembly does not request permission for the liberty of speech from the king, as is customary in the House of Commons, conveys a "constitutional dignity" because speech is in fact "one of the natural rights of man" (122). Since "artifice" has been replaced by a knowledge of the "proper character of men," the French constitution itself can thus be said to abide by "the natural order of things"—unlike the false dichotomy projected by the ministerial and opposition parties in Britain. Nonetheless, it is somewhat curious that despite Paine's lack of fluency in French, he sees fit to praise the rhetoric deployed by the National Assembly as "free, bold, and manly," commending its "right angled character of men" for spurning "the gaping vacuity of vulgar ignorance" and "sycophantic insignificance" (123). It would only be a matter of time until Louis XVI began to feel progressively hampered by the diminished authority and prerogatives accorded to him, particularly since he was only permitted a suspensive veto—one which was to be overridden at any event in constitutional and financial matters.

Here, it is worth examining some of Paine's claims more closely: to what extent was Parliament effectually governed by the King? Although Paine's remarks would appear to be contradicted by Parliament's upper hand during the reigns of Georges I and II, as mentioned earlier, they are not inaccurate where the first two decades of George III's reign are concerned.[78] Certainly, during the 1760s and '70s, George III was determined to exercise a greater degree of influence than his predecessors in the choice of a prime minister; in fact, the young king's choice of the Earl of Bute in 1762 proved controversial partly because George II was frequently humiliated in his attempts to select his own ministers (Pares, 63). By contrast, as George III procured a larger share of executive power through the 1770s, complaints began to materialize, culminating in John Dunning's famous resolution of February 1780, "the influence of the crown has increased, is increasing, and ought to be diminished." Moreover, as late as 1784, George III had threatened members in the House of Lords, warning them that anyone who voted for Burke's East India Bill would earn his enmity. But it is also worth noting that, as recent historians have argued, the king's interactions with members of Parliament—whether by means of influence or bribery—may actually have signaled a tacit acknowledgment of the latter's power; the very fact that Parliament did not exist merely to register the king's decrees and accede to new taxes as in France, but instead, formed a cohesive constitutional settlement and stable aristocratic democracy most likely facilitated the creation of a National Debt and public credit after 1694. Indeed, the French king's notorious capacity to repudiate debts, not to mention the lack of a viable parliamentary and constitutional government,[79] helped foster a collective impression of financial instability, thereby hindering the nation from borrowing at the low rates enjoyed by the British and Dutch. Without a central treasury or publicly supported bank, credit could not be so easily procured—thereby resulting in interest rates that were nearly twice as much enjoyed by the British (Bien, 40); it was as such that by 1788, 51% of national income was absorbed by the interest on debt (Vovelle, 76).

VII THE NATIONAL ASSEMBLY

At first glance, it may appear puzzling to find Paine delivering an account of the convocation of the Estates-General and the subsequent creation of the National Assembly in June 1789 so many paragraphs and pages after his initial description of the events surrounding the fall of the Bastille. Did he assume that the examination of a new, more democratically-oriented government could only be better appreciated in light of an overall consideration of natural rights and the inherent flaws of the establishments? Although it is initially tempting to gloss over Paine's brief narrative of the years leading up to the convocation of the Estates General, given the multitude of accounts since 1789, such an oversight can cloud our understanding of the ideas and events which informed *Rights of Man*—and by extension, the overall achievement of Part 1.[80] By ignoring them, we fail to grasp just how Paine crossed the political bridge, so to speak, from Whiggish reform to popular radicalism as noted by Gregory Claeys, J.G.A. Pocock, and James Epstein.[81] It is telling, for instance, that Paine's criticisms of Louis XIV and XV are relatively light in comparison with those invoked by other British reformers and radicals: rather than dwell on the numerous wars of aggression waged by Louis XIV or the military and financial losses accumulated under his successor, Paine focuses more on popular adulation of the monarchy. He finds it infinitely more troubling that the people had "lost all sense of their own dignity," in contemplating that of their "Grand Monarch" prior to suffering a "lethargy" under his successor, Louis XV (125). Paine thus implies that danger is more likely to arise from the populace's ignorance or toleration of kingly errors than from the king's actions: a point that harks back to his commentary on public esteem of titles. The true danger, as it were, lies in uncritical admiration of the powers that be. Even if it is possible that Paine may have not been entirely cognizant of Louis XV's distinct lack of popularity amongst his subjects—one that bordered closely on general detestation—it is striking that he deems plebeian admiration far more damaging.

But perhaps more interesting here is Paine's muted assessment of the possible influence of Montesquieu, Voltaire, Rousseau, Raynal, Quesnay, and Turgot despite the general brevity of his observations. Here, it is worth returning to Burke's assessment of Rousseau, Voltaire, and the French enlightenment in *Reflections*:

> We are not the converts of Rousseau; we are not the disciples of Voltaire; Helvetius has made no progress amongst us. Atheists are not our preachers; madmen are not our lawgivers. We know that *we* have made

no discoveries, and we think that no discoveries are to be made, in morality; nor many in the great principles of government, nor in the ideas of liberty, which were understood long before we were born.

In short, they have gone too far in their own nation but have fortunately failed to corrupt Britons, given their lack of interest in new-fangled ideas. Not surprisingly, Paine arrives at a very different conclusion. Damning Montesquieu, Voltaire, Rousseau, Raynal, and Turgot with faint praise, he slights Voltaire for cherishing less than altruistic motives, while dismissing Rousseau and Raynal for their failure to address the recovery of liberty. Turgot and the Physiocrats, in turn, are viewed as half-hearted economists more interested in "the administration of the government rather than the government itself" (127).

More than two hundred years later, we can't help but wonder if Paine did not unduly underestimate the influence of Voltaire, Montesquieu, Rousseau, and Turgot. There is no question, for instance, that regardless of Voltaire's satiric turn of mind, his decades-long criticisms of Catholic avarice and persecution paved the way for the toleration of Protestants and Jews shortly before and after the fall of the Bastille. Nor is there any question that the ideas of Rousseau and Montesquieu eventually contributed to the accentuation on general sovereignty during the drafting of the Declaration of Rights and the temporary overthrow of aristocratic government; indeed, Rousseau's conceptualization of general sovereignty would also play a significant role in the shaping of Paine's ideas as stated in the conclusion to Part 1: namely, that "Sovereignty, as a matter of right, appertains to the Nation only, and not to any individual" and "Every citizen is a member of the Sovereignty, and, as such, can acknowledge no personal subjection" (175). For just as Rousseau had execrated a system where "children should command old men, fools wise men, and that the privileged few should gorge themselves with superfluities, while the starving multitude are in want of the bare necessities of life" (*Discourse on Inequality*), Montesquieu—not unlike Harrington—had warned of the dangers posed by aristocratic states, specifically, "extreme inequality between those who govern and those who are governed," while demanding the abolition of primogeniture and stipulating that nobles should have little role in levying taxes since they were liable to abuse their power (Book 5, Chap. 8). Nor can it be denied that Turgot was at least several steps ahead of many political thinkers when he advocated a unicameral legislature—much like Paine—in addition to paving the way for the end of feudal privileges. The Six Edicts issued by Turgot in 1776 which included demands for a free trade of grain and the replacement of the corvée (i.e., peasant labor on road construction) by taxes on land would come to fruition in August 1789 with the formal eradication of feudalism. Noting that a tax "imposed by force upon the weak" would be comparable to a "government founded only on the right of conquest,"[82] Turgot stigmatized nobles as

> the common enemy of the society; the strongest would defend themselves as they were able, the weak would succumb and be wiped out. ... That is not the idea one has of a paternal government, based on a national constitution whereby the monarch is raised above all in order to assure the welfare of all ....

> If the question is considered from the humanitarian side, it is extremely difficult to congratulate one's self upon being exempt from taxes, as a nobleman, when one sees them snatched from the copper pot of the peasant.

Not surprisingly, Turgot's proposals were initially greeted with horror by the *parlements*, leading to his replacement by Necker in 1781, while subsequent attempts to renew them by Calonne and Brienne in 1787 and 1788, as we have seen, fared no better. Regardless of their rejection or general lack of favor, it is difficult to accept Paine's claims that Turgot's ideas were centered merely on "the administration of the government rather than the government itself."

Nonetheless, it is also possible to see why Paine underestimated their collective influence: for the fact is that few of these writers pushed the issue of rights of men as vigorously as members of the Third Estate ultimately did in 1789. For instance, the pragmatic strain in Voltaire's *Treatise on Toleration*, inspired by the case of the Protestant merchant Jean Calas, articulates a position that falls short of the ideals upheld by such men as Price and Priestley with its less than complete acceptance of civil liberties for Protestants and other religious minorities. Similarly, despite Montesquieu's general awareness of the inequities and abuses practiced by the aristocracy, particularly "extreme inequality between those who govern and those who are governed" such that "laws should prevent or check result from these two inequalities" (Book V, Chap. 8), there is little evidence that he sought to abolish titled distinctions but rather continued to uphold the protection of their political interests as he recommended that they form an upper house in legislation not unlike the House of Lords, retaining a "right to check the enterprises of the people, as the people have the right to check theirs" (Book 11, Chap. 6). Much the same can be said for Turgot who defended titled distinctions even as he checked their privileges and called for a unicameral legislature. In short, while supportive of reform, few were prepared to take the plunge into radicalism by expunging every source of injustice.

At the same time, even as Paine's lofty estimation of the American revolution invites some degree of skepticism given his own personal activism and his sentiments for his newly adopted nation, his verdict remains largely correct. If anything, it might even be contended that just as the writings of Voltaire, Rousseau, Montesquieu, Turgot served to enhance the image of America, Benjamin Franklin played an even larger role in his savvy cultivation of the simple Rousseauvian man of nature to the hilt, particularly when he vouched for the success of Turgot's physiocratic ideals in the colonies; as Condorcet explained, "Men whom the reading of philosophic books had secretly converted to the love of liberty because enthusiastic over the liberty of a foreign people while they waited for the moment when they could recover their own."[83] Indeed, while Americans presented their colonies as a vindication of French enlightenment ideals in practice, French soldiers in America would in turn burnish the overall impression of American egalitarianism with their eyewitness accounts.

But nowhere is Paine's veneration for the American revolution more apparent than in his representation of the conflict among king's ministers, Lafayette, the *parlement* (referred to as Parliament by Paine),[84] and the Assembly of Notables, as well as the ensuing battles during the meetings of the National Assembly. Not unlike his earlier delineation of the fall of the Bastille, Paine continues to recreate the contours of the American revolution, highlighting a ministry bent on raising taxes and its various opponents including the *parlement* of Paris, the newly convoked Third Estate, and not least, Lafayette, the presiding hero. Paine's interpretation, however, is not free of errors as it reveals his yet less than complete comprehension of the forces at work in France. Although a considerable portion of the populace had long supported the *parlement* of Paris as a defender of their rights against monarchical power, what is glossed over in Paine's narrative is the nature of the protest over new taxes. In reality, the battle waged by the Assembly of Notables and the *parlement* against the ministry arose not only from a stamp tax, but as we have seen, the nobility's opposition to new taxes imposed upon land as proposed severally by Turgot, Necker, Calonne, and Brienne, with some going so far as to denounce the rationale for taxes as "class warfare." Even more ironically, it was the perceived spendthrift, Calonne, who defended the taxes on the nobility with populist rhetoric, demanding greater parity in taxation as he announced "Privileges will be sacrificed! Yes justice desires it, necessity demands it." It was a call that would precipitate a reactionary argument on the part of the *parlement* for the preservation of class distinctions even as members professed some concern for common interests.[85] Here, it is also somewhat ironic that Lafayette was initially anything but the daring defender of popular rights as presented by Paine in *Rights of Man*. The young marquis' first response to the call for provincial assemblies in 1787 was certainly less broadminded than Calonne's proposed idea of permitting membership and offices to all eligible voters; Lafayette was also to brush aside the latter's demand for the ending of noble tax privileges as "rabble-rousing."[86] Moreover, when it was announced in March 1787 that the Estates-General was the only entity that could levy new taxes, Lafayette remained silent; it was not until May, that the contentious exchange between Lafayette and d'Artois over the calling of the three Estates took place.[87] Finally, Louis XVI is similarly represented as a stalwart supporter of the Third Estate when in reality he was far more hesitant, sanctioning the propositions of the most conservative nobles and agreeing that their privileges must be retained while calling for votes by order on June 23, 1789.

Equally striking is what is left out in Paine's brief credit to Marie Antoinette. While taking notice of her popularization of all things American, he refrains from commenting on her reputation, much of it highly negative. Widely mocked by the French as "Madame Deficit," she was hardly less censured by Thomas Jefferson in his letters to Madison (June 1789) and by critics of Burke. Was this reticence an effort on Paine's part to exculpate her for promoting America more than a decade earlier—not unlike his praise for her husband? Or was Paine simply unaware of the prevailing perception that her notorious spending on clothes and entertainment had bankrupted the nation, not to mention the damaging repercussions of the scandal surrounding the Diamond Necklace Affair in 1786 which continued to reverberate? Equally surprising in this context is Paine's overall oversight of the numerous popular pamphlets that castigated the royal court, the clergy, and nobles, much of which injected a dose of populist anti-aristocratic criticism, adding fire to the circulation of ideas promulgated by the philosophes. For instance, there is no mention of Sieyès highly influential pamphlet, "What is the Third Estate?" a work which Jefferson had likened to *Common Sense* as one "which had electrified that country" in terms of popularity and appeal; indeed, it can be said to recombine the ideas of Rousseau, Montesquieu, and Turgot while introducing a more militant strain of class consciousness in much the same way that *Common Sense* had radicalized Locke and later British reformers. Did Paine's estimation for the American revolution blind him from acknowledging these phenomena?

Yet, even as Paine misconstrued the nature of the conflict between Louis XVI and the *parlement*, he would lend a dramatic quality to the conflict between the Second and Third Estates by showing how liberals in the Second and Third estates challenged conservatives. In fact, the very intensity of the conflicts between conservatives and liberals, on top of those between nobles and commoners, may explain not only why Paine adopted a much harsher tone on the aristocracy in *Rights of Man* than in his earlier writings, but also why he called for the eradication of titles and privileges. The friction that began with the pushback against Comte d'Artois' privileging of monarchical power and the notion of an aristocratic "constitution" and "feudal rights" would result in a struggle for a doubling of the number of deputies in the Third Estate before eventually yielding a unification of the First, Second, and Third Estates: even as conservative nobles and high ranking clergy fought changes to the 1614 procedures tooth and nail during the winter and spring of 1789. Here, let's examine Paine's words on the attitudes displayed by the Second Estate:

> On the other hand, the Nation disowned knowing anything of them but as citizens, and was determined to shut out all such up-start pretensions. The more aristocracy appeared, the more it was despised; there was a visible imbecility and want of intellects in the majority ... while it affected to be more than citizen, was less than man ... This is the general character of aristocracy, or what are called Nobles or Nobility, or rather No-ability, in all countries. (139)

That Paine may not have been exaggerating is reinforced by the observations of Madame de Staël. She noted a "certain aristocratic self-complacency, that can hardly be imagined ... a mixture of frivolity of manners and pedantry of opinion; and all this combined with an utter disdain for ideas and intelligence" (qtd. in Tackett, 136).[88] As modern historians have noted, the Third Estate was far more willing than the Second Estate to urge change—while the latter were more likely to demand a broad retention of the seigneurial system (Tackett, 99–109), thereby intensifying the fault lines; in fact, anti-noble sentiment quickly emerged as the most prevalent sentiment amongst deputies of generally divergent views.[89] If Lafayette himself had referred to the largely noble Assembly of Notables as "the not-ables," the nobility was denigrated by others as "a body of parasites living off the labors of the people," a "monstrous feudal aristocracy," and a "political monstrosity" (Tackett, 107–10): as such, it may have not been entirely fortuitous that Paine referred to the aristocracy at large as a "monster" and the "no-ability."

VIII MISCELLANEOUS CHAPTER AND CONCLUSION

Thus far, we have seen that Paine was not by any means the first to discover the inefficiencies and problems entailed by town charters, inadequate political representation, aristocratic government, religious toleration, and monarchical influence in Parliament. Nor in a longer historical context were his claims for equal rights that dated back to the creation of Man and republican governments. Yet, what distinguishes *Rights of Man*, Part 1 not only from other replies to Burke, but from other reformist and radical writings was a thoroughgoing, if not broadly comprehensive reorientation of government around the basic concepts of rights: a reorientation that allowed Paine to forcefully challenge the sources of civil, economic, and political inequality across Britain. It is as such that he criticized not only game laws, chartered towns, and inadequate representation, but also hereditary government. To a greater extent than other writers, Paine would also associate hereditary governments with the past and representative governments with the present and future. Only with the total eradication of the vestiges left by the Norman Conquest—whether privileges of birth, sect, or town—could Britain finally become an egalitarian land of liberty.

In short, it is as if Paine had begun to gather and recombine the ancient and early modern ideas of rights that had variously surfaced through the centuries, from Gratian and Ockham through the uprisings of 1381, 1549, the Civil War, and Interregnum through the American revolution and British reform movements, to convey a powerful new message all while rebutting Burke's "*established* church, an *established monarchy*, an *established* aristocracy, and an *established democracy*" and veneration for the past. Although Paine, as we have seen, had not quite accepted the idea of universal suffrage yet or thoroughly repudiated the idea of monarchical government in Europe, he had already begun to revise his earlier idea of an opposition between society and government as articulated in *Common Sense*. What he was just discovering from the American and French revolutions was the Rousseauvian possibility that society and government did not have to remain opposed to one another; that such an opposition was instead a symptom of corruption deriving from monarchical, conquest-based governments. Not unlike the Levellers, Diggers, Nedham, Harrington, and Sidney, Paine came to acknowledge that governments needed to do a better job of administering to the general needs and concerns of society: and that in England, a government that embraced commonalty with a dose of common sense was to be preferred to a government still founded on the prototype established by William the Conqueror. If *Rights of Man*, Part 1 can be read as a bridge of sorts from Whiggism to popular radicalism, the Miscellaneous Chapter and Conclusion can in turn be viewed as the midpoint of that bridge with Paine arriving at a new analysis of monarchical government that is far bolder than the earlier sections of Part 1.

Here, as in earlier pages of Part 1, he reiterates his observation that hereditary government is anything but a "contrivance of wisdom," being ultimately a form of usurpation that entails slavery on future generations in all but name. The present argument harks back to that advanced in his *Four Letters on Interesting Subjects* (1778) where he fulminates against the charter granted by Charles II to William Penn, appointing the latter and his heirs the "perpetual and absolute" governors of Pennsylvania:

> Where there are no people, there can be no government; it is the people that constitute the government; and to give away a government is giving away the people, in the same manner that giving the proprietaryship was giving the soil. What right could Charles the Second, a deceased tyrant of the last century, have to appoint a governor for the present generation, or declare that the heirs of William Penn should be the Lords and Masters of persons to be born a thousand years hence?

The subjects of a monarchy are hardly any more different: when a family is established as a monarch, future generations are naturally precluded from making any choice of a monarch. As such, if government is supposed to be a "contrivance of human wisdom," according to Burke, what guarantees of wisdom can a monarchical or mixed government possibly offer? Can everyone descended from one particular line be a Solomon in his or her own right? Similarly, Paine suggests, not all men are going to be sufficiently wise or even mentally fit for the task of governing: a judgment that was certainly borne out by George III's episodes of insanity after 1788 as well as Louis XVI's shyness and indecisiveness when he was forced to ascend the throne after the death of his older brother. If anything, it could even be argued that the hapless Louis XVI was the quintessential victim of hereditary government as Paine's attempt to rescue him from the guillotine in 1793 failed narrowly. Paradoxically, then, monarchies are not only despotisms at large, but also nominal forms of slavery.

Arguably more problematic is the issue of monarchical duty and its significance, not to mention the costs involved. In certain respects, it is ironic yet strangely fitting to locate affinities between Burke's and Paine's opinions on Pitt's handling of the Regency crisis of 1788 when George III suffered his first bout of insanity. For just as Burke and the Opposition decried the Parliamentary act of affixing the royal seal to the bill as a virtual mark of George III's approval, referring to the procedure as a "phantom," Paine similarly construes the action as implied evidence of the monarchy being little more than a fiction, observing that if "Royal Authority is a Great Seal, it consequently is in itself nothing" (163). Interestingly enough, this sense of a virtual monarchy also became glaringly obvious to Louis XVI, albeit for different reasons, as he discerned that his role in the new constitutional monarchy was reduced to that of a ceremonial figurehead, having lost the bulk of his powers and prerogatives. In this context, it is hardly fortuitous that Paine addresses the subject of the extraordinary costs involved in the maintenance of a monarchy. Why should so much of the nation's wealth be squandered on a royal court and national policies dictated by a king's personal interests? That Paine was not inaccurate at all in his assessment is proven by the fact that the rising costs of war contributed substantially to the sharp rise in taxation, especially on consumables. Moreover, since wars and battles occupied no less than half of the century, it is not astonishing that a significant portion of tax revenue was spent on maintaining the army, navy, and accumulating interest.[90] It is worth pointing out, however, that when attempting to contrast the relative poverty of England to France, with the hints that the drain on gold and silver could be attributed to George III's siphoning of funds to Hanover,[91] Paine was off the mark since the source for his information on the French economy—namely, Jacques Necker's *Compte Rendu* (1781)—had conveniently omitted the substantial costs involved in the American war: the French economy was far worse than Paine had imagined as it continued to deteriorate with the circulation of *assignats* in 1791. Not least, Paine adds, monarchies entail a bundle of contradictions. It is ironic, after all, that in spite of the contempt for foreigners and despotic governments displayed by the English, monarchs from 1688 have been mostly foreign born. How strange, he muses, "that although the people of England have been in the habit of talking about kings, it is always a Foreign House of kings; hating foreigners, yet governed by them" (152). He ponders on the seeming contradiction of "uniting in the same person the principles of Freedom and the principles of Despotism"; as such, it is ludicrous to have a King of England who is also a German Elector, a man who exemplifies "Arbitrary Power" and "despotism."

If the institution of the monarchy is vexed, the idea of a mixed government is arguably even more so, according to Paine. Claiming the use of the word "Constitution" in Britain to be no more than a "cant word," being "one thing" today, and "something else" tomorrow, he issues an even harsher refutation in the Conclusion, pointing at the lack of accountability amongst the highest members of the government as functions and duties are obfuscated:

> In mixed Governments there is no responsibility: the parts cover each other till responsibility is lost ... When it is laid down as a maxim, that a King can do no wrong, it places him in a state of similar security with that of idiots and persons insane, and responsibility is out of the question with respect to himself. It then descends upon the Minister, who shelters himself under a majority in Parliament, which, by places, pensions, and corruption, he can always command ... In this rotatory motion, responsibility is thrown off from the parts, and from the whole.

> When there is a Part in a Government which can do no wrong, it implies that it does nothing; and is only the machine of another

> power ... as the Cabinet is always a part of the Parliament, and the members justifying in one character what they advise and act in another, a mixed Government becomes a continual enigma; entailing upon a country by the quantity of corruption necessary to solder the parts. (173)

It is worth noting that his discomfort with the blurred and shifting relationships amongst the king, prime minister, cabinet, and Parliament looks forward to Vernon Bogdanor's current observations on those between the prime minister and Parliament which he claims to be constitutionally undefined. Having recourse once again to the idea of Burkean show and artifice, Paine doubts that such a "pantomimical contrivance" can take place in a "well-conditioned republic"; it is an inefficiency that reinforces the idea that the present British government is anything but "a contrivance of human wisdom."

If his contemplation of a republic places him beyond the most radical Whiggish thinkers who dared to imagine a commonwealth or even a republic, as in the case of the Earl of Shelburne, it is Paine's exposition of the uses of wars in monarchical governments that offers a groundbreaking vision of an ideal polity—beginning with the identification of a chasm between "the interest of Governments" and that of nations—that might be said to push him out of Whiggism altogether: even if many had already censured the idea of military conquest (e.g., Burgh, Price). Here, Paine ventures even further by claiming that it is not so much monarchs or even monarchies themselves which are to be blamed, but the fact that such a system relies on a state of war in order to reap revenues for royal and other government expenses. Of course, this was not an entirely new idea since Adam Smith had already hinted at the use of war as a means for raising taxes in *The Wealth of Nations*: "When a nation is already overburdened with taxes, nothing but the necessities of a new war, nothing but either the animosity of national vengeance, or the anxiety for national security, can induce the people to submit, with tolerable patience, to a new tax" (522).[92] But Paine would make this connection much more explicit:

As war is the system of Government on the old construction, the animosity which Nations reciprocally entertain, is nothing more than what the policy of their Governments excites to keep up the spirit of the system. Each Government accuses the other of perfidy, intrigue, and ambition, as a means of heating the imagination of their respective Nations, and incensing them to hostilities. Man is not the enemy of man, but through the medium of a false system of Government. Instead, therefore, of exclaiming against the ambition of Kings, the exclamation should be directed against the principle of such Governments ....

In short, Paine may be said to anticipate the modern notion of the "military industrial complex," variously developed by Daniel Guerin, C. Wright Mills, and most famously by President Dwight Eisenhower in the mid-20th century. Similarly, by reviving (the French) Henry IV's plans for a "European Congress," one with "delegates from several Nations, who were to act as a Court of arbitration in any disputes that might arise between nation and nation" (176), he would also usher in the idea behind the United Nations. Yet, it is ironic, as we will see later, that his assumption on the avoidance of war in republics would be ultimately disproved by American history in which only 29 years were not spent in any battle or war; the fact that the U.S. presently spends more on the military than any other nation and more combined than the thirteen nations ranking just below in expenditure arguably attests more to Alexander Hamilton's view in the sixth Federalist paper that commerce fuels, rather than dampens, the appetite for war.

It is equally important to examine Paine's rhetoric in these chapters. Even if some of the elites sneered at Paine's grammar as Horace Walpole did, others must have winced at his swift, perspicacious observations where he frequently spits Burke's words back in his face: Paine, as Olivia Smith has noted, "had not only to write a political vernacular prose ... but to write in a manner that would refute the political implications of the literary skills represented by Edmund Burke."[93] Not surprisingly, much of what Burke defends is almost always presented by Paine as the exact reverse of all it is supposed to be, beginning with the opening sally. It is Burke, for instance, not the French revolution itself—

which presents a "mob of ideas tumbling over and destroying one another" (149). Paine proceeds to thumb his nose at the latter's already much derided statement of government as a "contrivance of human reason," with "Political reason" frequently operating as a "computing principle; adding—subtracting—multiplying—and dividing, morally, and not metaphysically or mathematically, true moral demonstrations"; such discourse is little more than "learned jargon" (150), designed to fool the masses. Moreover, just as Paine had alluded to the unnaturalness and insubstantiality of the aristocracy and church, he extends his reasoning here, summoning up the chimerical world of fairy tales and pantomimes when questioning the practical uses of monarchy in this powerful passage. Note how he takes Burke's observation on government as a "contrivance of human wisdom," turning it around to suggest that this contrivance is applied purely for disingenuous purposes in its raising of taxes "from a nation under specious pretences":

> But, after all, what is this metaphor called a crown, or rather what is monarchy? Is it a thing, or is it a name, or is it a fraud? Is it a "contrivance of human wisdom"... Is it a thing necessary to a nation? ... what service does it perform, what is its business, and what are its merits? Does the virtue consist in the metaphor, or in the man? Doth the goldsmith that makes the crown, make the virtue also? Doth it operate like Fortunatus's wishing-cap, or Harlequin's wooden sword? Doth it make a man a conjurer? In fine, what is it? It appears to be something going much out of fashion, falling into ridicule, and rejected in some countries, both as unnecessary and expensive.

The steady stream of questions, beginning with the question of actual worth and culminating in the comparisons to a wishing-cap and wooden sword accentuate the impression of absurdity, while the final sentence serves to deflate the idea once and for all. It is perhaps not surprising that Burke found this passage objectionable.[94]

Alternatively, the elites may have felt intimidated by Paine's truths, mostly delivered in a clear, no-nonsense manner that indicated knowledge of the most recent scientific discourse—in spite of his lack of a formal education: one immediately apparent in his vindications of progress and revolution. Even if the call for change was hardly unique to him, he would articulate a forceful rationale for change while resisting the temptation to retread familiar arguments by contemporary writers. Instead, in keeping with his "unnatural" branding of the Burkean philosophy, he asserts his disbelief that anyone will cling to outdated notions for such would defy any understanding of science or human nature:

> The mind, in discovering truth, acts in the same manner as it acts through the eye in discovering objects; when once any object has been seen, it is impossible to put the mind back to the same condition it was in before it saw it. Those who talk of a counter-revolution in France, show how little they understand of man ... it has never yet been discovered how to make man unknow his knowledge, or unthink his thoughts.

Paine provides an even stronger defense of revolution in his conclusion, contradicting Burke every step of the way. In fact, we may even wonder if this very defense did not also revolutionize connotations of revolution—especially as he goes further by suggesting that there can be such a thing as a revolution produced by "reason and accommodation" rather than by convulsion.

> What were formerly called Revolutions, were little more than a change of persons, or an alteration of local circumstances ... But what we now see in the world, from the Revolutions of America and France, are a renovation of the natural order of things, a system of principles as universal as truth and the existence of man, and combining moral with political happiness and national prosperity.

It is no wonder even today that "revolution" continues to have a positive "buzz" in a popular sense even if the idea of political revolution is still feared by many. The irony, as we will see in Part 2, was that Paine had underestimated the force of habit and prejudice as discerned by Burke: not only were the masses fondly protective of George III, but were easily goaded by the likes of the local aristocracy and gentry into burning effigies of Paine across England.

Not least, if reformist-minded working-class readers enjoyed Paine's humour, the elites may have been taken aback by his markedly plebeian colloquialisms, irreverent humour and mockery of elite, formal rhetoric, all of which can be said to signal a nonchalant lack of deference duly expected from men of his class. Note how Paine points out merrily that Burke, "To use a sailor's phrase," has "swabbed the deck, and scarcely left a name legible in the list of Kings" (149). One might also take his description of William I, for instance, with its bold irony and insult: "*There is the head of the list! there is the fountain of honour!* the son of a prostitute, and the plunderer of the English nation" (151). It is equally remarkable to see how deftly Paine spins Burke's denial of the role of the populace at large in the selection of William III. If Burke informs the reader that "His Majesty's heirs and successors, each in their time and order, will come to the crown with the same contempt of their choice with which His Majesty has succeeded to that he wears" (153), Paine pushes this idea of contempt in a populist direction, observing "it is saying too much even to the humblest individual in the country; part of whose daily labour goes towards making up the million sterling a year" (153). They may have been shocked too by Paine's pun and use of scatological humour when he observes that "a band of interested men, such as Placemen, Pensioners, Lords of the bed-chamber, Lords of the kitchen, Lords of the necessary House, and the Lord knows what besides can find as many reasons for monarchy as their salaries, paid at the expense of the country" (159).

NOTES

1 Albert Mathiez, *The French Revolution* (New York: Russell and Russell, 1962) p. 10.
2 Eric Hazan, *A People's History of the French Revolution*, trans. David Fernbach (London: Verso, 2012, 2014) p. 42.
3 A *lit de justice*—translated as "bed of justice"—was an event intended to assert the king's power over the *parlements*.
4 The *cahiers* were notebooks citing grievances which were submitted to Louis XVI in March and April 1789.
5 Cited in Hazan, p. 58.
6 Qtd. in F.P. Lock, *Edmund Burke*, Vols. 1–2 (Oxford: Oxford University Press, 2006) 2, p. 204.

7 Qtd. in John Keane, *Tom Paine: A Political Life* (New York: Little, Brown, 1995) p. 283.

8 *The Annual Register for 1794* (London) p. 267.

9 See: http://oll.libertyfund.org/titles/price-a-discourse-on-the-love-of-our-country. All subsequent quotations from *Discourse* are drawn from this site.

10 Qtd in Jane Hodson, *Language and Revolution in Burke, Wollstonecraft, Paine, and Godwin* (London: Ashgate, 2007) p. 75.

11 Edmund Burke, *Reflections on the Revolution in France*, in *The Writings and Speeches of Edmund Burke*, ed. L.G. Mitchell (Oxford: Oxford University Press, 1989) 8, p. 66. All references to *Reflections* are drawn from this edition.

12 Even though the passage had already been roundly scorned by his friend, Philip Francis, for its "foppery," Burke obviously thought highly enough of it to retain it for publication.

13 This argument had already been anticipated by Rousseau in *The Social Contract*, Book 2, Chapter 4.

14 William Windham had made a similar observation a few months earlier in Parliament when questioning the appeal for parliamentary reform, announcing that he must protest "against the strange mixture of metaphysics with politics, which we are witnessing in the neighboring country." Qtd. in Jenny Graham, *The Nation, the Law and the King, Reform Politics in England, 1789–1799*, Vols. 1–2 (Lanham, MD: University Press of America, 2000) 2, p. 159. Interestingly, on the other side of the Channel, the conservative attorney and deputy to the National Constituent Assembly, Pierre Victor Malouet, also expressed reservations against the "metaphysical discussion" of rights. See Speech of August 1, 1789 (Qtd. in *The French Revolution and Human Rights: A Brief Documentary History*, ed., trans., and Intro. by Lynn Hunt, p. 75).

15 See: http://avalon.law.yale.edu/17th_century/england.asp

16 Thomas Paine, *Rights of Man*, ed. Claire Grogan (Toronto: Broadview Press, 2011) p. 72. All subsequent quotations from *Rights* are drawn from this edition.

17 See: http://www.let.rug.nl/usa/presidents/thomas-jefferson/letters-of-thomas-jefferson/jefl81.php. In my private conversations, some (e.g., Martha Spiegelman) have rightly noted that Jefferson did not apply this reasoning to the ownership of slaves.

18 Capel Lofft, *Remarks on the Letter of the Rt. Hon. Edmund Burke, concerning the Revolution in France* (London, 1790) p. 20. Subsequent quotations from this pamphlet are drawn from this edition.

19 Catharine Macaulay, *Observations on the Reflections of the Right Hon. Edmund Burke of the Revolution in France* (London, 1790) p. 14.

20 Sir Brooke Boothby, *A Letter to Burke* (London, 1790) p. 59.

21 Jenny Graham, *The Nation, the Law, and the King, 1789–1799*, Vols. 1–2 (University Press of America, 1999) 1, p. 175.

22 Benjamin Bousfield, *Observations on the Right Hon. Edmund Burke's Pamphlet on the subject of the French Revolution* (Dublin, 1791) p. 20.

23 Paine's criticisms of Louis XVI are certainly more moderate compared to those of James MacKintosh in his *Vindiciae Gallicae*, 1791, published shortly after *Rights of Man*, Part 1.

24 For instance, Jack Fruchtman wonders if there was "something qualitatively different about him and his aristocratic minions that they could admire the rustic Benjamin Franklin? ...Was there an underlying appreciation of political reform ... when
they openly celebrated the success of the American victory?" See Fruchtman, *Political Principles of Thomas Paine* (Baltimore, MD: Johns Hopkins Press, 2009) p. 13.
In *Thomas Paine and the French Revolution* (Switzerland: Springer, 2018), Carine
Lounissi mentions that although Paine makes note of the *lit de justice* of August 6,
1787, he does not comment on Louis' arbitrary handling of that meeting (Kindle
Locations 1091–1095). It is also worth noting that Louis XVI could be very high-
handed in dealing with the *parlements*: when the *parlement* moved to declare *lettres
de cachet* illegal in 1788, the king summoned a *lit de justice* to nullify its decision.
Finally, not unlike Louis XV, Louis XVI attempted to neuter the *parlements* altogether. Nonetheless, it is also important to recall that the idea of republicanism was
nearly nonexistent prior to Louis' attempted escape from Paris in June 1791
according to Lounissi. For this reason, Paine may have softened his criticism of
Louis without urging an abdication of the monarchy (Kindle Locations 2373–2378).

25 Letter to George Washington May 1790, *Complete Writings of Thomas Paine*, Vols.
1–2, ed. Philip Foner (New York: Citadel Press, 1945) 2, p. 1303.

26 *Address to the People of France* in *CW*, 2, p. 539. Paine seems to have argued at
times, according to Gregory Claeys, that nations had no business interfering in
the internal affairs of another nation. In the *Eighteenth Fructidor*, Paine writes:
"That one nation has not a right to interfere in the internal government of
another nation, is admitted; and in this point of view, France has no right to
dictate to England what its form of government shall be. If it choose to have a
thing called a king, or whether the king shall be a man or an ass, is a matter
with which France has not business" (2, 608).

27 Timothy Tackett, *Becoming a Revolutionary: The Deputies of the French National
Assembly and the Emergence of a Revolutionary culture (1789–1790)* (University
Park: The Pennsylvania State University Press, 1996) p. 104.

28 Interestingly, Jack Fruchtman notes that while in France Paine had no contact
with the lower orders of French society but was constantly in aristocratic com-
pany. Could this explain the surprising paucity of details on the march and other
populist activity? See *Thomas Paine: The Apostle of Freedom* (New York: Four
Walls Eight Windows, 1994) p. 183.

29 See *Philotheodosius with a new character of Mr. Burke* (1790). In one of the more
famous responses to Burke, *Vindiciae Gallicae*, James Mackintosh writes: "it is vain
to expect that a people inured to barbarism by their oppressors, and which has
ages of oppression to avenge, will be punctiliously generous in their triumph, nicely
discriminative in their vengeance, or cautiously mild in their mode of retaliation."
He also notes that far more died in the English and American revolutions.

30 John Scott, *Observations on the Present State of the Parochial and Vagrant Poor*
(London, 1773) p. 134.

31 Interestingly, as Lounissi observes, Paine referred his readers to a more detailed
account, namely, of the *Révolutions de Paris*, in which economic factors
appeared, even if they were posited as subsidiary in relation to political issues. It

is also difficult to imagine that Lafayette did not inform Paine of the furor over bread prices (Kindle Locations 1895–1907).

32 Obadiah Hulme, *An Historical Essay on the English Constitution* (London, 1771) p. 4.
33 See Robert Lamb, *Thomas Paine and the Idea of Human Rights* (Cambridge: Cambridge University Press, 2015). Also, see J.C.D. Clark, *Britain, America and France in the Age of Enlightenment and Revolution* (Oxford: Oxford University Press, 2018) for an expansion of this idea.
34 See Jeremy Waldron, *"Nonsense upon Stilts": Bentham, Burke and Marx on the Rights of Man* (London: Routledge Revivals, 1987, 2015) 1. He writes: "It would be wrong, of course, to suggest that there is nothing new in the modern discussion of rights ... For example, modern rights-theorists are more interested than their 18th-century ancestors in what are now known as welfare rights and in the idea that rights may express claims about need and not merely individual freedom."
35 See the definition of "Natural Rights" in the Encyclopedia of Diderot d'Alembert in the Collaborative Translation Project at the University of Michigan Library: https://quod.lib.umich.edu/d/did/did2222.0001.313/–natural-rights?rgn=main;view=fulltext;q1=Jean-Fran%C3%A7ois+de+Saint-Lambert+ascribed
36 A similar notion appears in Thomas Clarkson's *An Essay on the Human Species, particularly the African, translated from a Latin dissertation* (London, 1786).
37 Richard Price, *Evidence for a Future Period of Improvement* (London, 1787) p. 30.
38 Glenn Burgess, *The Politics of the Ancient Constitution: An Introduction to English Political Thought, 1603–1642* (University Park, PA: University Park Press, 1993).
39 David Williams, *Letters on Political Liberty* (London, 1782) p. 48.
40 David Williams, *Lessons to a Young Prince* (London, 1791) p. 48.
41 See: http://thomaspaine.org/recently-discovered/four-letters-on-interesting-subjects.html
42 Problems associated with an unwritten constitution have loomed forth in the context of the recent Brexit crisis: https://www.newstatesman.com/politics/uk/2019/08/brexit-crisis-shows-why-uk-finally-needs-written-constitution
43 Anthony King, *The British Constitution* (Oxford: Oxford University Press, 2009) p. 4.
44 Vernon Bogdanor, *The Monarchy and the Constitution* (Oxford: Oxford University Press, 1995) p. 9.
45 Speech of Robespierre in *French Revolution and Human Rights: A Brief Documentary History*, ed. Lynn Hunt (New York: Bedford/St. Martin's, 1996) pp. 83–4, p. 83.
46 See Thouret, *Report on the Basis of Political Eligibility*, in Hunt, *French Revolution and Human Rights*, p. 82
47 Emmanuel Sièyes, *Political Writings: Including the Debate between Sièyes and Tom Paine in 1791*, ed. Michael Sonenscher (Indianapolis: Hackett, 2003) p. 164.
48 Jon Mee, *Print, Publicity and Radicalism in the 1790s: The Laurel of Liberty* (Cambridge: Cambridge University Press, 2016) p. 24.
49 See Keane, p. 14. According to Keane, Thetford was also one of the most rotten of boroughs, rife with aristocratic political intrigue.
50 Mary Wollstonecraft, *Vindication of the Rights of Men*: https://oll.libertyfund.org/titles/wollstonecraft-a-vindication-of-the-rights-of-men

51 John Butler, *Brief Reflections on the Liberty of the British Subject* (Canterbury, [n. d.]) p. 51. Though undated, it is believed to have been published no later than November 1790.

52 William Blake may have been inspired by this repetition of "chartered" as he wrote his poem, "London" (*Songs of Experience*), where he mentions the "charter'd street" and "charter'd Thames."

53 John Brewer, *The Sinews of Power* (Cambridge, MA: Harvard University Press, 1990) p. 73.

54 See Gail Bossenga, "Financial Origins of the French Revolution" in *From Deficit to Deluge: The Origins of the French Revolution*, ed. Thomas E. Kaiser and Dale K. Van Kley (Stanford, CA: Stanford University Press, 2011) pp. 37–66. The fact that the French king was able to repudiate collections of debt also lowered the national credit rating, thereby elevating interest rates on loans.

55 Jack Goldstone, "The Social Origins of the French Revolution Revisited" in *Deficit to Deluge*, pp. 74–85. Brewer also states that aggregate tax revenue had increased six-fold. See Brewer, *Sinews*, p. 89.

56 John Sinclair, *The History of the Public Revenue of the British Empire* (Dublin, 1785) p. 309.

57 George II complained in 1744 that "Ministers are the kings in this country." Cited in Bogdanor, p. 11. However, it could be said that the creation of the role of prime minister originated under his father, George I, who frequently skipped cabinet meetings. As his senior minister took his place, he thus came to be known as prime minister. It was then, according to Bogdanor, that monarchs would begin to play a more limited role in the determination of policy.

58 Lewis Namier, *England in the Age of the American Revolution* (London: Macmillan, 1930, 1961) p. 4.

59 Peter McPhee, *The French Revolution 1789–1799* (Oxford: Oxford University Press, 2002) p. 93.

60 "Because you are a great lord, you believe that you are a great genius! You took the trouble to be born, no more. You remain an ordinary enough man!"

61 Qtd. in Gary B. Nash, *The Unknown American Revolution: The Unruly Birth of Democracy and the Struggle to Create America* (New York: Viking, 2005) p. 450. Also, see chapters 1–3 in Amanda Goodrich, *Debating England's Aristocracy in the 1790s: Pamphlets, polemics, and political ideas* (Suffolk: Boydell Press, 2005).

62 See Jefferson's letter to James Madison, Oct. 28, 1785: http://press-pubs.uchicago.edu/founders/documents/v1ch15s32. And http://press-pubs.uchicago.edu/founders/documents/v1ch15s32.htmlhtml

63 Thomas Jefferson to John Adams Oct. 2, 1813: http://press-pubs.uchicago.edu/founders/documents/v1ch15s61.html "At the first session of our legislature after the Declaration of Independence [*sic*], we passed a law abolishing entails. And this was followed by one abolishing the privilege of Primogeniture, and dividing the lands of intestates equally among all their children, or other representatives. These laws, drawn by myself, laid the axe to the root of Pseudoaristocracy."

64 Philipp Ziesche, "Thomas Paine and Benjamin Franklin's French Circle" in *Paine and Jefferson in the Age of Revolution*, ed. Simon P. Newman and Peter D. Onuf (Charlottesville, VA: University of Virginia Press, 2013) pp. 121–36.

65 Keane, p. 254.

66 See: https://oll.libertyfund.org/titles/price-observations-on-the-importance-of-the-american-revolution

67 Ian Christie, *Stress and Stability in Late Eighteenth-century Britain* (Oxford: Clarendon Press, 1984) p. 56.

68 John Belsham, *Historic Memoir on the French Revolution, to which are annexed Strictures on the Reflections of the Rt. Hon. Edmund Burke* (London, 1791) p. 44.

69 [Aedanus Burke], (London, 1785) p. 10.

70 It is worth noting, however, that Paine does not identify as many privileges enjoyed by the British aristocracy as Sièyes did in his *Essay on Privileges*: here, the latter identifies exemptions from arrest for debt, infamous punishments, serving as sheriffs or on juries, but above all, "the exclusive and hereditary right to be Legislators and Judges, and the advisers and counsellors of the sovereign." Such are privileges "which ought to be the right of every citizen" and are actually "of a much higher importance than those of the late French nobility" (3).

71 That Paine's words on the aristocracy struck a nerve with Burke is evident in the latter's copious citation in his *Appeal from the New to Old Whigs*.

72 The phrases "pride and prejudice" and "prejudice and pride" were already used by Fanny Burney and Ann Radcliffe long before Austen. Notice the appearance of the phrase "national pride and prejudice" in Paine's *Common Sense*.

73 See: http://www.chronicle.com/article/10-Myths-About-Legacy/124561

74 Nor can American designers (e.g., Ralph Lauren) resist a general obsession with the "prep" look that is widely associated with the nation's de facto aristocracy, East Coast WASPs.

75 John Adams, *Defence of the Constitutions of the Governments of the United States of America*, Vols. 1–3 in *The Complete Works of John Adams*, ed. Charles Francis Adams, Vols. 4–6. Reprinted in the Online Library of Liberty. See: http://oll.libertyfund.org/titles/adams-the-works-of-john-adams-vol-4, 4. He even goes so far as to add: "Go into every village in New England, and you will find that the office of justice of the peace, and even the place of representative, which has ever depended only on the freest election of the people, have generally descended from generation to generation, in three or four families at most."

76 Across the Channel, there was similar criticism of the luxuries enjoyed by the bishops. One deputy of the Third Estate reported "We all rushed forward asking the right to speak out against [the bishops'] absurd expenses, their ridiculous luxury, their useless residence in the voluptuous society of Paris" (Tackett, 68).

77 Qtd. in Michel Vovelle, *The Fall of the French Monarchy 1787–1792* (Cambridge: Cambridge University Press, 1984) p. 114.

78 David Bien, "Old Regime Origins of Democratic Liberty" in *The French Idea of Freedom: The Old Regime and the Declaration of Rights of 1789* (Stanford, CA: Stanford University Press, 1994) pp. 23–71, p. 34.

79 The *parlements* were actually appellate courts, rather than legislative counterparts of the British parliament.

80 There have been recent claims made by J.C.D. Clark that this section of Part 1 was most likely written by Lafayette or someone other than Paine. Even if that were the case, Paine's decision to incorporate it into his text indicates a fundamental agreement with the ideas at hand. In her own recent monograph on Paine's years in France, Carine Lounissi denies "the alleged stylistic rupture" suggested by Clark. Since Paine probably relied on the letters and oral testimonies of Jefferson, Lafayette, and others, there was bound to be some difference in style even if he penned the account himself. See her *Thomas Paine and the French Revolution* (Springer). Kindle Edition. (Kindle Locations 806–810.)

81 See Claeys, *The Social and Political Thought of Thomas Paine* (Oxford: Routledge, 1989), Epstein, *Radical Expression: Political Language, Ritual, and Symbol in England, 1790–1850* (Oxford: Oxford University Press, 1994), and Pocock, *Virtue, Commerce, and History* (Cambridge: Cambridge University Press, 1985).

82 The corvée would be replaced by a tax on landowners in the Second and Third Estates. As Bailey Stone observes in his study of the *parlements*, it is evident that the *parlementaires* sought to protect their noble status and privileges—particularly exemptions from taxes. See chapter 4.

83 Qtd. in Durand Echeverria, *Mirage in the West: A History of the French Image of American Society to 1815* (New York: Octagon Books, 1966) p. 42. For historiography on the subject of American influences on the French revolution this subject, see also Allan Potofsky, in *Rethinking the Atlantic World: Europe and America in the Age of Democratic Revolutions* (Basingstoke: Palgrave Macmillan, 2009) pp. 17–45, p. 24. See also Lounissi's *Thomas Paine and the French Revolution*. She notes that in May 1790, Paine wrote to George Washington that "the principles of America opened the Bastille." Moreover, Jefferson may have discussed the ways in which the French soldiers who had fought alongside the Continental Army were "eventually placed in the school of Freedom, and learned the practice as well as the principle by heart." There were numerous essays on the influence of the American revolution, including such essays as Raynal's *Révolution de l'Amérique*, to which Paine had responded in 1783, Condorcet's *Influence de la Révolution américaine en Europe* (1786) or Brissot's *De la France et des Etats-Unis* (1787); newspapers such as Benjamin Franklin's *Affaires de l'Angleterre et de l'Amérique*. Not least, the idea that 1776 and 1789 were closely connected was quite common in replies to Burke: for instance, Joseph Priestley, who stated that 1789 sprang from 1776, and Benjamin Bousfield who believed that "the seeds of French liberty were sown in the forests of America." It is worth bearing in mind, however, as Lounissi points out, that Paine did not go as far to say that the American revolution had triggered off the French one but instead argued that 1776 had made new political principles and practices known in Europe and that only an "opportunity" was needed to apply them (Springer). Kindle Edition. (Kindle Locations 1010–1045; 1421–1424).

84 As noted earlier, the *parlement* actually began as a judicial court rather than a legislative body mostly by approving taxes and decrees issued by the king and

his ministers. However, over the course of the 18th century, its functions became increasingly political.

85 See Bailey Stone, *The Parlement of Paris: 1774–1789* (Chapel Hill: University of North Carolina Press, 1981) p. 162. It is also worth noting that pamphlets which sided with the ministry, as Dale van Kley observes, tended to accentuate equality and equal access while execrating "aristocratic domination" and "feudal anarchy." See "Origins of an Anti-historical Declaration in *The French Idea of Freedom,*" ed. Dale van Kley (Stanford, CA: Stanford University Press, 1994) pp. 72–113, p. 85.

86 Laura Auricchio, *The Marquis Lafayette Reconsidered* (New York: Alfred Knopf, 2014) p. 158.

87 Interestingly, the *parlement* had misgivings about convoking the Estates General. One judge supposedly predicted that "the first time that France sees the Estates General, she will also see a terrible revolution" (Stone, 158).

88 Arthur Young recorded comparable observations on his travels through France, noting that the nobles were "disgustingly tenacious of all old rights, however hard they may bear on the people" (qtd in Graham, *The Nation*, 1, p. 174.)

89 Many were opposed not only to the fiscal immunities, social privileges, and political leverage enjoyed by the nobility, but also to their perceived presumptuousness and condescension. In general, the Third Estate was delighted at the decrees of August 4, hoping that they would "take the nobles down a peg." Conversely, the great majority of nobles were opposed to the liberals amongst the Second Estate (Tackett, 109). Interestingly, too, as if reinforcing this impression of "no-ability," some nobles equally regretted a lack of fluency on their part.

90 Patrick K. O'Brien and Peter Mathias, "Taxation in Britain and France, 1715–1810: A Comparison of the Social and Economic Incidence of Taxes Collected for the Central Governments" in *Journal of European Economic History*, 5 (1976) pp. 601–50, 602–9. Both Britain and France were involved in war for much of the century, but Britain levied significantly higher taxes which partly explains why the former was able to avoid bankruptcy after the American war.

91 Paine notes the expenses on Hanover, suggesting that English monies have been wasted abroad. In *History of the Public Revenue of the British Empire*, Parts 1 and 2, however, John Sinclair disputes this belief, mentioning that it dates back to the days of George II (389). But even though "It is certain, that our connexions with that country necessarily involved us, more than otherwise would have been necessary in the affairs of the continent," he questions its truth, attributing the wasted fund to "mismanagement in our domestic affairs" since "Little care was taken to raise such a revenue as the nation could afford" (390).

92 Adam Smith, *The Wealth of Nations*, Vols. 1 and 2, ed. Andrew Skinner (London: Penguin Books, 1982) 2, p. 522.

93 Olivia Smith, *The Politics of Language 1791–1819* (Oxford: Clarendon Press, 1984) p. 41.

94 See his *Appeal from the Old Whigs to the New.*

2

RIGHTS OF MAN, PART 2, PREFACE–CHAPTER 3

"Tom Paine, No King—Damn the King"[1]

On July 8, 1791, the London newspaper, *The Oracle*, reported that Paine was writing a pamphlet to be titled Kingship and that "its object is to demonstrate the inutility of kings."[2] By the end of November, however, Paine had changed his mind, deciding to publish the new work as *Rights of Man*, Part 2, given the immense popularity of Part 1—even at the relatively steep price of three shillings. He also planned to print 100,000 copies each of Parts 1 and 2 at sixpence in order to make them readily accessible. Although Part 2 was supposed to have been completed by Christmas for the opening of the new parliamentary session, it did not appear until February 16, 1792, due partly to difficulties in procuring a printer for what was already anticipated to be a seditious text. Indeed, it was only days after its publication that a government spy was dispatched to keep an eye on him. As Part 2 broke every publishing record for the century, with widespread reports that it was found in the hands of crofters, miners, shoemakers, and other laborers, William Pitt issued a proclamation against "wicked and seditious writings" as well as a summons to court on May 21, 1792 for those very charges. Postponed to December out of fear that the popularity of *Rights* would make a martyr of Paine, the trial was ultimately held in absentia since he had already made his way to France in September after his election to the National Assembly as a representative of Pas-de-Calais (despite his inability to speak French). After a brief deliberation, Paine was declared guilty.

How and why did Part 2 become so radicalized and exceptionable—at least, according to the government and propertied elites? How and why did republicanism and anti-monarchical sentiment resonate so much more in Part 2? And again, just how progressive was Paine when compared to his contemporaries?

PREFACE AND INTRODUCTION

Although little more than a year had elapsed between the publications of Parts 1 and 2, much had transpired. In France, the most significant event was the attempt of Louis XVI and his family to flee from Paris disguised as servants. If Louis—unlike George III—had found himself stymied by the restraints placed on his power by the National Assembly, many of his subjects felt betrayed after his capture at Varennes: after all, he had just delivered a manifesto censuring the National Convention while pleading for assistance from his adherents shortly before his departure. In turn, the Declaration of Pillnitz signed by Marie Antoinette's brother, the Holy Roman Emperor Leopold II, and Frederick William II of Prussia less than two months later in August, would heighten the question of a monarch's role in governing a nation. Did the king always serve in the best interests of the people when other leaders and crowned heads could conspire with him against the general inclination of the nation?

Meanwhile, in Britain, the debate over the French revolution continued to brew as more writers leapt into the fray after the publication of *Rights of Man*, Part 1. Partly in response, Burke published two pamphlets, *Letter to a Member of the National Assembly* (May 1791) and *An Appeal from the New Whigs to the*

Old (August 1791). Indeed, it is worth taking a brief look at both texts since they may have informed Paine's themes in Part 2 at least as much as *Reflections* did in Part 1. Like *Reflections*, the *Letter* was aimed not so much for the acknowledged recipient (François-Louis-Thibaut de Menonville) but rather at a British audience so that the English could "estimate the wisdom of the plans" which were presented as a model.[3] Continuing his diatribe at the low social roots of the National Assembly and criticisms of Rousseau's "plan of levelling" for attempting to "establish their rights of men on a sure foundation," Burke stepped up his defense of monarchy. He remarked that its restoration in the shape of William III "was everything to us"; "without monarchy," no one would "enjoy either peace or liberty." Moreover, just as in *Reflections*, he reiterated his warning against excessive public scrutiny of a government, intimating that the French government had in fact lost "half its reputation."

By contrast, Burke's motive for writing *An Appeal* arose from a personal desire to vindicate himself after being accused of having abandoned Whig principles. Ridiculing the emerging emphasis on political representation as an indirect slap at Fox, Price, and other reformers whom he erroneously lumped together with a more radical Paine, Burke dug in his heels on the idea of tradition while castigating democratic practices even more vigorously. If certain men grumbled about older politicians with little awareness of "the rights of men" who lost their way "fumbling among rotten parchments and musty records,"[4] Burke protested that such ideas were on all counts preferable to "the pretended rights of men" and the "mischievous tendency of all such declarations to the wellbeing of men and of citizens." Here, too, despite denying that he was denigrating republican governments, he ridiculed the French for maintaining that their government must operate "wholly by popular representation." Why did they dismiss other forms of government as "an usurpation" or "atrocious violation of the indefeasible rights of man?" While Burke did not object to republican government in America, the fact was that such a government could only pose an "infinite detriment" to European nations; indeed, any republican elements should be safely founded upon "a real, not a nominal monarchy." He simply could not "rejoice at the destruction of a monarchy" coupled with "the tyranny of a licentious, ferocious, and savage multitude, without laws, manners, or morals."

The chief problem with the new Whigs was that they placed far too much unrealistic stock in the people:

> These new Whigs hold, that the sovereignty ... did not only originate from the people ... but that, in the people the same sovereignty constantly and unalienably resides; that the people may lawfully depose kings, not only for misconduct, but without any misconduct at all; that they may set up any new fashion of government for themselves ... magistrates have duties, but no rights: and that if a contract de facto is made with them in one age ... it only binds those who were immediately concerned in it, but does not pass to posterity. These doctrines concerning the people ... tend, in my opinion, to the utter subversion, not only of all government ... but to all the rules and principles of morality itself.

More specifically, however, Burke would also cite some of the most frequently quoted passages from *Rights of Man*, Part 1 without discussing them as if trusting that each quotation was sufficiently damning in itself. Likewise, he assumed that the likes of Fox and his followers sanctioned Paine's republicanism even though few of them did. The privileging of the people, he reiterated, would only destroy society.

> Discuss any of their schemes—their answer is—It is the act of the people, and that is sufficient. Are we to deny to a majority of the people the right of altering even the whole frame of their society ... They are masters of the commonwealth ... The French revolution, say they, was the act of the majority of the people ... The people are not to be taught to think lightly of their engagements to their governors; else they teach governors to think lightly of their engagements towards them. In that kind of game in the end the people are sure to be losers.

Burke would also continue to underscore the necessity of wiser, more affluent men governing those less so.

> To enable men to act with the weight and character of a people, and to answer the ends for which they are incorporated into that capacity, we must suppose them (by means immediate or consequential) to be in that state of habitual social discipline, in which the wiser, the more expert, and the more opulent, conduct, and by conducting enlighten [sic] and protect the weaker, the less knowing, and the less provided with the goods of fortune. When the multitude are not under this discipline, they can scarcely be said to be in civil society.

Burke's distrust of the majority in both paragraphs is telling. Although there is a vague sense of reciprocity between governors and the governed in his statement that "The people are not to be taught to think lightly of their engagements to their governors; else they teach governors to think lightly of their engagements towards them" because the people are bound "to be losers," Burke does not explain why. It is also telling that he presupposes "The wiser, the more expert, and the more opulent" to be less prone to self-interest and greed.

Not least is it important to consider Paine's own reactions to events from the same period, all of which can be construed as a collected foundation for Part 2. In the immediate aftermath of Louis XVI's escape, Paine lost whatever hope or forbearance he once placed on the hapless king as he joined other French republicans by issuing a counter manifesto, opening it with a bold question: "Did we require the most indubitable evidence that the presence of a king is rather a bane than a blessing, that as an element of the political system he is without force or value?"[5] Here, Paine rehearses the history of "cruelties and crimes" associated with monarchies, while returning to the more strident anti-monarchical sentiments of *Common Sense* and the *Crisis* papers. Leaning into the uncertain aspects of hereditary traits and capabilities, he points out that "an office that may be filled by a person without talent or experience" and can "consequently devolve on a madman, an imbecile, or a tyrant" was nothing short of "an absurdity." In other words, there is no telling how suitable an individual monarch may be for the throne. His ideas on the unpredictability of temperament and talents as well as the exorbitant expenses involved in supporting such governments are amplified in a reply to Sieyès' claim that greater liberty is more likely to exist under a monarchy than a republic: indeed, the manifesto and his reply to Sieyès can be said to form the basis for Chapter 3 in Part 2.

At the same time, Paine's *Answer to four questions on the legislative and executive power*, also written during the spring and summer of 1791, offers a rough blueprint for much of Chapter 4. In addition to highlighting the personal foibles of individual monarchs, Paine ponders the usefulness of two legislative chambers while urging the present legislative assembly to make provisions for future changes in the new constitution. With a revolution that is spinning "from West to East" and proving "quicker in its effects than the movement which once spread from East to West" (533)—a line that is reiterated in the Introduction to Part 2—he envisions a peaceful future when governments will no longer foment discord (529) but rely on "pacific methods and not by the ferocious horrors of war" (533). Broadly anticipating a United Nations, he imagined that a National Assembly would "call for a convention of the representatives of the various nations of Europe" and thereby "adopt measures for the general welfare" (533). Finally, in a speech delivered at the Thatched House Tavern in London on August 20, 1791, Paine would dwell more closely on the relevance of the French revolution to a Britain barely arisen from a "feudal system" (636). Taking a swipe at Burke by announcing his intention "to improve" and to eschew considerations of policy based on "the mere score of antiquity, or … the *old* Whigs or *new*" (636), Paine vowed to uphold the "sacred hereditary rights of man—rights which appertain to ALL, and not to any one more than to another." Wishing not only for "universal peace and freedom," he broached the idea of nationalized public welfare, declaring that the masses deserve a greater share of public monies than the privileged few as he points out the "very numerous poor"; no less worrisome are the "moral obligation of providing for old age" and "helpless infancy." This endeavor to help the masses, one that would be canvassed more thoroughly in Chapter 5, promised to be "far superior to that of supplying the invented wants of courtly extravagance" (535).

In this context, it is thus hardly surprising that the preface is anchored around the fundamental purpose of government: bearing in mind Burke's criticism of democratic principles and scrutiny of public officials, Paine delivers two arguments after quipping that Burke's refusal to contest the ideas from *Rights of Man* is a case in point of his lament that "the age of chivalry is gone." Firstly, the examination of laws should not be impeded if arbitrary power is to be averted. Since government is ultimately intended to benefit a nation, there is all the more reason for its citizens to examine and analyze its flaws. Maintaining that "It is for the good of nations, and not for the emolument or aggrandizement of particular individuals," he nudges the reader towards his claims that taxes have been expended chiefly to wage wars and reward the wealthy few instead of helping the plurality of citizens. Moreover, in distinct contrast to Burke's criticisms of Rousseau and his downplaying of popular politics, Paine more or less accepts the Rousseauvian premise that government is "not a convention between a superior and an inferior, but a convention between the body and each of its members" and as such, "legitimate, because based on the social contract" with "no other object than the general good, and stable."[6] Arguing that while "the operation of government is restricted to the making and administering of laws," Paine insists that it is the people who enjoy the right of "forming or reforming, generating or regenerating constitutions" since they pay taxes: a concept that he may have learned in America, as we will see in Chapter 4. A work investigating the flaws and weaknesses of government simply cannot be prosecuted because a "jury of twelve men is not competent to decide," particularly without witnesses or facts: indeed, "the only effectual jury" would be "a convention of the whole nation fairly elected" (187).

Observing that Burke is unable to contest the central ideas of *Rights of Man*, Paine doubts—almost exactly like Harrington in 1656—that "monarchy and aristocracy will continue seven years longer in any of the enlightened countries in Europe." Of course, Harrington and Paine would be proven equally incorrect in that regard.[7] Nonetheless, a reading of Burke's *Reflections* and *Appeal*—or Sieyès' published and unpublished writings on monarchy—displays a curious inability on the part of both writers to fully combat Paine's criticisms of hereditary government or explain the advantages offered by a monarchy. In *Reflections, A Letter*, and *Appeal*, for instance, Burke does not explain how or why a monarchy might be more effective without relying on his argument for tradition. Much the same can be said for Sieyès' confused defense of monarchy. Although he claims that all nations should have an element of representative government and that elective monarchies can be at least as troublesome as hereditary monarchies, he too fails to explain the purpose of either monarchy or show how they are superior to an entirely representative government.

In light of Burke's defense of tradition, it is also hardly fortuitous that Paine pushes back by devoting considerable attention to the power of enlightenment from the Preface through Chapter 3. If Paine had observed in the *Answers* that governments tended to create unnecessary wars (*CW*, 529), he closes the Preface by arguing that prejudices acquired from education and habit "have yet to stand the test of reason and reflection." The problem is that for too long, the English—and other nations—"have been imposed upon by parties" and by those "assuming the character of leaders"; as he states in the Introduction, "so deeply rooted were all the governments of the old world, and so effectually had the tyranny and the antiquity of habit established itself over the mind" (189). Quoting from *Common Sense* that "freedom hath been hunted round the globe," (189), Paine draws attention to the ironic lack of civilized progress in the supposed "Old World" countries. Indeed, he ventures beyond the language of Whiggish pamphleteering to decry that a "Great part of the old world" would appear "to be new, just struggling with the difficulties and hardships of an infant settlement." After all, it is the "old countries" which harbor "hordes of miserable poor" (190): countries that appear as if "they had not yet had time to provide for themselves"—a theme that is expanded on in Chapter 5. In the following paragraphs, Paine places repeated emphasis on variations of "universal civilization, peace, and commerce." If any of these goals are to be met, Old World governments must be radically transformed, including more advanced nations which are "apt to find the greedy hand of government thrusting itself into every corner and crevice of industry, and grasping the spoil of the multitude" (190) by means of wars and taxes. By contrast, the settling of the New World has proven to be more beneficent such that man learns to view "his species, not with the inhuman idea of a natural enemy, but as kindred" (190). The revolution in France, taking its cue from America, is no longer just a revolution confined to the borders of France, but rather a world revolution reversing the effects of "conquest and tyranny" that once "dispossessed man of his rights." Reiterating nearly word for word from his *Answer to Four Questions*, Paine remarks that "Government founded on a moral theory, on a system of universal peace, on the indefeasible hereditary Rights of Man, is now revolving from west to east, by a stronger impulse than the government of the sword revolved from east to west." In short, Paine's remarks provide a bold, diametrically different view from Burke who considered the revolution a savage and anarchic affair. For Paine, revolution establishes civilized order while sharply curtailing government corruption and improving human welfare.

Yet, however much most of us in the 21st century share Paine's enthusiasm for enlightenment and disapproval of prejudice, it is also easy to see that he was unfortunately not only too optimistic for his time, but for ours too. Although he was certainly correct in claiming that few cling to prejudices when wrong ideas are exposed for what they are, Paine can be said to underestimate the power of prejudice—that which was praised by Burke. It helps explain why numerous non-elites continued to admire George III in the immediate aftermath of the French revolution—just as there were counterparts across the Channel who supported Louis XVI. Conversely, we might wonder if Paine is overly generous in praising American colonists for their lack of prejudice; although they may not have regarded fellow white Americans as "a natural enemy," such cannot be said for their overall perception and treatment of African- and Native Americans. Moreover, even among whites, the less well-off frequently found themselves at the mercy of affluent men—who were supported by wealthy government officials in their attempts to defraud people of their land.[8] Nor were white Americans entirely tolerant of other whites belonging to different religious sects since several state constitutions excluded Catholics from holding office.[9]

CHAPTER 1

In anticipation of William Godwin, the first so-called anarchist, Paine states "The more perfect civilization is, the less occasion has it for government, because the more does it regulate its own affairs and govern itself" (194). Through much of the chapter, Paine privileges society over government, deeming it a far more important force in the preservation of order and stability. "The landholder, the farmer, the manufacturer, the merchant, the tradesmen, and every occupation, prospers by the aid which each receives from the other, and from the whole" (193). It is telling that much like Winstanley, he places emphasis on commonalty, adding that "Common interest regulates their concerns" and "laws"; in turn, "laws which common usage ordains, have a greater influence than the laws of government" (193). Although Paine's example of America governing itself successfully between 1776 and 1782 without the apparent trappings of government may not be altogether accurate since some states simply retained the workings of their decades-old state legislatures, his assertions bear a certain truth on a larger scale in light of the democratic process by which other state constitutions were created as we will see in Chapter 4. Here, too, Paine proceeds to highlight commonalty, stating that when formal government is abolished, society takes the reins with "common interest produc[ing] common security" (194). This sense of social engagement resurfaces in the following paragraph as he underscores "the great and fundamental principles of society and civilization—to the common usage universally consented to, and mutually and reciprocally maintained" (194). As such, there is little justification for a multiplicity of laws rather than laws of "common usefulness" (195).

If anything, Paine argues, it is government that provokes unrest—a response not unlike Burlamaqui's who maintained that "disorders" in the body politic frequently arose from the abuse of the sovereign power, or from the bad constitution of the state.[10] Citing the Gordon riots of 1780, during which Catholic churches and the residences of authorities who supported the Catholic Relief Act were burned, Paine blames the disturbances on a government that had long encouraged prejudice against Roman

Catholics, thereby proving itself the true "generating cause" of "riots and tumults" (195). In fact, if we glance through British and American history, we find that Paine is correct. Certainly, the imposition of a flat tax in 1381, when the poor and middling orders found themselves paying disproportionately higher taxes, was a significant source of aggravation that instigated a revolt. One might also consider how the American animus against Britain did not escalate until the passing of the Stamp Act in 1763. Similarly, on a smaller scale, within the states themselves, the Regulator uprising of North Carolina did not erupt until a planter elite, bolstered by wealthy government officials, well-educated attorneys, and the Royal Governor William Tryon, attempted to force poorer citizens off their land while engaging in tax extortion.

It is here that Paine arrives at a simple yet profound observation that has been proven largely correct not only throughout British and American history, but across much of the world:

> Excess and inequality of taxation, however disguised in the means, never fail to appear in their effects. As a great mass of the community are thrown thereby into poverty and discontent, they are constantly on the brink of commotion; and deprived, as they unfortunately are, of the means of information, are easily heated to outrage. Whatever the apparent cause of any riots may be, the real one is always want of happiness. It shows that something is wrong in the system of government, that injures the felicity by which society is to be preserved.

By contrast, Paine argues, America has set a happier record in spite of its diversity of national origins, languages, and religions: this, of course, overlooks the hardships suffered by African and Native Americans as mentioned earlier. Pointing out a lack of inequality rarely encountered in Europe or other parts of the world, he states: "There, the poor are not oppressed, the rich are not privileged. Industry is not mortified by the splendid extravagance of a court rioting at its expense. Their taxes are few, because their government is just." Indeed, current research shows that economic inequality in American history was at its lowest in the late 18th century while social mobility was also at its highest. In 1774, according to modern historians, colonial incomes were considerably higher than those in Britain and Wales as the wage advantage over Britain was even greater than the income per capita advantage due partly to labor scarcity and land abundance.[11] Similarly, inequality was also much lower than in other parts of Europe (*Unequal Gains*, 14).

CHAPTER 2

Chapter 2 proceeds to examine the problems with old government. Although Paine does not allude to England until the third paragraph, he begins by pinning the blame squarely on the Norman conquest; by now, it is probably not surprising that rather than mention the Saxons and their much vaunted democratic government as repeatedly alluded to by the likes of Cartwright, Hulme, and Sharp, Paine omits them altogether as he did in Part 1. Again, one wonders if Paine did so in order to stress the ubiquity of natural rights around the world or if he tended to dismiss the idea of Saxon government as one verging on the mythological. It is also possible that he wished to forego the concept of restoring Saxon rights altogether given his impatience with mouldy precedents. Unlike Hulme, for instance, who described Saxon government as one founded upon "the principles of liberty" and Norman government on "the principles of slavery," Paine focuses entirely on the latter. For Paine, the history of England is a history of brutality where violence begets violence: a vision similar to Mary Wollstonecraft's image of feudal barons fighting one another in her reply to Burke. According to Paine, the real origins of government begin with the "bands of robbers" which plundered one another, with the conqueror treating the conquered "not as his prisoner, but his property" (198). With the passing of time, their successors would assume "new appearances to cut off the entail of their disgrace" even as their "principles and objects remained the same" (199). In short, it is an interpretation that shares many affinities with Winstanley's ideas on monarchy, namely the notion that all laws promulgated by kings helped "confirm and strengthen the power of the Norman Conquest."[12] Paine proceeds to reflect on the benefits that might accrue to the ordinary person:

> What inducement has the farmer, while following the plough, to lay aside his peaceful pursuit, and go to war with the farmer of another country? or what inducement has the manufacturer? What is dominion to them, or to any class of men in a nation? Does it add an acre to any man's estate, or raise its value? Are not conquest and defeat each of the same price, and taxes the never-failing consequence?—Though this reasoning may be good to a nation, it is not so to a government. War is the Pharotable of governments, and nations the dupes of the game.

In other words, there are few advantages to be reaped from war. Many 21st-century philosophers, economists, and political scientists have likewise continued to question the benefits of war and high military spending, observing that such activities have mostly enriched the wealthiest who either invest in or have a direct hand in the trade of weapons, ammunition, and oil.

Yet, there is also an irony involved in the debate over the relevance of war to the ordinary person. Even if few were invested or stood to profit from it, there was certainly a solid proportion of the public which enjoyed hearing of Britain's military prowess. Adam Smith, for instance, suggested that funding which allowed wars to take their natural course regardless of length was actually sanctioned by a government all too cognizant of the popularity of war:

> In great empires the people who live in the capital, and in the provinces remote from the scene of action, feel, many of them, scarce any inconveniency from the war; but enjoy ... the amusement of reading in the newspapers the exploits of their own fleets and armies. To them this amusement compensates the small difference between the taxes which they pay on account of the war, and those which they had been accustomed to pay in time of peace. They are commonly dissatisfied with the return of peace, which puts an end to their amusement, and to a thousand visionary hopes of conquest and national glory from a longer continuance of the war.

Similarly, Sinclair points out that

> When money however can easily be procured, and the nation is only loaded with an annuity to pay the interest of the debt that is incurred,

war is a pastime to the people, which they are not desirous of giving up, whilst they are occasionally favoured with Extraordinary Gazettes, announcing the victories gained by their fleets and armies, and celebrating the valour of their troops and the conduct of their commanders.

In other words, war is not only easy to fund, but even entertaining to many sectors of the public. Such has proven to be no less the case more than 200 years later with the initial support of the Iraq war in 2003 when two-thirds of Americans backed George W. Bush's decision to invade. Yet, it is also worth pointing out that after two years, numerous Americans increasingly disapproved of the never-ending war while questioning its premises.

CHAPTER 3

Paine begins Chapter 3 by repeating his juxtapositions between old government and new, reminding his readers that old governments champion war and national prejudices. Again, like Winstanley, he underscores "the common benefit of society," suggesting once more, as in Chap 1, that it will be accomplished by means of "universal society" and "universal commerce." For Paine, the latter can only be achieved through representative government. Hereditary government, by contrast, cannot function properly because it is an "imposition on mankind" and "inadequate" to the purposes of government. Revisiting his argument from Part 1, he claims that "Man has no authority over posterity in matters of personal right" (202). Here, he backs his assertion by contending that the premises of hereditary government defeat the purpose of government altogether, beginning with a tendency to reduce its subjects to "heritable property." Paine's reasoning is not unlike Harrington's and Sidney's. Just as Harrington claimed that it was wrong for a people to be "number'd as the Herd and Inheritance of One" while Sidney believed kings regard their nations "as grazers do their herds and flocks, according to the profit that can be made of them," Paine construes the idea of inheriting a government as one nearly equivalent to "inherit[ing] the people, as if they were flocks and herds" (202).[13] Secondly, although government "ought to be in full maturity"—meaning that it must reflect experience and wisdom—it seldom does. If Nedham alleged that monarchs were guilty of levelling their subjects by destroying their property and wealth, Paine can be said to renew the charge of levelling, albeit in a different context. What bothers Paine is the "mental levelling" involved, by which the personal qualities of the ruler are brushed aside. "Vice and virtue, ignorance and wisdom" are all "put on the same level" as it matters "not what their mental or moral characters are" (202). Like Sidney and Rousseau, Paine highlights the uncertain and unpredictable nature and character of the king: will he be sufficiently mature and wise? Sidney, for instance, feared for the safety of a nation when the king "is sometimes a child, and sometimes overburden'd with years" or when "Some are weak, negligent, slothful, foolish, or vicious" (440), just as Rousseau lashed out against an irrational system where "children should command old men, fools wise men and … the privileged few should gorge themselves with superfluities, while the starving multitude are in want of the bare necessities of life" (*Discourse on Inequality*).[14] Not fortuitously then, Paine snappily points out how government under a monarchy may appear "under all the various characters of childhood, decrepitude, dotage, a thing at nurse, in leading strings, or in crutches" (202). There is little doubt that Paine shared Sidney's view that one of the most "brutal and abominable of all extravagancies" was to elevate someone "inferior to others," deeming it an inversion of "the laws of nature and reason" (Sidney, 89) to be governed "by children, fools, or vicious and wicked persons" (94): Paine too would regard monarchy as a reversal of "The whole wholesome order of nature." Moreover, as if recalling his own words from his manifesto that a monarchy can be "filled by a person without talent or experience" or "devolve on a madman, an imbecile or a tyrant," Paine was quick to add that the mental characters of kings are often "Below the average of human understanding," with one being "A tyrant, another an idiot, a third insane, and some all three together" (203). (It is possible that he may have been aiming a jibe at George III.)

Paine proceeds to add that monarchies are far from stable; after all, a glance at the history of France and England reveals that problems caused by uncertain succession often trigger war, with hereditary monarchies proving far worse than elective ones.

Recent research, however, has disproven Paine's claim, suggesting instead that Sieyès was correct when he claimed that elective monarchies were more of a risk to stability than their hereditary counterparts.[15] In the period between 1000 and 1799, civil wars that took place in the wake of a monarch's death actually declined with the institution of primogeniture and rise of dynasticism.[16] From here, Paine tackles the problem of hereditary characteristics. Just as Sidney observes that children don't always resemble their fathers (257), Paine questions whether talents can be passed on from one generation to another. It is striking that he takes what might be called a democratic view of personal characteristics as he purports that such gifts and talents are scattered randomly, frequently changing hands. The last statement in the paragraph implies that every family receives some measure of talent at one point or another:

> Experience, in all ages, and in all countries, has demonstrated that it is impossible to control Nature in her distribution of mental powers. She gives them as she pleases ... It would be as ridiculous to attempt to fix the hereditaryship of human beauty, as of wisdom. Whatever wisdom constituently is, it is like a seedless plant; it may be reared when it appears, but it cannot be voluntarily produced ... It rises in one to-day, in another to-morrow, and has most probably visited in rotation every family of the earth, and again withdrawn. (205)

Once more, there is an implication that hereditary government is a travesty and perversion of nature when Paine states in the following paragraph "As this is in the order of nature, the order of government must necessarily follow it" or "degenerate." Here, it is interesting to contrast John Adams' rationale for advantage by birth in the following passage:

> Wise men beget fools, and honest men knaves; but these instances, although they may be frequent, are not general. If there is often a likeness in feature and figure, there is generally more in mind and heart, because education contributes to the formation of these as well as nature. The influence of example is very great, and almost universal, especially that of parents over their children. In all countries it has been observed, that vices, as well as virtues, very often run down in families

from age to age. Any man may go over in his thoughts the circle of his acquaintance, and he will probably recollect instances of a disposition to mischief, malice, and revenge, descending in certain breeds from grandfather to father and son. (*Defense of the Constitutions*)[17]

Although Adams' remarks are not without reason—education can make a significant difference while parents can exercise influence by example, they can hardly be made a case for legitimizing the privileges of birth. After all, parents do not always rely on the same methods of education: a fact that is witnessed through the changing standards of parenting through the ages. It is also worth reiterating that family resemblances are not predictable as certain traits may skip generations.

Paine, however, attempts to strengthen this idea of democratic talent by comparing the world of politics to the "republic of letters": as Claire Grogan suggests in her note, Paine clearly equates the democratic market of publications with those of government, observing "the right of each to apply and for society to determine their individual worth" (205). Not least does Paine quip that he knows "not whether Homer or Euclid had sons"; but most likely if they did, their sons would not be able to finish whatever works that their fathers left unfinished (205). Even more damning is the "separation between knowledge and power" (210) particularly when the monarch is a child and the very nature of a regency detracts even more from a monarchy. Here, we are reminded of Rousseau who noted in Book III Chap. 3 of *The Social Contract* that the "lack of coherence" and "inconstancy of royal government which, regulated now on one scheme and now on another, according to the character of the reigning prince or those who reign for him, cannot for long have a fixed object or a consistent policy": all too frequently, kings were prone to reverse whatever was done by their predecessors—in contrast to republics which "advance towards their ends by more consistent and better considered policies." Paine similarly censures this randomness, maintaining that "A regency is a mock species of republic, and the whole of monarchy deserves no better description." It lacks the "stable character that government ought to possess" since "Every succession is a revolution, and every regency a counter-revolution." In short, given the lack of reason and knowledge involved in monarchies, Paine calls it a "silly contemptible thing" that is

> kept behind a curtain, about which there is a great deal of bustle and fuss, and a wonderful air of seeming solemnity; but when, by any accident, the curtain happens to be open, and the company see what it is, they burst into laughter.[18]

By contrast, the only form of government that is rational, according to Paine, is one that approaches democracy. It is the democracy of the Athenians in which there is "more to admire, and less to condemn," Paine explains, noting that the enactment of laws "in the first person" exhibited "public principle" (207). Nonetheless, it is striking that Paine rejects Athenian democracy, imagining that if the system of political representation were understood, early democracies might not have lapsed into monarchies and aristocratic governments. It is the republican form of government, as Paine describes a few pages later, that is the ideal government. The question, of course, that surfaces at this point, is what precisely is a republican government? In order to understand Paine's idea of a republic, it is necessary to compare it to his definition in an essay he wrote five years earlier, *Public Good*. In the earlier work, he not only explicitly identified it as one directed by the "fundamental principles of right and justice," thereby the complete opposite of despotism, but also highlighted its representative nature: "the administration is executed by a select number of persons periodically chosen by the people, who act as representatives and in behalf of the whole." He then adds "The public good is to be their object," which he defines as "the good of every individual collected." Its "foundation-principle" is also "justice." Interestingly, he would proceed to posit a republic as an ideal form that excludes despotism by either one man or a vast number: Paine may have dreaded a mob mentality nearly as much as Hamilton and Madison:

> In this pledge and compact lies the foundation of the republic: and the security to the rich and the consolation to the poor is, that what each man has is his own; that no despotic sovereign can take it from him, and that the common cementing principle which holds all the

parts of a republic together, secures him likewise from the despotism of numbers: for despotism may be more effectually acted by many over a few, than by one man over all.

Although Paine's views did not change drastically in 1792, he would make the case for republicanism more compelling, partly as a result of his debate with Abbé Sieyès. As Paine asserted in a public response to Sieyès' article in *Le Moniteur*, explaining that "I do not mean by Republicanism that which bears the name in Holland, or in some Italian States" but rather "simply as a Government by Representation" (Sieyes, 165), Sieyès countered this identification by suggesting that a monarchy and a purely representative government could both be regarded as republican governments since both may be equally supportive of "public interest": "When they call themselves Republicans, it should not be by opposition to Monarchy: they are Republicans because they are for the public interest, and certainly we are so."

In *Rights of Man*, Paine brings greater focus to the idea of the "public good" than in *Public Good*, while also replacing "despotism" with "monarchy." Note that his amplification of RES-PUBLICA serves to underscore at greater length what he believes to the true mission of government: tending to the needs of the people. As if taking his cue from Sieyès, he points out that a republican government is not necessarily representative but that "such a government is usually so" because republican government is government established and conducted for the interest of the public, "individually and collectively." There is no particular form of government associated with it, "but it most naturally associates with the representative form." Perhaps even more significantly, Paine overturns the centuries-long belief that republican governments are only appropriate for small countries:

Those who have said that a republic is not a form of government calculated for countries of great extent, mistook, in the first place, the business of a government, for a form of government; for the res-publica equally appertains to every extent of territory and population. And, in the second place, if they meant anything with respect to form, it was the simple democratical form, such as was the mode of government in the ancient democracies, in which there was no representation. The case, therefore, is not, that a republic cannot be extensive, but that it cannot be extensive on the simple democratical form ... What is the best form of government for conducting the RES-PUBLICA, or the PUBLIC BUSINESS of a nation, after it becomes too extensive and populous for the simple democratical form? It cannot be monarchy, because monarchy is subject to an objection of the same amount to which the simple democratical form was subject. (208)

The confusion arises from the fact that republics are often mistakenly assumed to be simple democracies where representation does not figure in at all. Instead, when compared with simple democracy and monarchy, republican government proves far superior given its access to "the various and numerous circumstances of a nation, its agriculture, manufacture, trade, commerce, etc., etc.," and representatives elected from a variety of professions and experiences. Such men would form "an assemblage of practical knowledge, which no individual can possess." Interestingly too, if monarchical government can only be limited "from the incompetency of knowledge," Paine faults "democratic government," for its tendency to "degenerate" into "confusion" with its "multiplicity of population." Here, he returns to his metaphor of the republic of letters in his assessment of republican government. If "simple democracy was society governing itself without the aid of secondary means," a republican government—a "grafting of representation upon democracy"—was a system of government "capable of embracing ... all the various interests and every extent of territory"; it was "as much superior to hereditary government, as the republic of letters is to hereditary literature." For Paine, "What Athens was in miniature America will be in magnitude"; because the new republican government in America is "ingrafted upon democracy," it will naturally avoid "the ignorance and insecurity of the hereditary mode, and the inconvenience of the simple democracy." This is a claim that puts him in the same political position as Madison and to the right of Rousseau who, as we have seen earlier, believed that representation did little to serve the people's needs—or at least, less so than simple democracy.[19] Perhaps Paine believed that the American system of representation would be more responsive than the British one given the wider disenfranchisement.

As Paine returns to berating monarchies, he adds that representative governments are always "in a state of constant maturity," and generally, "subject neither to nonage, nor dotage" while never becoming overly subject to "all the accidents of individual man" like a monarchy. The president of the U.S., for instance, cannot be under the age of 35 so as to ensure that he is mature and "Has lived long enough to be acquainted with men and things, and the country with him."[20] Unlike the unnaturalness of the British government, the American representative system is "always parallel with the order and immutable laws of nature, and meets the reason of man in every part." Paine would also note that the president was handsomely but not excessively compensated—again, unlike the monarch in Britain. But although Paine was generally correct in claiming that the U.S. government did not spend anywhere near as much as the British and French governments, this cost-effectiveness may be attributed to the fact that the young republic had not yet established a military budget—not to mention the important advantage of possessing ample lands for sale. Moreover, knowledge on the part of an informed electorate helps too, as Paine asserts that "the representative system diffuses such a body of knowledge throughout a nation, on the subject of government, as to explode ignorance and preclude imposition." It is a system of representative government that demands a reason for everything, particularly since "every man is a proprietor in government, and considers it a necessary part of his business to understand" (213). Indeed, a knowledge of government is necessary for his personal livelihood because it "concerns his interest" and "affects his property."

NOTES

1 This was scrawled on the shutters of a public house. See Mark Philp, *Reforming Ideas in Britain: Politics and Language in the Shadow of the French Revolution, 1789–1815* (Cambridge: Cambridge University Press, 2013) p. 67.
2 John Keane, *Tom Paine: A Political Life* (New York: Little, Brown, Co., 1995) p. 319.
3 See: http://oll.libertyfund.org/titles/burke-further-reflections-on-the-french-revolution
4 See: http://oll.libertyfund.org/titles/burke-further-reflections-on-the-french-revolution
5 Thomas Paine, "A Republican Manifesto" in *The Complete Writings of Thomas Paine*, Vols. 1–2 ed. Philip Foner (New York: Citadel Press, 1945) 2, p. 517.

6 Jean-Jacques Rousseau, *The Social Contract*, Book 2, Chap. 4, trans. G.D.H. Cole for Marxists.org. See: https://www.marxists.org/reference/subject/economics/rousseau/social-contract/cho2.htm#004

7 James Mackintosh was somewhat more guarded in his optimism: "Any reasonings on the influence of the French Revolution may therefore be supposed to be premature until its permanence be ascertained ... the decease of Gothic governments cannot be distant. Their maturity is long past, and symptoms of their decrepitude are rapidly accumulating. Whether they are to be succeeded by more beneficial or more injurious Governments may be doubted, but that they are about to perish, we are authorized to suppose ...." See: https://oll.libertyfund.org/titles/mackintosh-vindiciae-gallicae-a
nd-other-writings-on-the-french-revolution

8 See Chapter 2 in Gary Nash's *The Unknown American Revolution* (London: Penguin, 2005).

9 Many states imposed religious tests for public office. Sanford Levinson notes that "Maryland and Delaware were relatively liberal ... requiring only that one be Christian, though Delaware required a belief in the Trinity as well. New Hampshire, Connecticut, New Jersey, North Carolina, and Georgia specified that officeholders be Protestant; no Catholics need apply. Pennsylvania and South Carolina officials had to believe in one God and in heaven and hell. The outliers in this regard were Georgia, Virginia, New York, and Massachusetts." See *Framed: America's 51 Constitutions and the Crisis of Governance* (Oxford: Oxford University Press, 2013) p. 70.

10 See Burlamaqui, *The Principles of Natural and Politic Law*, Vols. 1–2, trans. Thomas Nugent, ed. Peter Korkman (Indianapolis: Liberty Fund, 2006). Online edition. Vol. 1, Part 2, Chap. 1, XXXIII–IV.

11 Peter H. Linder and Jeffrey G. Williamson, *Unequal Gains: American Growth and Inequality since 1790* (Princeton, NJ: Princeton University Press, 2016) p. 69.

12 Gerrard Winstanley, *A Letter to the Lord Fairfax*, in *CW*, 2, p. 49.

13 See Harrington, http://www.constitution.org/jh/oceana.htm; Algernon Sidney, *Discourses on Government*, ed. Thomas G. West (Indianapolis: Liberty Fund, 1990, 1996) p. 202.

14 Jean-Jacques Rousseau, *Discourse on Inequality*, Part 2. See: https://www.marxists.org/reference/subject/economics/rousseau/inequality/cho2.htm

15 See Andre Kokkonen and Anders Sundell, *The King is Dead: Political Succession and War in Europe, 1000–1799*, Working Paper Series 9: 2017, Quality of Government Institute, University of Gothenburg.

16 Kokkonnen and Sundell, p. 3.

17 Reprinted in the Online Library of Liberty. See: http://oll.libertyfund.org/titles/adams-the-works-of-john-adams-vol-4, 4.

18 One wonders if the directors of *The Wizard of Oz* (1939) had this quotation in mind when Dorothy's dog, Toto, moves the curtain aside to reveal a small man manipulating the thundering image of the seemingly wonderful wizard: after which he is called a "humbug."

19 In *Federalist* #10, Madison states: "Under such a regulation, it may well happen that the public voice, pronounced by the representatives of the people, will be more

consonant to the public good than if pronounced by the people themselves, convened for the purpose." Modern constitutional scholars such as Sanford Levinson seem to share Rousseau's ideas as he argues that "But why would one expect elected representatives to be more devoted to 'the public good' than "the people themselves"? Sanford Levinson, *Framed*, 90. Levinson proceeds to point out that many U.S. states as well as countries such as New Zealand, Switzerland, and Australia—all incorporate the possibility of direct democracy into their constitutional orders: "All would be described as adherents of representative democracy, but they incorporate features of direct democracy ... by which 'the people' are permitted to decide for themselves one or another vital issue—and not merely select those who are then given power to make such decisions" (120).

20 In *Framed*, 118, Levinson criticizes the seemingly arbitrary assignment of age to political representatives, suggesting that age limits can be changed. However one may agree, it is clear that age was deemed important to the Founding Fathers in order to avoid the problems associated with immature monarchs.

3

RIGHTS OF MAN PART 2, CHAPTER 4

In many respects, Chapter 4 can be said to pick up where *Common Sense* left off when Paine declared "a new era for politics is struck—a new method of thinking hath arisen" as he developed ideas from *Answers to Four Questions*, a work that he published in Paris during the summer of 1791. It is also here that we detect the first inklings of Abraham Lincoln's famous conceptualization of "government of the people, by the people, for the people" as Paine opens the chapter by pointing out that constitutions are written by the people—not the government—and that "government without a constitution, is power without a right" (214): ideas that reinforce earlier ideas from *Dissertations on Government* (1786):

> In republics, such as those established in America, the sovereign power ... remains where nature placed it—in the people; for the people in America are the fountain of power. It remains there as a matter of right, recognized in the constitutions of the country ... this sovereignty is exercised in electing and deputing a certain number

of persons to represent and act for the whole, and who, if they do not act right, may be displaced by the same power that placed them there.[1]

If people are "the fount of power," fears of instability and political disorder are unwarranted for the simple reason that elections provide an effective means for replacing unsuitable representatives. Having denied usurpation and antiquity as viable premises for government, Paine focuses on the people themselves by reiterating the importance of starting anew: that is, of "seeing government begin, as if we had lived in the beginning of time" without the "the errors of tradition." In other words, to quote *Common Sense*, there must be a means of starting the world over again. This idea, of course, was hardly unique to Paine since even the more conservative-leaning Alexander Hamilton equally denied in *The Federalist* that Americans "suffered a blind veneration for antiquity, for custom, or names" in place of "good sense" and "their own experience."[2] Having addressed the inconveniences and problems endemic to hereditary government in Chapter 3, Paine attempts to demonstrate in Chapter 4 just how much more democratic and constitutional the new American republic (and by extension, the new French government) stands in comparison to Britain, freed from the "errors of tradition" (214). Reflecting on the writing and ratification of the 1776 Pennsylvania constitution—a constitution that he admired all through his later years—Paine praises the scrupulous care taken in electing representatives from each county to create a constitution, a draft of which was to be published, "not as a thing established, but for the consideration of the whole people" (215). It is notable that Paine again highlights the participatory aspects of a constitution drafted at the convention while pointing to the important role played by the people at large, adding that the constitution was sealed and proclaimed "on *the authority of the people* and the original instrument deposited as a public record" (215).

Indeed, the apparently hands-on, democratic nature of constitution writing was widely lauded by his American contemporaries as they extolled the participatory nature of a constitution, positing it as a novel phenomenon unique to the New World: and it is entirely possible that Paine took his cues on the democratic nature of constitution writing from the creation of state constitutions as reported in pamphlets and newspapers not long after his arrival in Philadelphia. He may have gleaned a certain pride in the comments of such men as Oliver Wolcott, a congressional delegate from Connecticut, who marveled at America's constitution-making in 1776 as a "real" rather than "theoretical expression of the people's will," and in those of historian David Ramsay who proclaimed in near-Paineite phrasing that "We are the first people in the world who have had it in their power to choose their own form of government."[3] It was during this period that the people came to be stipulated as the source of "all constitutional authority" (Fritz, 33), not only in the preambles to the constitutions of South Carolina and New Jersey, but also in the bill of rights in Virginia's constitution which plainly alluded to the "power … vested in, and consequently derived from, the People" (qtd. in Fritz, 33). Likewise, over the course of the 1770s and '80s, a number of organized artisans and mechanics in New York disputed the right of a provincial congress to pass a constitution, a power which they argued belonged to "the inhabitants at large" because it was a "right" handed from God "to judge whether it be consistent with their interest to accept or reject a constitution."[4] A similar belief was shared by the attendees of a Pittsfield, Massachusetts meeting who determined that the first step for people in the restoration of a "Civil Government" was "the formation of a fundamental Constitution." Claiming that "the Approbation of the Majority of the people of this fundamental Constitution" was "absolutely necessary," they stipulated that a "Representative Body" could not "impose said fundamental Constitution upon a people" (qtd. in Adams, 63). Perhaps inspired by those state constitutions which implemented standard procedures for passing amendments and "alter or abolish" provisions,[5] Paine would encourage the election of a convention every seven years in order to accommodate "the benefit of experience" and "prevent the accumulation of errors" in the constitution: with these measures in place, the constitution would always remain relevant and up-to-date. Not least, the publication of other state constitutions in newspapers and the circulation of drafts for public commentary (Adams, 33), the printing of other state constitutions in newspapers and essays must have heightened the importance of a democratic process.[6]

If Paine refers to the constitution as a "political bible of state," tacitly aligning the American government with an equally approved Protestantism and the British government with a more popularly reviled Roman Catholicism, it is telling that he duly accentuates the transparent, accessible, and congregational nature of American government:

> Here we see a regular process—a government issuing out of a constitution, formed by the people in their original character; and that constitution serving ... as a law of control to the government. It was the political bible of the state. Scarcely a family was without it. Every member of the government had a copy; and nothing was more common, when any debate arose on the principle of a bill ... than for the members to take the printed constitution ... and read the chapter with which such matter in debate was connected. (216)

As Robert Lamb has recently suggested, it is for this reason that Paine's preoccupation with the importance of a written constitution is not mere quibbling:

> Constitutions function by empowering citizens: they display the equal status of citizens and their individual rights publicly ... They enable individuals to see and know both what rights they hold and, by implication, what duties they owe to others. Their existence is necessary for the democratic prosperity of a political community.[7]

After all, how can a political society function properly when its citizens are not fully cognizant of their laws?

Moreover, when observing that Congress went no further than to issue recommendations to the several provincial assemblies in September 1774 and May 1775, allowing the latter to adopt them at their own discretion, Paine highlights the notion of reciprocity between a government and the people, asserting that "the strength of government" lies in "the attachment of a nation, and the interest which a people feel in supporting it" (216). Again, since it is the people who are the true governing bodies, there is nothing more ludicrous than "the idea of a compact between the people on one side, and the government on the other" because a compact arises from the people "produ[cing] and constitut[ing] a government" (217). Here, again, Paine's attitude may have been colored at least in part by those state constitutions which promulgated the idea of the people as the *de facto* governing forces. After all, the Virginia Bill of Rights went so far as to establish the state residents rather than their government officials as the true sovereigns while the constitutions of Massachusetts and New Hampshire similarly deemed the officials no more than "substitutes and agents" for the people and "at all times accountable to them" (Fritz, 18, 19). Even Hamilton, with his broad distrust for democratic sentiment, was able to pay lip service to this idea in *The Federalist* Papers 22 and 78:

> It has not a little contributed to the infirmities of the existing federal system, that it never had a ratification by the *people* ... The fabric of American empire ought to rest on the solid basis of *the consent of the people*. The streams of national power ought to flow immediately from that pure, original fountain of all legitimate authority. (Hamilton, #22)

Such a rationale may explain why Paine was keen to remind his readers that there are no "rights" to be possessed exclusively by government but only "duties"; much less should it be instituted for "personal emolument" since it is "altogether a trust, in right of those by whom that trust is delegated" (217).

As Paine delves into the drafting and ratification of the U.S. Constitution, however, one is struck by the glaring discrepancies between his idealistic narrative of a democratically designed constitution and the actual account of its development. To what extent did Paine share the views of his somewhat less populist peers, particularly Alexander Hamilton and James Madison, that the states wielded too much power and the federal government "too little": even if he himself had once asserted that the states were bound together too loosely? Especially when he defended the creation of a new national constitution as well as the Pennsylvania constitution of 1776 by underscoring the idea of democratic consensus, stating that the proposed alterations of its state constitution were passed only after being approved by the people (219)? Indeed, what is particularly curious is how Paine glosses over the difficulties in ratifying the U.S. constitution, despite his acknowledgement that there was "much debate and division" involved in the ratification of the Constitution in Boston. Rounding off the section on the stages of ratification with unmistakable confidence, he praises representative governments for quietly "decid[ing] all matters by majority" (218). Equally curious too is his reticence on features of the Constitution that might be said to be as flawed as those of the British constitution. Perhaps these anomalies are not unduly astonishing since he had already sailed off to Europe on April 26, 1787—that is, three weeks prior to the first day of the Constitutional Convention at Philadelphia on May 14—so that he missed numerous details on the composition, discussion, and ratification of the Constitution in each of the thirteen states, a lengthy process which did not conclude until 1790. However bold and revolutionary the American constitution must have appeared to much of the Western world at the close of the 18th century, particularly in light of its elaborate checks and balances with its relative diminution of executive power, it was nonetheless perceived by many of Paine's American contemporaries as a reactionary, even conservative document. In fact, the rationale and ideals behind the constitution might be said to stand at odds against Paine's ideals for a transparent, democratic government as stated in *Common Sense* and other works. Here, it is worth examining a few similarities between the American constitution and its British counterpart as perceived by supporters of the former and its detractors, the Anti-Federalists. The latter are especially worth paying attention to not so much because they may have influenced Paine who was on his way to Europe—but rather because Paine may have been informed by the same train of thought that influenced them.

There is little doubt that the intent behind the constitution was nowhere nearly as open or democratic as Paine assumed. If anything, its creation might be said to represent the act of government protecting itself from the people—a rather far cry from Paine's remark that "there is no such thing as the idea of a compact between the people on one side, and the government on the other" (217). After all, the Constitution was initially borne out of frustration not only with the weak Articles of Confederation which prevented Congress from regulating foreign and interstate trade, but also out of anxieties aroused by Shays' Rebellion in Massachusetts and the ensuing measures for economic relief passed in the wake of the rebellion across various states.[8] In other words, it grew out of a profound distrust of populism. In 1787, for instance, the Connecticut legislature simply refused to pay Congress's latest requisition for taxes rather than risk the prospect of a Shays' Rebellion (Klarman, 98). Monied and propertied elites resented such relief measures, insisting that creditors had a right to be repaid what the government had borrowed from them in hard specie. They also took exception at other relief measures such as payment in produce and the amelioration of debt. Indeed, during 1785–6, Paine found himself on the wrong side of the populist argument when he argued for the establishment of the Bank of North America while deprecating the issuance of paper money, explaining that the latter was "both the bubble and the iniquity of the day" believing that "the whole system of safety and certainty" would be "overturned, and property set afloat."[9] In light of the general tendency of state governments to accede to populist impulses, Federalists decided that a stronger, more centralized government was necessary: namely, by preventing state governments from caving into the demands of the unruly mobs in the first place. Richard Henry Lee thus concluded that a departure "from simple democracy" was "indispensably necessary" while his cousin, Charles Lee, advised Washington that unless state legislatures could be rendered "more powerful and independent of the people," public and even private debts would be entirely cancelled (Klarman 86). As such, Madison would articulate his distrust of democratic tendencies, in *Federalist* #10, fearing that "When a majority is included in a faction, the form of popular government, on the other hand, enables it to sacrifice to its ruling passion or interest both the public good and the rights of other citizens." A more "independent" legislature— one not immediately beholden to the people—would thereby curb the desire for paper money, the abolition of debts, equal division of property or "any other improper or wicked project": thereby ultimately preserving the wealth of propertied elites.

In short, genteel Pennsylvanians hoped that, with the new ban on paper money and the requirement that debts be paid in gold and silver, the ratification of the Constitution would facilitate foreign investment and boost real estate.[10] The new Constitution would therefore be created expressly for the elite purpose of curbing populist demands deemed inimical to property rights and encouraging overall investment in the young republic. With the determination to contain popular pressures, Madison, Hamilton, and other Federalists advocated longer terms in office, larger constituencies, a bicameral legislature, and indirect elections: measures abhorred by the more democratically inclined. Larger constituencies were projected to ensure the election of distinguished large property holders—men likely to support legislative action that protected property rights (Klarman 171)—while indirect elections of the Senate, Presidency, or even the House of Representatives (which a few initially advocated) would preserve distance between elected representatives and the represented as another means of limiting influence of the people.[11] But even though the Virginia Plan and New Jersey Plan implemented the common practice of recall for congressional representatives, this idea was ultimately nixed as Hamilton deemed that such a practice would inevitably privilege state prejudices "rather than the good of the union" (Klarman 176). Likewise, the delegates also rejected the right of the people to "instruct" their representatives as stipulated in several state constitutions such as in New Hampshire (Klarman, 176). So far, then, what we have is an anti-populist vision of government that is almost the exact opposite of Paine's as proffered in *Common Sense* where he envisioned a system where

the ELECTED might never form to themselves an interest separate from the ELECTORS, prudence will point out the propriety of having elections often: because as the ELECTED might by that means return and mix again with the general body of the ELECTORS in a few months, their fidelity to the public will be secured by the prudent reflection of not making a rod for themselves. And as this frequent interchange will establish a common interest with every part of the community, they will mutually and naturally support each other, and on this, (not on the unmeaning name of king,) depends the STRENGTH OF GOVERNMENT, AND THE HAPPINESS OF THE GOVERNED.

In fact, Madison was deeply disappointed that the proposed measure for the federal powers to veto state laws failed: as such, the federal government would not be able to prevent state legislatures from succumbing to populist demands for debt relief (Klarman, 254–5).

Further safeguards would be placed against democracy in the form of a Senate, an entity serving as yet another corrective to democratic impulses in the House of Representatives. Not unlike much of the aristocracy and gentry in England, Hamilton voiced extreme wariness of the masses.

> All communities divide themselves into the few and the many. The first are the rich and well born, the other the mass of the people. The voice of the people has been said to be the voice of God; and however generally this maxim has been quoted and believed, it is not true in fact. The people are turbulent and changing; they seldom judge or determine right. Give therefore to the first class a distinct, permanent share in the government. They will check the unsteadiness of the second, and as they cannot receive any advantage by a change, they therefore will ever maintain good government.[12]

This skepticism was reinforced a year later by Hamilton in a speech on the floor of the U.S. Senate in 1788 where he doubled down on the necessity for "some permanent body" to correct the "prejudices," "passions," and to "regulate the fluctuations of a popular assembly." He feared that "despite good intentions," the people at large did "not possess the discernment and stability necessary for systematic government," since they were all too likely to be "misguided by ignorance, by sudden impulses, and the intrigues of ambitious men" (*On the Adoption of the constitution*).[13]

It was Madison, again, who clearly spelled out his fears for the undoing of property rights of the haves under a potential plurality of have-nots in the distant future: a belief radically divergent from Paine's resentment of a wealthy aristocracy that legislated for its own interests. If the landed interest should ever shrink to a minority, he assumed it would require protection from the desires of the less wealthy to "redistribute." Like Hamilton and John Adams, he preferred a limited British-style electorate in order to "protect the minority of the opulent":

> The man who is possessed of wealth, who lolls on his sofa ... cannot judge of the wants or feelings of the day laborer. The government we mean to erect is intended to last for ages. The landed interest, at present, is prevalent; but in process of time, ... will not the landed interest be overbalanced in future elections ... ? In England, at this day, if elections were open to all classes of people, the property of the landed proprietors would be insecure. An agrarian law would soon take place. If these observations be just, our government ought to secure the permanent interests of the country against innovation. Landholders ought to have a share in the government ... They ought to be so constituted as to protect the minority of the opulent against the majority. The senate, therefore, ought to be this body; and to answer these purposes, they ought to have permanency and stability.[14]

No less telling is his other assumption that the demise of the landed class would spell the inevitable end of government as if he presumed the latter to be wholly comprised of the former: again, a stipulation very different from Paine's. He went even so far as to argue for a senate out of anxiety that the have-nots might demand a redistribution of wealth, fretting that those who "labour under all the hardships of life," would "Secretly sigh for a more equal distribution of its blessings" and exhibit "symptoms of a leveling spirit" which was already being manifested.

In order to disguise such nakedly anti-populist fears, however, the rationale for a senate was framed in substantially different terms by Hamilton in *The Federalist Papers* #62 where he claimed that body of senators might serve an important purpose if the House of Representatives ever "forg[ot] their obligations to their constituents and prove[d] unfaithful to their important trust." Unlike Paine who, as we will see, continued to recommend a unicameral legislature, a number of delegates were thus eager to erect a senate as an American counterpart to the House of Lords.[15] Since the "democratic parts of our constitution" posed great danger while state charters provided insufficient "checks against the democracy," according to Edmund Randolph, a delegate from Virginia, a "firm Senate" was necessary to counteract "the democratic licentiousness of the state legislatures."[16] It was as such that John Dickinson of Pennsylvania proposed that senators should be selected on account of their social rank and wealth so as to bear as strong a resemblance to the "British House of Lords as possible" with Charles Cotesworth Pinckney of South Carolina concurring on the necessity of wealth (qtd in Klarman, 210). To further prevent a capitulation to political populism, the terms of senatorial elections were to be lengthened and staggered: whereas those in the upper houses of state legislatures and governors served on an annual basis, senators would serve much longer six-year terms. Not least, even though the president would not wield nearly as much power as the British king, he was to be vested with far more executive power than any state governor:[17] he would have veto power and the predominant share of the appointment power in addition to becoming commander-in-chief of the armed forces with the necessary authority to negotiate treaties and pardon criminals. While some went so far as to propose lifetime tenure, others—most notably, George Mason and James Madison—feared that it would bear too much of the qualities of a monarchy.

Paine's erstwhile support for the Constitution—at least in *Rights of Man*—is thus all the more puzzling when his strong disapproval of aristocratic government, suspicion of secrecy, inadequate representation, and irregular proceedings are weighed. Although the anti-Federalists did not necessarily share all of Paine's characteristic concerns and antipathies, many of their relatively egalitarian views can be said to bear great affinities to his; it is difficult not to conclude that Paine and the Anti-Federalists were swayed by similar ideas on government. Writing as a "Columbian Patriot," for instance, Mercy Otis Warren found the size of the House of Representatives "very inadequate" (*Observations on the New Constitution*)[18] while the Pennsylvanians who penned *The Address and reasons of dissent of the minority and of the convention of the state of Pennsylvania to their Constituents* (Dec. 17, 1787), also regretted the "inadequate" and "unsafe" level of representation. Since the "various climates, products, habits, interests, and opinions" simply could not be collected in so small a body, what was to be most feared "from the mode of election and appointment" was that the candidates would be inevitably drawn from the most elite class of men, thereby forming a de facto aristocracy.[19] Others drew attention to the fact that the number of members was exceeded not only by individual states but even by the British House of Commons (Klarman, 355). The real crux of the problem, however, was the lack of a truly democratic representation. In his *Objections to the Constitution*, George Mason fretted that the House of Representatives would fail to respond to the needs of the people, complaining that there was only the "shadow" of representation, "not the substance"; he feared that laws would be made by men "little concerned in, and unacquainted with their effects and consequences."[20] It was therefore all too likely that the government would begin as a "moderate aristocracy" before culminating in a "monarchy," the number of representatives limited to one per 30,000 men,[21] the pool of most eligible candidates would inevitably be drawn from men most distinguished for "birth, education, talents and wealth" (as noted earlier, such indeed was the intention of Madison). If representatives "should be a true picture of the people," sharing their "circumstances and their wants" in addition to being capable of "sympathiz[ing] in all their distresses,"[22] it was all too predictable that "the farmer, merchant, mechanick, and other various orders of people" would fail to be truly represented.

On the other hand, as he noted, it was too probable with a limited house of representatives that only the wealthiest merchants would be represented while "The great body of the yeomen of the country" would not. Given the gaping distance "between the people and their representatives" and the fact that the most well-off were generally "ignorant of the sentiments of the middling class of citizens" and their particular "wants and difficulties," representatives would most likely be ignorant of the "pains and labour" required to acquire wealth and property; nor could they imagine the challenge "arising from the payment of small sums." The writer feared a serious liability for the people with a legislature of such "an imperfect representation," knowing that there would be little security in such a miniscule body of representatives against "bribery, and corruption." Not to mention that elites were less personally suitable; if anything, they were arrogant and standoffish, holding "themselves above the common people" while "fancy[ing] themselves to have a right of preeminence in everything." In short, they behaved with more or less "the same feelings" and "same motives of a hereditary nobility" (New York Ratifying Convention, June 21, 1788). Instead, it would be far preferable to have government presided over by the yeomanry:

> A representative body, composed principally of respectable yeomanry is the best possible security to liberty.—When the interest of this part of the community is pursued, the public good is pursued ... And because the interest of both the rich and the poor are involved in that of the middling class. No burden can be laid on the poor, but what will sensibly affect the middling class. Any law rendering property insecure, would be injurious to them.—When therefore this class in society pursue their own interest, they promote that of the public, for it is involved in it.

It is worth noting that Smith's remarks might be said to be more radical than Paine's since the latter did not specify any class to serve as representatives—even if he felt a largely propertied elite set of MPs to be ignorant of public concerns.

Opinions on the proposed senate and electoral college system ran along similar lines. For Mercy Otis Warren, the selection of senators by state legislatures was "nearly tantamount to the exclusion of the voice of the people." Censuring the extremely limited number of representatives for its all too certain lack of awareness of "the wants, local circumstances, and sentiments of so extensive an empire," she predicted that the senate would become a "*permanent* Aristocracy," prey to "corruption and undue influence" (*Centinel* 1).[23] She also disapproved of the limited number of men on the electoral college system for the selection of the president, regarding it as an "aristocratic junto." Given these collected criticisms, it is hardly astonishing that *The Federal Farmer* castigated the Federalists for their attachment to "the principles of monarchy and aristocracy" and an "Aversion to democratic republics," while predicting that the "democratic branch" was sure to be "weak and small," offering few "genuine friends" to the people. In short, a government that was accrued in the hands of the wealthiest could not be trusted by the people:

> Without scrutinizing into the particulars of the proposed system, we immediately perceive that its general tendency is to collect the powers

of government, now in the body of the people in reality, and to place them in the higher orders and fewer hands ... the body of the people evidently feel there is something wrong and disadvantageous to them; both descriptions perceive there is something tending to bestow on the former the height of power and happiness, and to reduce the latter to weakness, insignificance, and misery. (*Federal Farmer* #9)[24]

Again, although it is difficult to ascertain whether Paine was acquainted with any of these Anti-Federalist writings, it is none-theless highly probable that the political beliefs shared by Paine and the Anti-Federalists were guided alike by the strong current of populist politics in the young republic. It was not until at least a decade later that Paine would register his disapproval of the 1787 U.S. Constitution and the newly reformed Pennsylvania constitution of 1792 (revised to align more closely with the fed-eral constitution by accommodating wealthier citizens).

But the balance of power in the hands of the elites was hardly the only shortcoming in Anti-Federalist eyes. Many found fault with Congress' powers to alter regulations for the time and place of elections—much like Marat did in 1774. The Anti-Federalists at the Pennsylvania convention dreaded that the senators and representatives could potentially "prolong their existence in office, for life" by postponing elections and appointments "under var-ious pretenses"; instead, they contended that "the *time, mode*, and *place* of the election of representatives, senators and president-general of the United States, ought not to be under the control of Congress, but fundamentally ascertained and established" (*The Address and reasons of dissent of the minority of the convention, of the state of Pennsylvania*). It is a complaint that bears close resemblance to Paine's observations on Parliament throughout Part 1 and in the very pages of Chapter 4 where he claims that "Were a bill to be brought into any of the American legislatures" comparable to that passed by Parliament at the beginning of George I's reign, it would be denied because "the check is in the constitution" (229).[25] At the same time, Anti-Federalists found the legislative and executive branches too closely enmeshed—particu-larly where the senate and presidency were concerned: again, a criticism not unlike that of Paine's assessment of the relationship between Parliament and the King in Part 1. Both branches, according to Warren, were "so dangerously blended" and the language governing their conduct "is couched in such … vague and indefinite expression" (*Observations on the New Constitution*).[26] Just as George Mason feared that senatorial "influence" on the executive branch would "destroy any balance in the government" and "enable them" to usurp "the rights and liberties of the people" (*Objections to the Constitution*),[27] the writers of the *Address and Reasons of Dissent* disapproved of "the undue and dangerous mixture of the … same body possessing legislative, executive, and judicial powers."[28] Particularly objectionable was the fact that the senate, as part of the legislature, enjoyed "judicial power in judging on impeachments" while helping the president appoint principal officers. Citing Montesquieu, the writers worried that the combination of legislative and executive powers could potentially "bias the judgments of the senators," screening "great delinquents from punishment." However, Anti-Federalists differed among themselves in regard to the source of lethal influence: if Elbridge Gerry anticipated that such a dangerous integration of powers enabled the president to obtain "undue influence over the legislature,"[29] an Anti-federalist from North Carolina conversely assumed that the president would be unable to prevail against the Senate (Klarman, 370). Not least was the problem of future revisions and alterations. As Christian Fritz notes, even though Madison proposed to remind the nation that all power is vested in and derived from the people, with the added provision that they "have an indubitable, unalienable, and indefeasible right to reform or change their government," these ideas never entered into the bill of rights: this reticence stood in opposition to the many state bills of rights that not only outlined the powers of the sovereign but also articulated how the people as the ruler of the state could exercise collective rights (Fritz, 145).

But perhaps most surprising in light of Paine's detestation of slavery is his silence on the safeguards for its continued practice. Although several northern delegates to the Philadelphia convention played prominent roles in their states' antislavery movements, no northern legislature instructed its delegates to take action against slavery (Klarman, 262). Moreover, if the Three-Fifths Clause, the

Foreign Slave Trade Clause, and Fugitive Slave Clause lent tacit support for slavery, the provision granting permission to the national government for the suppression of "domestic violence"—which could include a slave insurrection as much as a Shays' rebellion—could easily be understood as yet another means of support (294). Similarly, as already noted, the ban on congressional export taxes was a concession to southern planters whose slaves primarily produced agricultural goods for export (see Klarman, 115, 262, 294).

At the same time, far from being a publicly transparent affair as presented by Paine, the entire process behind the convening, drafting, and ratification of the Constitution was shrouded in secrecy from beginning to end. It is telling that the election of George Washington by the delegates of the constitutional convention as president of the convention itself was not quite the democratic process implied by Paine when he claims that the convention "did not, like a cabal of courtiers, send for a Dutch Stadtholder, or a German Elector" but "referred the whole matter to the sense and interest of the country" (218): Washington was simply chosen as a delegate from Virginia before being unanimously voted by other delegates—rather than the people at large—as president of the convention. Moreover, when convening at the Pennsylvania State House, the delegates took care to have the doors and windows shut and sealed tightly with all curtains drawn even during the hot summer months. Jefferson was later to complain to Adams that he was "sorry they began their deliberations by so abominable a precedent as that of tying up the tongues of their members" in addition to "displaying their ignorance of the value of public discussions" when he learned of the prohibition of the printing or publication of the proceedings (Klarman, 136). None of this was accidental, of course, as the *Federalist Papers* defended its actions, explaining their reluctance to stir the "public passions" (Hamilton or Madison, #49). Not least, while Paine asserts in the opening lines of the chapter that "a constitution is not the act of a government, but of a people constituting a government" (214) and "Government has not right to make itself a party in any debate respecting the principles or modes of forming, or of changing, constitutions" (217), the writing of the Constitution might be said to fall under those very circumstances since a majority of the delegates to the Constitutional Convention in Philadelphia were either members of their state legislatures or appointed by them (i.e., in South Carolina, they were appointed by the Governor) even if they were not members of Congress. In fact, some of the delegates had already played instrumental roles in their state legislatures by resisting what they referred to as the "iniquitous system" of paper money. It is telling that John Rutledge wondered if very different "Characters would have been preferred," had "this convention had been chosen by the people in districts" (qtd. in Klarman, 246).

Madison justified the secrecy by rationalizing it as a practice not only in all state legislatures but also the British House of Commons, explaining that "no constitution would ever have been adopted ... if the debates had been public." Perhaps not surprisingly, it was roundly castigated by Anti-Federalists who frowned on the provisions allowing Congress to publish the journal of its proceedings on an occasional basis, exempting parts which "may in their judgment require secrecy." Mercy Otis Warren suspected "fraudulent designs"[30] while lambasting the idea of a "secret conclave"; it was an elitist concept that betrayed the very "genius of aristocracy" which compelled the delegates to require extreme secrecy in the form of keeping doors locked and forbidding members to publish extracts (Klarman, 252).[31] The process of ratifying the Constitution was similarly anything but transparent or even-handed. In Pennsylvania, for instance, Federalists relied on stealth and unpredictability to get the Constitution passed with minimal public debate by announcing a state ratification convention before any opposition had a chance to organize.[32] On September 28, just ten days after the first public reading of the new Constitution—and a few hours before Congress called on the states to ratify it—George Clymer, a Philadelphian banker and war debt speculator, proposed that ratification elections be held in just twelve days: such a quick turnaround was also obviously intended to allot insufficient time for a rider to deliver copies of the Constitution to the western counties for a sustained debate. During the month before elections, Pennsylvanian Federalists managed to circulate a one-sided stream of pro-Constitution editorials and news items while gagging the opposition. Violent threats were even issued against Anti-Federalist printers as *The address and reasons for dissent* censured the measures taken to intimidate critics of the constitution and the ways in which newspapers issued threats against them—with some going so far to propose tarring and feathering.

Ultimately, despite the ratification of the Constitution, there was widespread opposition—particularly from the lower and middling classes—coupled with a fear that America would revert to British-style tyranny of the 1760s and '70s.[33] At the Massachusetts ratifying convention, Amos Singletary, a representative in the Massachusetts General Court and a supporter of Shays' rebellion, remarked that "if anybody had proposed such a Constitution as this in 1775, it would have been thrown away at once" (Bouton, 384). Indeed, a Pennsylvania Anti-Federalist reported that west of the Susquehanna River, at least nine out of ten people were "as willing to oppose the Constitution as they were the British in their late designs" (Bouton, 378–9). But perhaps this is not astonishing since the aims and ideals of colonial propertied elites were perceived to resemble those of the British during the 1760s and '70s.[34] As several modern historians suggest,[35] the Constitution wound up eradicating popular reforms that ordinary citizens had tried to implement as Article I section 10 prohibited states from issuing their own paper currencies—thereby putting an end to state-run land banks and public, long-term, low-cost credit while laws "impairing the obligation of contracts" and moratoriums on debt repayments could no longer be enacted. Nonetheless, as Eric Foner points out, the Constitution was not universally condemned by non-elites. Artisans in Philadelphia, for instance, were not absolutely certain that the state alone could encourage manufacturing or provide "sustenance to our starving mechanics" (Foner, 205). One writer denied that the Constitution was aristocratic, insisting that it embodied the conditions of life of many Philadelphians, adding that "We common people are more properly citizens of America than of any particular state" (206). It is in this context alone that Paine's enthusiastic support for the Constitution seems less puzzling.

For the remainder of Chapter 4, Paine displays far greater approval of the U.S. Constitution and government than its British counterpart. After providing his sketch of the Philadelphia convention and the ensuing state ratifications, he returns once more to the disadvantages of hereditary governments. Again, Paine dwells upon the idea of a constitution-less Britain, noting that none of the famous documents credited for forming part of the British constitution are constitutional in any sense of the word. For instance, Magna Charta "did not create and give powers to government in the manner a constitution does" but instead was "of the nature of re-conquest"; as we will see in Chapter 5, Paine would assign greater credit to Wat Tyler than the barons at Runnymede because they took the first step in commodifying the commons (i.e., the land) into private property that could be bought, sold and mortgaged.[36] Only by renouncing its legacy of Norman usurpation, "as France has done its despotism," could Britain form a real constitution (221). Yet even if we are inclined to agree with Paine's laudatory assessment of Tyler and the rebels of 1381, it is nonetheless possible to view Magna Charta itself as one of the sources of the British constitution since the barons not only attempted to construct a more stable and regularized government but also established the idea of the rule of law which governed beggar and king alike.[37] Recent historians have argued that by defining the king's relationship with his subjects in a written document, the barons were able to transform personal grievances and customary law based on feudal norms into a true legal system while redressing general charges of misgovernment (Turner, 52, 67). Even if the barons were more concerned with reinforcing limitations and regulations from existing documents rather than creating new rules and laws, they displayed a burgeoning awareness of their collective rights and the possibility of communal identification by introducing numerous articles which were of little benefit to them but advantageous to those below them—knights, lesser freemen, merchants, townsmen, and even villeins.[38] Indeed, to a greater extent than its continental parallels, Magna Charta acknowledged non-baronial interests.

No less does Paine criticize the Bill of Rights of 1689, referring to it as a "Bill of Wrongs." Although some historians have concurred with his assessment of the convention parliament as a "thing that made itself, and then made the authority by which it acted" (221)[39]—perhaps not unlike the crafting of the American Constitution, others have shared his view that the Bill was little more than "the granting of concessions to a conquered people by a new William the Conqueror."[40] There is a general belief—as in the case of Magna Charta—that the Bill of Rights bears constitutional significance not only because of its creation of a constitutional monarchy but also for its clearly defined notion of a liberty to be enjoyed by the people under their government. The Bill, according to Elizabeth Wicks, offered the first clear signal "that the constitution must serve to protect the people from sovereign power."[41]

From here, Paine shifts to deprecating the operations of the British government, particularly the powers and liabilities of the executive branch. With a taxation that is nearly four times as much as in France per head, the problem is that "the government of England" (as opposed to what he calls "the English government," with all of its connotations of a government that has arisen directly from the English) heaps nearly all advantages onto a relatively small number of people comprised mostly of the monarchy and others on the Civil List. Returning to a point made towards the conclusion of Part 1 on the influence of the Crown, Paine observes that even with elections, despotism is a feature of the government since parliament essentially enjoys "unlimited powers" particularly when elections become "separated from representation": it is a criticism that bears some resemblance to Anti-Federalist criticisms of the U.S. Constitution as we have just seen. Here, Paine seethes at the "astonishing" mass of taxes paid by Britons, with the government enjoying perpetual recourse to "new loans and taxes" despite the execution of the civil government by means of "parish officers, magistrates, quarterly sessions, juries and assize." Instead, the government is "so completely engrossed and absorbed by foreign affairs"—mostly in the shape of wars—while negligent of "domestic concerns." The source of the problem, as Paine postulates, is that most governments, particularly in the Old World, are not founded on the rights of man but rather on "the doctrine of precedents" (224): yet, this emphasis on the "doctrine of precedents" was no less salient in the American Constitution as designed by Hamilton and Madison. In order to attack monarchy all the more effectively, Paine resurrects the familiar metaphor of Roman Catholicism once more, declaring that "This political popery, like the ecclesiastical popery of old, has had its day…The ragged relic and the antiquated precedent, the monk and the monarch, will smoulder together." Using rhetoric from *Common Sense*, Paine declares that Britain witnesses the nation and government at loggerheads with one another: with the former looking forward and the other backward as government proceeds "By precedent" and nations "by improvement." This assessment, however, may not have been entirely accurate given the scale of popular opposition to Paine after the publication of *Rights of Man* Part 2.[42] If Paine is assured that "Government is nothing more than a national association" where the object is "the good of all, as well individually as collectively," it is equally striking that he expects a competent government to foster a decent standard of living for the nation:

> Every man wishes to pursue his occupation, and to enjoy the fruits of his labours, and the produce of his property in peace and safety, and with the least possible expense. When these things are accomplished, all the objects for which government ought to be established are answered. (226)

But Paine's assumptions, of course, rely heavily on the intelligence, knowledge, and honesty of the electorate and representatives alike: unlike Adams, Hamilton, and Madison or those who opposed universal male suffrage in Britain, he had few fears or latent apprehension of the people at large. The failure to acknowledge the rights of man—namely, the rights to maintain oneself—is to pretend that the people are no more than wild beasts: which harks back to Sidney's remarks on the monarchical inheritance of herds and flocks. Again, whether this is not entirely inapplicable to the United States after the ratification of the Constitution is debatable.

For Paine, there is simply little rationale for an executive branch—let alone a monarchy.[43] Indeed, he goes so far as to deny the necessity of an upper house (for instance, the Senate or House of Lords): as such, Paine was closer to a Turgot than an Adams, Hamilton or Madison. If Paine had already voiced his reasons for his fundamental opposition to the idea of a bicameral legislature in *Answer to Four Questions*, where he suggested that it was best to "separate the legislature into two bodies" prior to any discussions because such an arrangement was preferable to being held in one chamber or distributed between two (525), he would reiterate this idea near verbatim in Chapter 4. Here, anticipating the arguments of modern constitutional scholars, Paine questions the usefulness of a bicameral legislature, stating that neither house can necessarily offer a proper correction to the other:

> Thirdly, that two houses arbitrarily checking or controlling each other is inconsistent; because it cannot be proved, on the principles of just representation that either should be wiser or better than the other. They may check in the wrong as well as in the right,—and therefore, to give the power where we cannot give the wisdom to use it, nor be assured of its being rightly used, renders the hazard at least equal to the precaution.[44]

Moreover, it is absurd that as one house debates an issue, the issue can be open to new interpretations while the procedure itself can easily culminate in a situation where a majority is overruled by a minority (thereby violating a principle of democracy). By contrast, Paine would propose dividing the House of Representatives into two or three parts to be rotated through annual elections in order to keep "the representation in the state of constant renovation" (229). (Note that the reasoning behind this scheme differs dramatically from that planned by the Federalists.)

If Paine regards the judicial branch as the true executive branch on account of its "power to which every individual has appeal; and which causes the laws to be executed" (227), there is thus no genuine function for kings since they have largely relinquished their judicial capacity from the Middle Ages. Much like how dukes and earls have no readily perceived role in society or government as a "duke" or "earl," according to Paine, the executive "is either a political superfluity or a chaos of unknown things" (234). Kings (or queens) are simply unnecessary for the functioning of government: a conclusion that was reached separately by George III and Louis XVI when the former briefly considered abdicating the throne and the latter found himself reduced more or less to a figurehead after 1790. Indeed, presumably reflecting back on the regency crisis of 1788–9 or Louis XVI's attempted escape in the guise of a servant—or both, Paine asserts that nothing "presents a more degrading character of national greatness, than its being thrown into confusion by anything happening to, or acted by, an individual" particularly when the "ridiculousness" is heightened by the natural insignificance of the person by whom it is occasioned (230): therefore, no individual should possess any "extraordinary power" so as to cause undue anxiety at his "death, sickness, absence, or defection" in a rational government (230). The potentially perilous combination of extraordinary power and pay often yields a power of "creating and disposing of places" that comes at the great expense of the nation while weakening its state of liberty (231). Altogether, it is thus unnecessary for any one person to receive exceptional compensation—especially when positions in government do not require remarkable talent. Here, it is worth bearing in mind that Paine's acceptance of Jonathan Swift's notion that "Government is a plain thing, and fitted to the capacity of many heads" indicates a far more populist orientation when compared to the assumptions held by his contemporaries on both sides of the Atlantic including Burke, Priestley, Hamilton, Jefferson, and Madison: many of whom expected elected representatives to have a high level of formal education.

Similarly, it is also worth noting Paine's suggestion that those in the legislative branch deserve compensation as much as the executive branch "for it is inconsistent to pay the one, and accept the service of the other gratis"—an idea that was observed in America but not immediately in Britain:[45]

> In America, every department in the government is decently provided for; but no one is extravagantly paid. Every member of Congress, and of the assemblies, is allowed a sufficiency for his expenses. Whereas in England, a most prodigal provision is made for the support of one part of the government, and none for the other, the consequence of which is, that the one is furnished with the means of corruption, and the other is put into the condition of being corrupted. (234)

The question that naturally arises, bearing in mind the idea that no stupendous talents are needed for governing, let alone for those who don't even play an instrumental role in governing, is why should so much be expended on kings—especially when there is a great deal of poverty in the nation?

> It is inhuman to talk of a million sterling a year, paid out of the public taxes of any country, for the support of any individual, whilst thousands who are forced to contribute thereto, are pining with want, and struggling with misery. Government does not consist in a contrast between prisons and palaces, between poverty and pomp; it is not instituted to rob the needy of his mite, and increase the wretchedness of the wretched. (note on p. 232)

The overall problem with monarchical government—if not hereditary government—is its tendency to support those at the top with little regard to everyone else. It is not just the king who enjoyed the power of creating positions, but wealthy aristocrats like the 3rd Duke of Richmond, who received a grant for every cauldron of coal as Paine exclaims with some indignation in a footnote:

> Humanity dictates a provision for the poor; but by what right, moral or political, does any government assume to say, that the person called the Duke of Richmond, shall be maintained by the public? Yet, if common report is true, not a beggar in London can purchase his wretched pittance of coal, without paying towards the civil list of the Duke of Richmond. Were the whole produce of this imposition but a shilling a year, the iniquitous principle would be still the same; but when it amounts, as it is said to do, to no less than twenty thousand pounds per annum, the enormity is too serious to be permitted to remain. This is one of the effects of monarchy and aristocracy.

By contrast, Paine argues, the qualifications for the President of the United States are more rational than those for an English monarch. Unlike the monarch who can ascend the throne at the age of 18 with little knowledge of the nation, the president must be a relatively mature 35. Moreover, unlike an English king or queen who is either "half a foreigner" (such as in the case of William III, George I, and George II) and "always married to a foreigner" (George I, George II, and George III) the American president must be born in the United States. The great irony is that given the issues of the monarch's birth and marriage alliances, s/he is seldom truly independent—which, in turn, can diminish national independence;[46] here, Paine cites the example of the Stadtholder of Holland, explaining that the marriage of the latter to the daughter of the Prussian king, meant that "Holland, by marriage, is as effectually governed by Prussia, as if the old tyranny of bequeathing the government had been the means" (233). This idea would be strengthened not long after the publication of Part 2, as France declared war on Austria and Prussia after discovering their conspiracy to save the royal family. In short, European monarchs were unlikely to have the nation's best interests in mind considering the multiplicity of demands from attachments to their own country of birth and their spouses. In the same footnote, Paine repeats the idea that it is not party that matters, but government: "whether the parties are in the ministry or in the opposition, it makes no difference: they are sure of the guarantee of each other" (232).

This is not to say that Paine remained blithely oblivious to the problems in the Constitution. Far from a John Adams who venerated the "English constitution" as "the most stupendous fabric of human invention" for which "Americans ought to be applauded instead of censured,"[47] Paine execrated it in 1796, less than a decade later. It is possible that he only supported the Constitution then, as he explains in a bitter letter to George Washington in 1796, on account of the general weakness of the federal government at a time when he still believed that "it contained the means of remedying its defects by the same appeal to the people by which it was to be established" (691). Indeed, he would claim that the federal Constitution was in many respects nearly as contemptible "as the original of the form of the British Government" with many similar vices (693–4).[48] Given the strong link between "form and practise," it is only natural that "to adopt the one is to invite the other" (693–4). In particular, he objected to the Executive branch, preferring a small council to a single man and a shorter term for the Senate (692). It would thus not be difficult for him to envision a highly unequal America in future years. But perhaps even more telling, Paine would express a profound distaste for the Pennsylvania constitution of 1790, revised on the model of the federal Constitution as the unicameral House was transformed into a bicameral one.[49] Since "the fundamental principle in representative government is that the majority governs," but when "there are two houses of unequal numbers, and the smaller number negativing the greater, it is the minority that governs, which is contrary to the principle." Preferring annual elections, he complained that a four-year senatorial term was far too long as he reiterated the significance of a body of representatives "accountable to those who elected him" (998).

NOTES

1 Thomas Paine, *Dissertations on Government*, ed. Philip Foner in *Complete Writings of Thomas Paine*, Vols. 1–2 (New York: Citadel Press, 1945) 2, p. 367.

2 *Federalist* #14. See: https://avalon.law.yale.edu/18th_century/fed14.asp. All further references to *The Federalist Papers* are drawn from this site: https://avalon.law.yale.edu/subject_menus/fed.asp66

3 Cited in Christian Fritz, *American Sovereigns: The People and America's Constitutional Tradition Before the Civil War* (Cambridge University Press, 2009) pp. 16–17.

4 Cited in Willi Paul Adams, *The First American Constitutions: Republican Ideology and the Making of the State Constitutions in the Revolutionary Era*, trans. Rita and Robert Kimber (London: Rowman and Littlefield, 2001) p. 62.

5 Fritz notes that some of these "alter or abolish" provisions echoed the traditional right of revolution as, for instance, in Maryland and New Hampshire. Even "conservative" constitutions of the post-revolutionary period retained the idea of alter or abolish, including the 1780 Massachusetts constitution, the 1790 Pennsylvania Constitution, the Preamble to Delaware's 1792 Bill of Rights, and the 1818 Connecticut Constitution. See p. 24. This populist belief was certainly shared by fellow Pennsylvanian James Wilson who held that the people can "change the constitutions whenever and however they pleased" since they were sovereign (Fritz, 30).

6 Marc Kruman, *Between Authority and Liberty: State Constitution-making in Revolutionary America* (Chapel Hill: University of North Carolina Press, 1999) p. 18.

7 Robert Lamb, *Thomas Paine and the Idea of Human Rights* (Cambridge: Cambridge University Press, 2015) p. 95.

8 With large debts owed to foreign creditors and wealthy wartime speculators who held 90 percent of government securities, both of whom wanted their monies and profits returned to them in hard specie (i.e. gold and silver), states raised taxes: an act which put extraordinary pressure not only on farmers and other poor and middling citizens, but even worse, veterans who had not yet received compensation for their wartime services. Shays' rebellion—named for Daniel Shays—and other similar uprisings erupted as foreclosures and bankruptcies rose in response to the increased taxes and demand for hard specie. In September 1786, Shays and other

leaders in western Massachusetts led several hundred men in forcing the Supreme Court in Springfield to adjourn. As Klarman states, the Constitution was very much a reaction to the economic relief measures enacted by most states in the mid-1780s. See *The Framers' Coup: The Making of the United States Constitution*, Kindle Edition (Oxford: University Press, 2016) p. 74.

9   See Eric Foner, *Tom Paine and Revolutionary America* (Oxford: Oxford University Press, 1977, 2004) pp. 197–8. The poor and middling classes supported the dissemination of paper money for the most part. However, Foner suggests that Paine's dislike of paper money may have had a populist rationale. Paine appears to have believed that "manufacturers and mechanics" were among those whose "immediate interest paper money operates the strongest." Paper money not only reduced their income but also banished "all the hard money which the exports of the country brought in," sending it abroad "to purchase foreign manufactures and trinkets" (200).

10 Terry Bouton, *Taming Democracy: The People, the Founders, and the Troubled Ending of the American Revolution* (Oxford: Oxford University Press, 2007) p. 179.

11 Sherman, for instance, preferred that state legislatures choose members of the lower house because he considered the people unqualified to do so (170). While professing opposition to "an undue aristocratic influence in the Constitution," Pinckney nonetheless thought it essential that national officeholders "be possessed of competent property to make them independent and respectable." He proposed that the Constitution fix the property requirements and suggested $100,000 for the president and half that for federal judges and members of Congress—thresholds that 99 percent of the population could not have satisfied. Even though most of the delegates strongly supported property qualifications for federal officeholding, they wound up not authorizing Congress to do so (182).

12 https://founders.archives.gov/documents/Hamilton/01-04-02-0098-0004

13 June 24, 1788, https://www.bartleby.com/268/8/20.html

14 June 26, 1787, https://founders.archives.gov/documents/Madison/01-10-02-0044

15 For a brief period when Paine was in the midst of chartering the Bank of North America, he lost confidence in a single legislature, one founded "on a hope that whatever personal parties there might be in a state, they would all unite and agree in the general principles of good government ... and that the general good, or the good of the whole, would be the governing principle of the legislature." However, when under the control of one party, it "is capable of being made a compleat aristocracy for the time it exists" (201). That the Senate was viewed as the American counterpart to the British House of Lords has also been underlined by Sanford Levinson in *Framed: America's 51 Constitutions and the Crisis of Governance* (Oxford: Oxford University Press, 2012) p. 137. "A well-organized state would therefore make sure that those with significant property were well represented in at least one house of the legislature. We would not call them 'lords,' but we would, nonetheless, recognize that possession of property brought with it certain prerogatives, including some special role in governance."

16 See Madison debates, June 12, 1787, http://avalon.law.yale.edu/18th_century/debates_612.asp

17 Levinson notes in *Framed* that "In sum, the Philadelphia convention created an extraordinarily powerful executive, especially given that just a decade earlier Americans had felt so aggrieved by the abuses of the British king that they eviscerated state executives in the constitutions they wrote during the Revolution" (137).

18 See: https://constitution.org/cmt/mowarren/observations_new_constitution_1788. html

19 See: http://www.constitution.org/afp/pennmi00.htm. It is striking that even today, members of the Senate are disproportionately wealthy. As Sanford Levinson states, a 2009 blog post in the *New York Times* entitled "Your Senator Is (Probably) a Millionaire" reported that a full two-thirds of senators were millionaires. See: http s://economix.blogs.nytimes.com/2009/11/25/your-senator-is-probably-a-milliona ire/. The 2010 congressional elections, viewed by many as a "populist insurgency" against elites, brought a number of newcomers to both the House and Senate. The Center for Responsive Politics found that "sixty percent of Senate freshman and more than 40 percent of House freshmen are millionaires." See *Framed*, p. 137.

20 George Mason, "Objections to the Constitution," October 1787, http://www. constitution.org/gmason/objections.html

21 Today that proportion is 1 Representative to 700,000 voters.

22 Melancton Smith, New York Ratifying Convention, http://press-pubs.uchicago. edu/founders/print_documents/v1ch13s37.html

23 See: https://teachingamericanhistory.org/resources/ratification/mcmasterstone/ chaptervii/

24 See: https://www.constitution.org/afp/fedfar09.htm

25 Paine had already stated this idea in *Answer to Four Questions* (1791). See *Complete Writings*, 2, p. 526.

26 https://www.constitution.org/cmt/mowarren/observations_new_constitution_1788. html

27 https://www.constitution.org/gmason/objections.html

28 https://teachingamericanhistory.org/resources/ratification/mcmasterstone/chap tervi/

29 Response to Elbridge Gerry's Objections by Rufus King and Nathaniel Gorham (November 3, 1787), http://www.consource.org/document/response-to-elbridge-gerrys-objections-by-rufus-king-and-nathaniel-gorham-1787-11-3/

30 http://oll.libertyfund.org/titles/ford-pamphlets-on-the-constitution-of-the-united-states-1787-1788

31 According to George Mason, secrecy was "a necessary precaution to prevent misrepresentations or mistakes."

32 Bouton, 180–1. See also THE ADDRESS AND REASONS OF DISSENT OF THE MINORITY OF THE CONVENTION OF THE STATE OF PENNSYLVANIA TO THEIR CONSTITUENTS Dec. 17, 178**7.**

33 Bouton, 87. In the end, the gospel of moneyed men bore a striking resemblance to that of British colonial governors of the 1760s and '70s. The policies were similar, as were the justifications for limiting democracy and the easy dismissal of criticism by the public. Like British officials and the Penn family, Morris and others believed that power over money and credit needed to be removed from

democratic control because popularly elected governments supposedly could not manage finances. Like Britain, they killed the land-bank system without offering a viable alternative for getting money and credit to ordinary folk. When the latter complained about a scarcity of money, the revolutionary elite called the charges unfounded and said the public was lazy, greedy, and ill informed—just as Britain had. And like Britain, the revolutionary elite enacted new taxes payable in gold and silver to fund the war and government expenses.

34 Bouton, p. 87. Note in the address of dissent how the writers describe the delegates from Pennsylvania: "It was composed of some men of excellent characters; of others who were more remarkable for their ambition and cunning, than their patriotism; and of some who had been opponents to the independence of the United States."

35 See Klarman as well as Woody Holton, *Unruly Americans and the Origins of the American Constitution* (New York: Macmillan, 2007).

36 Thanks to Ed Dodson (School of Cooperative Individualism) for pointing this out.

37 Ralph V. Turner, *Magna Carta* (London: Pearson Education, 2003; London: Taylor & Francis, 2003, 2014) p. 2. Interestingly, John Cartwright viewed the Magna Charta as evidence of a constitution already in place, denying that it was a "foundation of English liberties" and "the English constitution." However, it was "a glorious member of the superstructure," but never "would never have existed, had not the constitution already had a basis, and a firm one too" (*American Independence*, 39).

38 Claire Valente, *The Theory and Practice of Revolt in medieval England* (London: Taylor & Francis, 2003) pp. 50–65.

39 See Mark Kishlansky, *A Monarchy Transformed—1603–1714* (London: Penguin Books, 1996) p. 283, where he states that "the convention parliament was summoned in the name of William III, and therefore can be viewed as a Fig-leaf for William's power."

40 J. Morrill, "The Sensible Revolution" in Jonathan Israel, *The Anglo Dutch moment—Essays on the Glorious Revolution and Its World Impact* (Cambridge: Cambridge University Press, 1991) p. 87. See also W.S. Holdsworth, *A History of English Law*, Vol. 6 (London: Methuen Co. 1924) p. 241. "We look in vain for any statement of constitutional principle in the Bill of Rights."

41 Elizabeth Wicks, *The Evolution of a Constitution: Eight Key Moments in British Constitutional History* (Oxford and Portland, OR: Hart, 2006) p. 30.

42 Although *Rights of Man* was admired by many radicals, there was also considerable opposition to his work: it is difficult to determine the extent to which it was influenced by the Church and King mobs and encouragement from local authorities. see the Conclusion.

43 Levinson appears to share some of Paine's reservations on the executive branch. Here, he wonders "why one would expect devotion to 'the public good' to be found so much more often in a single president than in an *aggregate* Congress ... What is it about a president that makes him or her more trustworthy about judgments of 'good' and 'bad' than others in the polity, or the executive branch?" In short, Hamilton, according to Levinson, shared the same

mistaken assumptions of the British, believing that presidents differed from members of Congress "in the way that lords were different from commoners and the king ultimately different (and better) than either?" (168).

44 In *An Answer to Four Questions*, Paine writes "However skilfully a constitution may be framed, it is impossible to decide previously, when there are two chambers, how far they will act as a check upon each other. They may come to an agreement not to avail themselves of this power of mutual restraint, either for good or evil; still, if the Constitution makes provision for such restraint, the result is sure to be advantageous." He adds that he did not favor two chambers "which have each an arbitrary veto on the action of the other." After all, there was nothing to prove that one body would be wiser than the other (*CW* 2, 128). Contemporary constitutional scholars such as Sanford Levinson are likewise not completely convinced of the necessity for a second house. In *Framed*, he notes that Jesse Ventura, former governor of Minnesota, once called for the abolition of that state's upper house, claiming that it contributed nothing to the overall legislative process. He rejected the argument that bicameralism provided Minnesota with "efficiency gains" while pointing to Nebraska's single-house legislature. Levinson adds that Ventura could have also pointed to New Zealand, a country with a population of approximately 4.3 million, stating "There is no evidence that Nebraska or New Zealand pays a significant cost for its unicameralism" (140).

45 British M.P.s did not receive a salary until 1911.

46 Of course, Paine could not predict that foreign influence on national politics would eventually increase with developments in communications and technology. Consider American involvement in elections around the world, particularly the Middle East and Latin America—or more recently, alleged Russian interference in the American presidential election of 2016.

47 John Adams, *Defence of the Constitutions of the Governments of the United States of America*, Vols. 1–3 in *The Complete Works of John Adams*, ed. Charles Francis Adams, Vols. 4–6. Reprinted in the Online Library of Liberty, see: http://oll.liber tyfund.org/titles/adams-the-works-of-john-adams-vol-4, 4.

48 He makes a similar point in *Constitutions, Governments, and Charters*, p. 989: "The general defect in all the constitutions is that they are modeled too much after the system, if it can be called a system, of the English government, which in practise is the most corrupt system in existence, for it is corruption systematized."

49 The state did not allow for the constitution to be voted on (Bouton, 195).

4

RIGHTS OF MAN, PART 2, CHAPTER 5

The idea that governments should provide for the well-being of its people was hardly a novel concept by the time Paine began writing *Rights of Man*. It was certainly already in existence when Algernon Sidney declared that "governments are not set up for the advantage ... of one or a few, but for the good of the society"[1] and Montesquieu that the state "owes to every citizen a certain subsistence, a proper nourishment, convenient cloathing [*sic*]" and a life "not incompatible with health" (Book 23, Chap. 29).[2] More generally, Granville Sharp upheld "*the Good of the People*" as the "principal end of all *legal* Human Governments" because "*all Men are naturally equals*" in *A Declaration of the People's Natural Right to a Share in the Legislature* (xiv). So it is not altogether fortuitous that Paine similarly declared the sense of "general happiness" a paramount consideration for governments. By contrast, one which "create[s] and increase[s] wretchedness in any of the parts of society" requires "reformation." What is more unusual, however, is how Paine attempted to address this problem on a much more comprehensive scale.

This assessment begins with Paine's radical reconceptualization of civilization. According to Rousseau, equality is a distinctive feature of "savage" life while inequality is more characteristic of civilization: a primary reason for his veneration of primitive life. In *Discourse on Inequality*, he praises less modern civilizations for their higher degree of empathy:

> In fact, commiseration must be so much the more energetic, the more intimately the animal, that beholds any kind of distress, identifies himself with the animal that labours under it. Now it is evident that this identification must have been infinitely more perfect in the state of nature than in the state of reason.[3]

Indeed, it was readily apparent that if "the prodigious variety in the education and manner of living" was compared to "the simplicity and uniformity that prevails in the animal and savage life," "every inequality of institution" must also heighten "the natural inequalities of the human species." Or simply put, civilization exacerbates the contrasts between rich and poor with inequality escalated by the rich who legislate in a manner to increase their own wealth, thereby binding "the fetters of the weak, and the strength of the rich."[4] Natural liberty would be "irretrievably destroyed" so that "artful usurpation" would effectively be changed "into an irrevocable title." This interpretation can be said to prefigure both Paine's interpretation of monarchy as described in Chapter 2, where "the power originally usurped, they affected to inherit" (199) and his criticisms of legislative control by propertied elites. All "natural compassion," according to Rousseau, was bound to lose influence over societies at large, with the exception of those "great souls, who consider themselves as citizens of the world." For Rousseau, the very clash between "moral inequality, authorised by positive right alone" and "natural right" was pervasive in "all civilised countries"; but, of course, moral inequality would eventually prevail in the form of topsy-turvy natural power, one where "children should command old men, fools wise men," while "the privileged few" feed on "superfluities" and "the starving multitude are in want of the bare necessities of life."[5] In other words, government was responsible for eradicating natural rights and perpetuating inequality by protecting the interests of the wealthy.

Chapter 5 may be read as an endeavor to confront and alleviate these inequalities. Paine begins by observing the irony inherent in the fact that "a great portion of mankind, in what are called civilized countries, are in a state of poverty and wretchedness, far below the condition of an Indian" especially since primitive society seldom placed restrictions on hunting or farming as found in English game laws: the obvious implication of this idea, of course, is that civilization should provide a higher standard of living for all people given the amount of progress made over the centuries. Certainly, Paine was far from being the first or only English writer to articulate this sentiment. In *Observations on the Present State of the Parochial and Vagrant Poor* (1773), Scott claimed that "Rags and vermin ... extravagance of luxury in food, dress, equipage, and architecture, perhaps never exceeded by the wanton prodigality of Asia or Rome in their pristine opulence, exhibited together in one picture, form a contrast too striking to escape the attention" of "the most inattentive."[6] Likewise, in *Observations on the Poor Laws on the Present State of the Poor and on Houses of Industry*, Robert Potter noted:

> Whilst we are rolling thro' the kingdom in our post-coaches ... the high culture of our lands gives us the idea of a *Ferme bien orné*, our nobility live in palaces, our gentry in villas, commerce has made us a nation of gentry ... and the whole is one delightfull [sic] scene of convenience, plenty, elegance, splendor, and magnificence. Mean time our interior police is disgrac'd with the number of our starving, naked, unshelter'd miserable Poor; this is an ulcer in our vitals.[7]

The visiting German writer Gebhard Friedrich August Wendeborn would likewise remark on the contrast between the sights of "the seats of the noble and the rich" and those of "so many poor persons half naked and starving around them":[8] an observation to be echoed two years later by George Dyer in *Complaints of the Poor People of England*. It would be left to Paine to find a means of mitigating such extreme differences between the rich and poor.

Indeed, in a speech delivered at the Thatched House Tavern in London on August 20, 1791, Paine had already begun to tackle the problem of inequality by suggesting that governments provided most generously to the wealthiest—namely, the royal court. The French revolution was relevant to all Britons because the English were

> oppressed with a heavy national debt, a burden of taxes, and an expensive administration of government, beyond those of any in the world. We have also a very numerous poor; and we hold that the moral obligation of providing for old age, helpless infancy, and poverty, is far superior to that of supplying the invented wants of courtly extravagance, ambition, and intrigue.[9]

As he notes some paragraphs later, a government is "nothing more than a NATIONAL ASSOCIATION" and one that is expected to secure "to every man his rights" while promoting "the greatest quantity of happiness with the *least expence*" (*CW*, 536). If modernization ought to necessitate a general improvement in living standards, according to Paine, societies that fail to do so are in fact uncivilized when they wage war while neglecting the masses.

> ... governments being yet in an uncivilised state, and almost continually at war, they pervert the abundance which civilised life produces to carry on the uncivilised part to a greater extent. By thus engrafting the barbarism of government upon the internal civilisation of a country, it draws from the latter, and more especially from the poor, a great portion of those earnings, which should be applied to their own subsistence and comfort.

So ironically, while European nations are the wealthiest and most civilized by virtue of their progress in science and technology over the course of the century, they are, in fact, far from being constructed "on the principle of universal civilization, but on the reverse of it." Because modern governments disregard the divine rights of man, they are "like so many individuals in a state of nature" (238), thereby defeating "the general felicity of which civilization is capable" (238). What's more, as Paine observes, European governments have perpetuated this evil through constant war and taxes which burden the middle classes and poor. Paine would delineate the stark differences between rich and poor even more dramatically in *Agrarian Justice* (1797) essentially agreeing with Rousseau's assessment of civilized society while blaming government for its perpetuation of extreme hardship:

> Whether that state that is proudly, perhaps erroneously, called civilization, has most promoted or most injured the general happiness of man, is a question that may be strongly contested. On one side, the spectator is dazzled by splendid appearances; on the other, he is shocked by extremes of wretchedness; both of which it has erected. The most affluent and the most miserable of the human race are to be found in the countries that are called civilized.
> Poverty, therefore, is a thing created by that which is called civilized life. It exists not in the natural state. On the other hand, the natural state is without those advantages which flow from agriculture, arts, science and manufacturers.[10]

Even more succinctly, he blamed "Civilization" for making "one part of society more affluent," and "the other more wretched, than would have been the lot of either in a natural state": this continues to remain the case centuries later, as we will see in the Conclusion, even when a supposed meritocracy has more or less come to replace birth and pedigree as a determining factor in the attainment of wealth. The fact is that the Western world has come to accept Paine's premise that a more civilized society—one founded on the "general happiness of society" (237)—should guarantee a higher standard of living so that all members of the populace can feed and maintain themselves without undue struggle.

That Paine may not have been exaggerating in his indictment of government in the perpetuation of poverty is evident from a glance at the list of public expenditures in 1788 as recorded by John Sinclair (Table 1).

It is clear that 53% of the expenditures was spent on the interest of the funded debt, the charges of managing the public debt, and the sum appropriated for the reduction of the national debt, 12% on the expenses associated with customs and excise, 25% on the military, 4.6% on the Civil List. Although it is difficult to ascertain the actual make-up of the miscellaneous services, they comprise a scant 4% of the £19,591,885. If Paine identified two

Table 1 General View of the Public Expenditure for the Year Ending 5th April 1789[11]

I. Expense of Collection, and other Deductions before the Produce of the Taxes reaches the Exchequer

1	Salaries, fees, and incidents in the custom[*sic*]-house	£506,548
2	Bounties payable out of the customs	429,818
3	Charges of the Excise	410,515
4	Bounties paid by the excise and salt office	39,572
5	Expenses of the stamp office	51,691
6	Expenses of the miscellaneous taxes	276,436
7	Charges of the levying the taxes in Scotland	135,182
8	Bounties payable in Scotland	66,790
9	Expense of levying the land tax	53,574
10	Expense of the militia	116,137
11	Other deductions from the land tax	14,000
12	Deficiencies of land and malt, including the interest of the Exchequer bills issued on the credit of those taxes	250,000
		£2,350,263

II. Ascertained and permanent expenses

1	Expenses of the civil list	£900,000
2	Interest of the funded debt, exclusive of tontine 1789	9,150,138
3	Interest and charges of Exchequer bills	180,419
4	Charges of managing the public debts	156,634
5	Expenses attending the lottery	13,600
6	The sum unalienably appropriated for the reduction of the national debt	1,000,000
7	Charges on the consolidated fund	68,000
8	Appropriated duties	31,859
9	Expenses of Greenwich hospital	75,200
10	Permanent grants to individuals	37,500
		£11,613,350

III. Annual Grants of Parliament

1	Navy	£2,348,118
2	Army	2,038, 852
3	Ordnance	484,507
4	Miscellaneous services	756,795

(Continued)

I. Expense of Collection, and other Deductions before the Produce of the Taxes reaches the Exchequer

	£5,628,272 [12]
Total sum	£ 19,591,885

facets of government, one of which is "local and useful to the people," operating more locally "at home" as civil government, while the other comprises "the court or cabinet government," i.e., "on the rude plan of uncivilised life," it is clear that Sinclair's enumeration of expenditures leans towards the latter with the bulk of expenses centered on the collection and servicing of taxes and debts. Moreover, the lack of a government-appointed police force, prosecutors, and other magistrates meant that they were not publicly funded or at least not directly. As Paine points out that civil government requires "little charge" while the Civil List entails "boundless extravagance," he also attempts to show how government can improve the general welfare of the people.

Once more, Paine reiterates his belief from Chapters 2 and 3 that a reformed society should be grounded in commerce, rather than on war—an interpretation that diverges sharply from Winstanley's equation between war and commerce, even if both men shared the fundamental belief that war destroys "abundance." That which Winstanley deplored as "buying and selling" is celebrated by Paine as a means of "promoting the civil intercourse of nations, by an exchange of benefits" (239). If war leads to the loss of commerce, peace enhances its "own natural operations" (240). As a means to "universal civilisation," Paine's desire for commerce would also appear to reinforce Winstanley's plea for "Universal Peace in the earth."[13] Indeed, broadly speaking, Paine's theory still holds true, not only through much of the 18th century when trade was reduced during the wars of Queen Anne's War (1702–13), the war of Jenkins' Ear and the war of the Austrian Succession (1739–48), the Seven Years' War (1756–63), and particularly the American Revolution (1775–83), but also more than two centuries later as consumers remain reluctant to spend during early or uncertain stages of a war, particularly on larger purchases.

Nonetheless, it is also equally true that wars also helped widen overseas markets[14]—not to mention the fact that the aforementioned wars were triggered in part by trade violations and disagreements. Moreover, if Alexander Hamilton was cognizant that an active commercial nation required a navy, he was equally aware that commerce could be a significant source of war.

> What are the chief sources of expense in every government ... that enormous accumulation of debts with which several of the European nations are oppressed? The answers plainly is [*sic*], wars and rebellions ... The expenses arising from those institutions which are relative to the mere domestic police of a state ... are insignificant in comparison with those which relate to the national defense.

> In the kingdom of Great Britain, where all the ostentatious apparatus of monarchy is to be provided for, not above a fifteenth part of the annual income of the nation is appropriated to the class of expenses last mentioned; the other fourteen fifteenths are absorbed in the payment of the interest of debts contracted for carrying on the wars in which that country has been engaged, and in the maintenance of fleets and armies.[15]

Indeed, unlike Paine, Hamilton was nearly as apt to blame commerce and popular opinion as a cause of war in Britain as monarchical succession.

> In the government of Britain the representatives of the people compose one branch of the national legislature. Commerce has been for ages the predominant pursuit of that country. Few nations, nevertheless, have been more frequently engaged in war; and the wars in which that kingdom has been engaged have, in numerous instances, proceeded from the people.

> There have been, if I may so express it, almost as many popular as royal wars. The cries of the nation ... have, upon various occasions, dragged their monarchs into war, or continued them in it, contrary to their inclinations, and sometimes contrary to the real interests of the State. In that memorable struggle for superiority between the rival houses of *Austria* and *Bourbon* ... it is well known that the antipathies of the English against the French, seconding the ambition, or rather

the avarice, of a favorite leader, protracted the war beyond the limits
marked out by sound policy ....

The wars of these two last-mentioned nations have in a great measure
grown out of commercial considerations,—. (23)

Instead, what is more striking are Paine's efforts to present
trade and commerce as an egalitarian phenomenon where all gain
and lose equally—unlike the consequences of war. For Paine,
trade is a mutual activity; if "there can be no such thing as a
nation flourishing alone in commerce" (240), it is no less true that
"the great support of commerce consists in the balance being a
level of benefits among all nations" (241), an egalitarian view of
trade unlike Winstanley's:

If a merchant in England sends an article of English manufacture
abroad which costs him a shilling at home, and imports something
which sells for two, he makes a balance of one shilling in his favour;
but this is not gained out of the foreign nation or the foreign merchant, for he also does the same by the articles he receives, and neither has the advantage upon the other. The original value of the two
articles in their proper countries was but two shillings; but by changing their places, they acquire a new idea of value, equal to double
what they had first, and that increased value is equally divided.

There is no otherwise a balance on foreign than on domestic commerce. The merchants of London and Newcastle trade on the same
principles, as if they resided in different nations, and make their balances in the same manner: yet London does not get rich out of
Newcastle, any more than Newcastle out of London: but coals, the
merchandize of Newcastle, have an additional value at London, and
London merchandize has the same at Newcastle.

Here, too, Paine reiterates Adam Smith's and Sir John Sinclair's
criticisms of empire, asserting that "The most unprofitable of all
commerce is that connected with foreign dominion" since "The
expense of maintaining dominion more than absorbs the profits
of any trade" in addition to "the significant cost of navies." Both
statements, however, would be disproved, not only because the

wars of 1713 and the Seven Years' War arose from conflicts arising over imperial trade, but because British commerce was
already outpacing other European economies; the profits of
empire would also grow exponentially over the following century
as the strength of the navy facilitated and enhanced trade:
whereas Britain conducted most of its trade with the Continent at
the beginning of the 18th century, the balance had shifted to its
colonies abroad.

With the anticipated loss of monarchies in Europe, Paine imagined fewer motivations for war and a return to a new concern
for the improvement of life—a vision not unlike Winstanley's:
both men clearly desired a world of "universal civilization" that
would allow man to "inherit his rights" without a predatory
government obstructing his efforts at self-sustenance. Some of
these ideas would be promulgated by John Scott as he complained of mean-spiritedness towards the poor:

> With some who have written on this subject of the poor, the diminu-
> tion of the expence to the maintainers, rather than the production of
> benefit to the maintained, seems intrinsically if not professedly the
> grand desideratum. But what is this expence that it should be so
> grudged and this tax that it should be so heavily complained of; while
> other expences, and other taxes, infinitely more unnecessary and
> infinitely more oppressive, are spontaneously incurred and implicitly
> complied with? ... Is not the air we breathe, the ground we tread on,
> and the food we eat, taxed to maintain a regular system of political
> corruption; to support the administrators of our government, and
> their innumerable dependents, in the most enormous extravagance
> of pomp and luxury? Why then should the poor alone be envied a
> trivial portion of that wealth, so profusely dissipated by ourselves?
> (Scott, 55–6)

In *A Republican Manifesto*, which Paine wrote shortly after the
capture of Louis XVI at Varennes, he reflected on the thirty millions of francs to be saved upon the eradication of the monarchy:
if this sum were to be applied to "the diminution of taxation,
what a relief it would be to the overburdened nation." After all,
"the greatness of a people is not, as the monarchs claim, based on

the magnificence of a king, but in the people's sense of its own dignity" (518–19). Here, in *Rights of Man*, Paine proceeds to launch what is arguably the most searing indictment of social and economic inequality—one that holds true even today. It is hard to disagree with his view that ostensibly affluent societies are anything but civilized when the most vulnerable live precariously:

> When, in countries that are called civilised, we see age going to the workhouse and youth to the gallows, something must be wrong in the system of government. It would seem, by the exterior appearance of such countries, that all was happiness; but there lies hidden from the eye of common observation, a mass of wretchedness, that has scarcely any other chance, than to expire in poverty or infamy ....

> Civil government does not exist in executions; but in making such provision for the instruction of youth and the support of age, as to exclude, as much as possible, profligacy from the one and despair from the other. Instead of this, the resources of a country are lavished upon kings, upon courts, upon hirelings, impostors and prostitutes; and even the poor themselves, with all their wants upon them, are compelled to support the fraud that oppresses them.

As we will see in the Conclusion, this problem is one that has persisted into 21st-century America and Britain with numerous pundits and scholars weighing in on the growing numbers of senior citizens who continue to work after the age of 65 and urban minority youths who are disproportionately incarcerated, while bailouts and tax cuts are lavished on banks, corporations, and the wealthiest 0.01%.

Paine, of course, was hardly the first in the 18th century to consider the problems posed by poverty since Scott had proposed solutions for the amelioration of workhouse conditions, not to mention the construction of cottages for the poor, in *The Parochial and Vagrant Poor*, as did Potter who reiterated some of the same ideas.[16] Nor was Paine the first to point out the fact of child poverty; in his *Observations*, Potter inquires why "poor children" were "expos'd to nakedness, hunger, and ignorance," going from "uninstructed youth thro' idleness, insensibility, and poverty, to obduracy, violence, and vice, burdens to themselves, pests to society, and aliens from God?" (28) However, Paine was unique among the respondents to Burke in proposing solutions to poverty, as if combining Digger ideas on economic justice with Leveller ideas on political and civil rights. Questioning "Why is it that scarcely any are executed but the poor?" Paine reflects upon the inadequacy of resources for the indigent: indeed, throughout the course of Part 2 in the main text and footnotes, he grapples multiple times with the question of adequate resources for their sustenance, arriving at increasingly generous solutions. Nonetheless, Paine goes further, explaining that it's not merely the fact the poor are "bred up without morals" or even because they are the "exposed sacrifice of vice and legal barbarity": the crux of the problem is government oversight of their ills—an observation not unlike that in Part 1 where he claimed that old governments "distortedly exalt" some men while leaving the rest distortedly debased such that "a vast mass of mankind are degradedly thrown into the background of the human picture to bring forward the puppet-show of state and aristocracy" (92). As such, much of Chapter 5 continues to tackle this predicament as Paine seeks a means of alleviating want and educating indigent children for a better future. The underlying problem is that "millions" are "superfluously wasted upon governments" when more can be expended on the basic needs of the impoverished. Advocating "the Rights of Man," Paine opens the discussion with a brief sketch of his own life, partly embedded in a footnote, portraying himself as a man who overcame the odds of financial hardship to become a political writer, "the most difficult of all lines to succeed and excel in," that "which aristocracy with all its aids has not been able to reach or to rival": a declaration that replicates James Murray's criticism of the elite assumption that the "vulgar are not qualified to judge of matters of state" (*Ministers*, 57). The lessons to be drawn not only debunk Burke's idea of the elite as the Corinthian column, but also serve as a tacit encouragement for education and personal improvement—even though Paine does not broach education until a few pages later; his emphasis on independence in his personal narrative of the American revolution equally serves to undercut the traditional assumption that aristocrats are more impartial and disinterested on account of their wealth. Yet, while claiming his cognizance of "the value of moral instruction" and that he has witnessed "the danger of the contrary," Paine does not pursue the issue of personal instruction or the abundance of opportunities for all men to remake themselves in America as one might expect, but instead to the defects of English government in an effort to demonstrate how the lives of ordinary Britons are blighted from the very beginning.

The problem is inherent in the limitations imposed by corporation towns and charters, with corporation towns restraining the entrance and egress of inhabitants and charters reserving rights for a minimal number of persons: a subject touched upon in Part 1 but pursued more rigorously here. Because one's rights are frequently confined to one's native town or parish, a person can only move to another town by undergoing naturalization—in much the same fashion that a foreigner becomes a naturalized citizen of another country. Inhabitants enjoy few rights within the towns themselves since the privileges of enfranchisement are granted to a miniscule number of men; here, Paine applies a reasoning deployed by Sieyès in an essay on privileges originally written in 1788, but not translated into English until 1791:

> The grant of any exclusive Privilege to any person, with respect to that which belongs to all, would be, to wrong the whole community, for the sake of an individual; which is an idea at once the most unjust and the most absurd.

> All Privileges, then, from the very nature of things, are unjust, odious, and contradictory to the supreme end of every political society.[17]

Paine spells out the injustice of privileges even more clearly:

> It is a perversion of terms to say that a charter gives rights. It operates by a contrary effect—that of taking rights away. Rights are inherently in all the inhabitants; but charters, by annulling those rights, in the majority, leave the right, by exclusion, in the hands of a few ... such charters would, in the face, be charters not of rights, but of exclusion. The effect is the same under the form they now stand; and the only persons on whom they operate are the persons whom they

> exclude ... They do not give rights to A, but they make a difference in favour of A by taking away the right of B, and consequently are instruments of injustice.

The slow growth and lack of commerce in corporation towns relative to that found in cities such as Manchester, Birmingham, and Sheffield can be directly attributed to the limited rights proffered by corporation towns: a view which would be affirmed more than a century later by Sidney and Beatrice Webb in their study, *English local government from the Revolution to the Municipal Corporations Act* (1907–22). Moreover, given the sizable number of members of Parliament elected from such towns, it's hardly unexpected that local vices were transplanted into the House of Commons whereby privileges enjoyed by a miniscule number of people in a chartered town may have influenced aristocratic privileges. Interestingly enough, however, Paine bypasses the consequences of this corruption and its ramifications apart from stating that a "successful candidate for Parliament" is generally "destitute of the qualities that constitute a just legislator" (250). Instead, he briefly mentions Burke as an example of a representative who remained in the ranks of the Opposition for much of his career: the presumed point being that Burke himself was unscrupulous in his post-revolutionary alignment with Pitt and George III.

From here, Paine shifts to zero in more closely on the aristocracy, highlighting the injustice of a legislature that tends exclusively to its own interests. If workers from other occupations—for instance, bakers and brewers—are denied the opportunity to pass laws according to their needs, why are those whose lives revolve around letting, leasing, or renting out land permitted to form their own legislative body? It is a view akin to that of Burgh's in *Crito* where the latter observed

> We, in our great wisdom, restrain the poor baker to a certain limited profit; but we allow the landlord, the exporter of corn, the farmer ... and the other encroachers, to load the necessaries of life with whatever unjust profits they, in their great eagerness for money, and indifference about the miseries of the poor, may think proper.[18]

The Abbé Sieyès, as we have seen in Part 1, had also questioned the justice of a hereditary body of men forming a part of Parliament.

But whereas Burgh blames the private actions of individual dukes, earls, and counts, taking them to task for "raising the *rents* of his land ... *to an immoderate rate, or to unpeople the country, by laying half his estate into lawns and* parks," Paine takes a bolder step by blaming an aristocratic legislature for shifting the weight of taxes from themselves onto the less well-off.

To what extent was Paine's allegation true? Here, it is worth pointing out that unlike French and German nobles, British aristocrats were not exempt from taxation: nonetheless, they paid disproportionately less than the vast majority of Britons relative to their income. At first glance, since land was mostly taxed at a rate of 3 or 4 shillings per pound (with the exception of the 1730s when it was reduced to 1 shilling a pound by Walpole in an attempt to ingratiate himself with wealthy property owners), Paine's claims may appear flawed in light of the fact that the land tax continued to fluctuate between 3 and 4 shillings in the pound through much of the century. Nonetheless, it is clear that the amount of land-tax was dramatically reduced from 1696 to 1791 as noted by Paine in a footnote[19] with the purposeful devaluation of land by those who supported the Stuarts (Sinclair, part III, 7) upon William III's accession to the Crown: a possible reason for the relatively low rates for land-tax is that a higher tax was feared to enrage the more conservative Tory-leaning gentry against the ministry.[20] Meanwhile, luxury taxes on wine, coaches, horses, gold and silver thread, and silver plate served only to disguise the disproportionate weight of taxes on the less well-off. The fact that land taxes were collected locally rather than centrally as in France meant that taxes were even more underassessed. Similarly, in America, Hamilton would point out the "Herculean task" involved in "obtaining a valuation of the land" particularly "in a country imperfectly settled and progressive in improvement" (98).

Paine, however, was hardly alone in remarking on the low valuation of land; in 1781, the author of the land reform treatise, *An Essay on the Right of Property in Land*, William Ogilvie, would also comment on the relatively light taxes faced by landowners; large farms and short leases deserved to be taxed as well as increased rents.[21] In fact, both men remarked upon the outdated assessment of land; thus, Ogilvie recommended that land valuation "ought to be renewed from age to age" (207) while Paine points out that the value of land has not been reassessed since 1692 even as the number of items bearing excise taxes have proliferated over the course of the century. Nonetheless, although the rate of the land tax did not actually decrease steadily over the course of the century, it did comprise a diminishing proportion of the taxes collected (Table 2).

Table 2 Net Receipts of Customs, Excise, and Land Tax as Portions of Public Income, 1690–1790[22]

	Customs	*Excise*	*Land and assessed taxes*
1688–91	0.22	0.28	0.36
	£1,920/£8,613	£2,430/£8,613	£3,172/£8,613

[The total intake of receipts in thousands was £8,613; customs was £1,920, excise £2,430, and land £3,172]

	Customs	*Excise*	*Land and assessed taxes*
1700	0.35	0.23	0.34
	£1,523/£4,344	£1,030/£4,344	£1,483/£4,344
1710	0.25	0.29	0.39
	£1,338/£5,248	£1,548/£5,248	£2,074/£5,248
1720	0.26	0.39	0.24
	£1,673/£6,323	£2,478/£6,323	£1,537/£6,323
1730	0.26	0.45	0.25
	£1,601/£6,265	£2,810/£6,265	£1,558/£6,265
1740	0.25	0.49	0.22
	£1,420/£5,745	£2,817/£5,745	£1,252/£5,745
1750	0.20	0.60	0.39
	£1,537/£7,467	£3,454/£5,745	£2,212/£5,745
1760	0.23	0.46	0.26
	£2,113/£9,207	£4,218/£9,207	£2,407/£9,207
1770	0.25	0.45	0.18
	£2,841/£11,373	£5,139/£11,373	£1,796/£11,373
1780	0.22	0.49	0.20
	£2,774/£1,2524	£6,081/£12,524	£2,523/£12,524
1790	0.20	0.45	0.18
	£3,462/£17,014	£7,698/£17,014	£2,993/£17,014

There may be various reasons for this. As Thomas Piketty explains, Britons who had the means loaned what the state demanded for the high level of public debt served the interests of the lenders and their descendants well: it was simply more advantageous to lend to the state in the form of government bonds and thereby receive interest on their loans rather than paying taxes without compensation: in other words, it was a win–win situation for the government and its lenders. Moreover, the fact that the government's deficits increased the demand for private wealth naturally increased the return on that wealth.[23]

As Paine reminds his reader, the taxes levied on beer do not affect the aristocracy since they brew their own: a commentary that recapitulates Smith's remarks in *The Wealth of Nations* on economic injustice. Stating that "many middling and almost all rich and great families" are able to save a substantial sum of 9 or 10 shillings (*Wealth of Nations*, II, 484–5), Smith observed that "the exemption which this superior rank of people at present enjoy from very heavy taxes which are paid by the poor labourer and artificer" was "surely most unjust and unequal, and ought to be taken away" (II, 490). More strikingly, just as Smith blames elite interest for "prevent[ing] a change of system that could not well fail both to increase the revenue and to relieve the people" (490), Paine dwells upon this at greater length, returning to a point made in Part 1 that the interests of the Houses of Commons and Lords are tightly intertwined; these colluding interests of the propertied elite explain why the tax on beer collected in 1788, an amount of £1,666,152 (Sinclair, Part 3, 110, 125) that is nearly the same as the land tax—£1,909,053. As such that, collectively speaking, the poor and the middle classes pay more in taxes. Asserting that such people "are more injured by the taxes … on articles of consumption than they are eased it by warding it from landed property," Paine adds that they not only consume more taxable articles in proportion to their property but also tend to live in towns where they pay poor-rates: in other words, quite unlike the aristocracy which tends to live on private, relatively secluded estates. This legalized evasion of taxes, Paine elaborates, is equivalent to a scenario where "a combination acts to raise the price of any article for sale, or rate of wages." In doing so, the Lords and Commons are essentially practicing exactly they've forbidden laborers from collective action by enacting their own union of sorts. The "landed interest" is little more than "a combination of aristocratical landholders, opposing their own pecuniary interest to that of the farmer, and every branch of trade, commerce, and manufacture." For instance, if there were a house of farmers, game laws would not be passed to favor the interests of aristocrats and gentry who hunted while running roughshod over the farmer's crops. Likewise, a house of manufacturers or merchants would not impose such unequal or excessive taxes. (It is worth bearing in mind, according to Smith, that such would result in additional bounties.)

Although Sinclair observed in his *History of the Public Revenue* that "The landed interest endeavoured to throw off the burden of the State from their own shoulders" by stipulating that "no money should be raised upon land, without the special leave of the House" (358), it is telling that Paine underscores this shifting of burdens with marked emphasis, observing that with the "power of taxation" wielded by landowners, the burden of taxation has shifted to those who are less well off: a belief that harks back to Gilpin's strongly worded sermon of 1552 which intimated that "mightie men, gentlemen and all riche men" intended "to robbe and spoile the poore,"[24] Thomas More's words on "a kind of conspiracy of the rich, who are aiming at their own interests under the name and title of the commonwealth," as well as Rousseau's observations on "the privileged few" gorging "themselves with superfluities, while the starving multitude are in want of the bare necessities of life." Nor were Paine and Sinclair the only ones who discerned this injustice. The German visitor Wendeborn had also complained that the British paid insufficient regard "to the different classes of people and their circumstances" particularly when "The rich, when compared to the poor, pay too little"; like Paine, he believed that this injustice could be directly attributed to the fact that "The members of parliament, are mostly people of fortune, and the taxes are laid on by them" (*View*, 109–10).

Here, too, Paine doubles down on his criticism of the aristocracy. Is the peerage truly "the pillar of security to the landed interest" (*Appeal to the Whigs*, 60) and "the Corinthian capital of polished society" (*Reflections*) as claimed by Burke? Certainly not, Paine suggests. First of all, the idea of "a landed interest" is fatuous since all humans must eat to survive, "the same ploughing, sowing, and reaping would go on." Secondly, the aristocracy are not the actual farmers "who work the land, and raise the produce," but the mere "consumers of the rent," a set of "drones, a seraglio of males, who neither collect the honey nor form the hive, but exist only for lazy enjoyment" (253). Such men constitute only a larger version of a "rotten borough," having little accountability on account of its hereditary nature. Here, it is worth taking a glance at Burgh's discussion of the public offices enjoyed by the aristocracy before comparing it to Paine's:

It has often been proposed, That, for the advantage of the sinking fund, places and pensions should be taxed ... The heaping of pensions, to the amount of many thousands a year, on persons in easy, often in affluent circumstances, to be continued from generation to generation, and the keeping up innumerable needless posts and palaces, with exorbitant salaries annexed to them, at an enormous national expence, to the great encouragement of idleness ... and to the heavy detriment of the arts, manufactures and commerce, while the state is almost swallowed up in debt; is so directly contrary to the policy we ought to observe ... so barefaced an acknowledgment of a total indifference about the public interest ....

It is reasonable enough, that those, who apply the whole of their time, and labour hard in the service of the public, be maintained by the public. But why must a gentleman of fortune, or a man of quality ... and at exorbitant wages, to do what may be dispatched in a few hours a-day, or perhaps a-week and will scarce defile the tip of his finger, or discompose one curl of his full-bottom ... But if the King has occasion for a person of fortune and rank to superintend the weighty affairs of state, must he pay the nobleman with the same dirt which pays the sordid artizan? ... But then, let not the tinselled thing pretend the least superiority over the shoemaker. They both serve their King for money. They are both alike hirelings.

Every industrious subject has a right at least to complain, where he sees the fruit of his labour devoured by a set of overgrown bloodsuckers; such are all those placement and pensioners, who ... receive, on any pretence, any of the public money in times of public exigency. (*Crito*, Vol. 1, 59–61)

Although Burgh's indignation is palpable from his deprecatory references to the elites—"tinselled thing" and "overgrown bloodsuckers"—Paine's approach to this issue is arguably even more caustic with his matter-of-fact description of the corruption at hand, one that has been perfected into a system that profits at the expense of the public:

There are but few of its members, who are not in some mode or other participators, or disposers of the public money. One turns a candle-holder, or a lord in waiting; another a lord of the bed-chamber, a groom of the stole, or any insignificant nominal office to which a salary is annexed, paid out of the public taxes, and which avoids the direct appearance of corruption. Such situations are derogatory to the character of man; and where they can be submitted to, honour cannot reside.

To all these are to be added the numerous dependants [*sic*], the long list of younger branches and distant relations, who are to be provided for at the public expense: in short, were an estimation to be made of the charge of aristocracy to a nation, it will be found nearly equal to that of supporting the poor. The Duke of Richmond alone (and there are cases similar to his) takes away as much for himself as would maintain two thousand poor and aged persons. (253–4)

Here, Paine contrasts himself once more to the aristocracy. Again, diverging from Burke's assessment of such men possessing "a character of weight and consequence," Paine counters that "the case appears to me directly the reverse": it is notable, however, that he does not provide any instances of poor personal behavior on the part of propertied peers and gentry so frequently mentioned by earlier writers such as James Murray. The aristocratic character is "an attaint upon character," an illegitimate "sort of privateering on family property": the use of the word "privateering," of course, lends a touch of the burlesque. Claiming that his parents were unable to provide a shilling "beyond what they gave me in education" such that "they distressed themselves," he opines on his success, reminding his readers that he possesses "more of what is called consequence, in the world, than any one in Mr. Burke's catalogue of aristocrats": a fact that is arguably borne out today by Paine's relative fame.

From here, Paine turns abruptly to the monarchy, affirming some of his earlier observations, namely that a king may be "wise or foolish, sane or insane, a native or a foreigner"—so long as the people expect to worship someone with "superstitious ignorance": a point he had made as early as 1778 in *A Serious Address to the People of Pennsylvania* where he linked the decline of superstition with the decline of monarchy. The problem is that the Crown no longer serves the purpose it once did when the king served as a judge or performed other customary duties. Altogether, there is only "an appearance of consequence to empty forms" which serve only to increase expenses. Why, then, must a monarchy be retained when it no longer serves a viable purpose? It is evident, Paine claims, that unlike their ancestors, present-day Britons are no longer keeping a careful eye on their government. Their predecessors, he surmises, "were a people who would not be imposed upon, and who kept governments in awe as to taxation, if not as to principle." After all, why were taxes substantially lower between 1066 and 1466: £400,000 in 1066, £200,000 in 1166, £150,000 in 1266, £130,000 in 1366 and £100,000 in 1466? Why did they rise sharply to £500,000 in 1566, £1,800,000 in 1666, and £17,000,000 in 1791 (also see Sinclair, pages xiii and xiv)—particularly when "the pay of the army, the navy, and of all the revenue officers, is the same now as it was about a hundred years ago?" There are, of course, other causes for the decreases and increases in taxation, with changes in population being perhaps a marked factor, particularly with the Black Death in the 1350s (Table 3).

Table 3 Population Set Against Tax Yield, 1066–1790

	Population	Taxes
1066	1,700,000	£400,000
1166	3,000,000	£200,000
1266	4,200,000	£150,000
1366	2,550,000	£130,000
1466	2,000,000	£100,000
1566	3,200,000	£500,000
1666	5,320,000	£1,800,000
1790	8,000,000	£17,000,000

Interestingly, Paine glosses over Sinclair's attribution of lower taxes between 1066 and 1566 to the monarchy's reliance on the practice of scutage, temporary grants, and "compulsive loans" to the Crown until the reign of Elizabeth (*History of the Public Revenue in the British Empire*, Parts 1 and 2, 5), most of which were drawn from the wealthiest subjects.

It is equally striking too that unlike Sinclair who accepted the basic premise of a British empire (as indicated in the very title of his book), Paine did not. Viewing the English discovery of the East and West Indies as a factor responsible for planting "the seeds of that political system" that necessitated "greater pecuniary aids" (141) as well as resources devoted to the development of the navy (308), Sinclair distinguishes the period following the Revolution as a drastically different one whereby the state "assumed the appearance of a great corporation" by borrowing money "to cultivate, to defend, or to acquire distant possessions" in hopes of producing "an extensive and a powerful empire" (5): hence, the rise in expenditures from £100,000 to £500,000 between 1466 and 1566. No less crucial a factor in the increase of expenses was the growing sophistication of weaponry after 1466 when guns and cannons were introduced, as Sinclair observes. Moreover, the greatly heightened costs of naval shipbuilding and the trebling of manpower in the army and navy from 1680 to 1780 (Brewer, 29), not to mention the growing duration of wars

(Sinclair, I, 307), were significant factors: as historians have noted, between 75% and 85% of annual expenditure was devoted to the army, navy and ordnance or to pay debts incurred from earlier wars.[25] These figures indicate that Britain devoted comparable commitment to military expenditure as any contemporary European power. Even if expenditures associated with the payment of national debt are excluded, current wartime military expenditure accounted for somewhere between 61% and 74% of public spending.[26] Yet, if Sinclair, like Paine, deplored the large sums of money "wasted in war" (III, 29), in addition to regretting the "rage for acquisition by the mode of colonization" by which subjects are sent forth to "cultivate and improve distant regions, instead of improving and cultivating at home" (III, 35), his overall assessment of the British economy—unlike Paine's—remained largely positive:

> From 1760 to 1789, though a space of only 28 years, such sums have been paid into the public treasury ... Nothing can more clearly demonstrate the immense wealth and resources of Great Britain; and had any considerable portion of that money, instead of being wasted in war, been laid out in cultivating the arts of peace, the nation would perhaps have grown too rich and powerful .... (Part 3, 29)

By comparison, Paine's attitude towards war is far less equivocal. Altogether rejecting the premise of colonialism, he dismisses "the idea of having navies for the protection of commerce" as "delusive" and blames the Glorious Revolution in addition to the arrival of George I for "the destructive system of continental intrigues, and the rage for foreign wars and foreign dominion." Nonetheless, as noted earlier, Paine omits the fact that the War of Jenkins' Ear, the Seven Years' War and the American Revolution, all of which were fought partly for the protection of British trade and commerce. More strikingly, Paine ventures much farther than other contemporary writers by proposing what might be regarded as a blueprint for a NATO-type alliance among England, France, and the United States. In his optimistic prediction that the French revolution will guarantee amicable relations between the peoples of France and England (a vision that would be quickly dispelled, as we will see later), he envisions a reduction of expenses for war in Britain and France with general spending brought down from £5,771,477 closer to the levels of that enjoyed by the spendthrift Charles II, at approximately £1,500,000 (261) (Table 4).[27]

Given a new post-revolutionary peacefulness between France and Britain, neither republican France nor republic-to-be Britain, according to Paine, will require as many fleets and armies; certainly, Britain will no longer be so easily "allured and alarmed into taxes" with the "clamour of French intrigue, arbitrary power, popery." But even if annual spending were to be substantially slashed from £1,500,000 a year (261), he claims, it will still exceed that of America six times over. However, it is worth bearing in mind that the population of America was only a half of Britain's and that military expenses for the new republic were minimal, particularly after the war for independence ended in 1783. In fact, the predominant desire for peace led to the disarmament of the Continental navy in 1785 which was not rebuilt until 1794 when eleven American ships were captured by Barbary pirates.

Here, too, Paine contests Burke's views of popular uprisings, particularly the peasant revolt of 1381, as presented in *An Appeal from the New Whigs to the Old*. According to Burke, the dynamics behind the French revolution did not differ substantially from those of "Cade, Ket, and Straw," all of whom "did no more than exert, according to the doctrines of ours and the Parisian societies, the sovereign power inherent in the majority"; there is some degree of self-satisfaction as Burke states, "we call the time of those events a dark age." Burke drips with irony as he praises the "Abbé John Ball" for understanding "the rights of man as well as the Abbé Gregoire" since

Table 4 Comparison of Expenditures

Condensed expenditures of 1788[28]		Paine's proposed expenditures	
Navy	£2,348,118	Navy	£500,000
Army	£2,038,852	Army	£500,000
Ordnance	£484,507	Expenses of Government	£500,000
Civil List	£900,000		£1,500,000
	£5,771,477		

> That reverend patriarch of sedition, and prototype of our modern
> preachers, was of opinion with the national assembly, that all the evils
> which have fallen upon men had been caused by an ignorance of their
> "having been born and continued equal as to their rights."

Burke proceeds to suggest that the modern counterparts of Ball
are loathe to quote him not only because they would not appear
as original, but also because "he was not successful." Rather than
address the subject of the revolt in the main text perhaps out of a
belief that it would appear extraneous to a chapter on contemporary problems and solutions, Paine contests Burke's statements in a footnote with a pointed rebuke, observing that it is not
surprising that the memory of Wat Tyler "should be traduced by
court sycophants, and all those who live on the spoils of a
public." Here, Paine also points out the injustice of a poll tax that
charges the poor proportionately more than the rich (257), going
so far as to claim the superior merit of the peasants when compared to the barons contesting John at Runnymede: the proposals
made to Richard II were

> more just than those which had been made to John by the Barons ...
> notwithstanding the sycophancy of historians, and men like Mr.
> Burke, who seek to gloss over a base action of the court by traducing
> Tyler ... If the Barons merited a monument to be erected in Runny-
> mede, Tyler merits one in Smithfield (257).[29]

Just as he once demanded in the *American Crisis* paper of
November 21, 1778, "Whether it is not a shame for a man to
spend a million a year and do no good for it, and whether the
money might not be better applied," Paine voices frustration with
the popular impulse to "be governed like animals." Noting caustically that "To read the history of kings" one would assume that
"government consisted in stag-hunting, and that every nation
paid a million a-year to a huntsman," he daringly stipulates that
none be paid more than £10,000 a year because no one should be
overcompensated for his duties. Since public money is drawn
from all sectors of the populace—including "the hard earnings of
labour and poverty" and "even from the bitterness of want and

misery"—it is wrong for the poor to support the rich as "Not a beggar passes, or perishes in the streets, whose mite is not in that mass." Paine would be arguably the first writer to express this unpopular truth in so stark and plaintive a manner before suggesting that it is only proper for a limited number of officeholders, with three positions paying £10,000 a year, ten at £5,000, 20 at £2,000, and 40 at £1,000.

Even more far reaching, however, is Paine's general scheme for public welfare, one to be created from a three-quarters reduction in military spending and a half of other government expenditures. The idea of public welfare was itself not an altogether novel one in 1792; as J.C.D. Clark points out, the very premise of the Poor Law was itself a scheme grounded on the idea of providing for the poor in spite of its localized orientation. Nonetheless, the 18th century would witness a number of attempts to redress poverty on a more national scale. In 1766, Burgh had already proposed a plan in *Crito* that would provide for the poor as he recommended that £50,000–£100,000 be collectively allotted on an annual basis to indigent families (I, 52–3). Nine years later, Paine himself would arrive at a scheme that aimed to bestow monies upon young couples and the elderly when he penned a letter to the editor of the *Pennsylvania Magazine*, suggesting "a fund for the purpose of portioning off young married people with a reasonable sufficiency to begin the world with, who would otherwise have nothing" and another "for the purpose of supporting us in our old age." Fifteen years later, John Sinclair would recommend a bipartite division of taxes drawn from consumption: one was to be remitted to the various counties for "exported manufactures" and the other to poor families "in proportion to the number of their children" in addition to the elderly who are "unable, from sickness or age, to maintain themselves." Only then could the "situation of that valuable class of men … be rendered as comfortable as the imperfection of human nature will allow" (Part 3, 128). Others, such as John Scott, commented on the uneven provisions for the poor, finding that "In some parishes," there was "not more than 2 shillings, or one shilling and sixpence, perhaps less, in others four, five, and it has been said, six and seven shillings in the pound per annum" allotted to the poor (35, footnote);

indeed, he would argue that given the "inequality of expence in different parishes," it was clear that "Taxation, therefore, should be no longer local and arbitrary, but general and uniform, limited like the land tax to a certain standard" (68–9).[30]

In Part 2, Paine pushes Burgh's and Sinclair's ideas considerably further. If Burgh regretted that "this method of managing our poor" causes "an enormous burden" to fall "upon a parish, in which there are many poor, and few rich, while a rich parish is almost free" (II, 89–90), Paine, like John Scott, took the next logical step by specifying that poor rates be funded nationally rather than locally in order to avoid uneven distribution. In Paine's view, the poor could be easily provided with twice as much—4 as opposed to 2 million pounds a year. Assuming England to have a population of 7 million in 1791 (modern estimates for 1791 are closer to 8 million) and those requiring further pecuniary assistance to comprise no less than 1/5th of the population,[31] Paine imagined the number of the latter to be 1,400,000, with the aged poor making up a tenth of this number at 140,000. It is worth noting, however, that Burgh provides greater largesse to recipients—perhaps because he underestimated the population of the poor. Rather than issuing £25 per 4,000 young people to marry (to which Burgh adds "might be given as a reward of attested industry and good behaviour")—a sum that was also at least partly intended as a means to encourage population growth, Paine proposes an annual sum of 20 shillings apiece for 20,000 marriages, 20 shillings apiece for 50,000 births (Paine assumes that a quarter of 200,000 annual births will require some financial assistance), £4 per child for schooling and 10 shillings for each child belonging to families which are only slightly better off, with an additional 2 shillings, 6 pence for spelling books and paper per child for six years. As if following up on the widespread lack of education that he mentioned in Part 1, he observes that "ignorance will be banished from the rising generation" such that the numbers of the poor will be reduced "because their abilities, by the aid of education, will be greater." Paine may have been reflecting back on his five years of education at Thetford—that for which his parents "distressed themselves"—in his observation that "Many a youth, with good natural genius, who is apprenticed to a mechanical trade, such as a carpenter, joiner, millwright … is prevented getting forward the whole of his life, from the want of a little common education when a boy" (267).[32] At the same time, while pointing out in a footnote the necessity for more readily accessible schools, Paine astutely reminds readers in his main text that a greater number of schools benefits not only children but also prospective teachers. Certainly, the tuition paid by parents would be appreciated by widows of distressed clergymen (270, n. 1) Altogether, he explains, a well-governed nation "should permit none to remain uninstructed." It is only "monarchical and aristocratical government" that "requires ignorance for its support" (270).

Although we may not be inclined to view Paine's recommendations for universal child education as particularly radical in our age of compulsory schooling, such a concept was nonetheless a highly uncommon one at a time when many disapproved of education for the poor, or at the very least, believed only a minimal amount to be necessary. It is striking, for instance, that Potter's otherwise sympathetic view of the poor offers little in the way of education beyond basic knowledge of the Bible and manual skills:

> a proper school should be established in every parish, under the direction of well qualified persons … Much learning is not necessary; but they should be taught to read the Bible; they should be impressed with an early knowledge and veneration of God … of his goodness in the redemption of the world; of the necessity of holiness to happiness; of the resurrection from the dead … In this school all the females should be taught to knit and sew … The boys, in like manner, under the direction of some sober man advanced in years, should some hours each day be employed abroad; they might at proper seasons gather stones, pull up weeds …. (Potter, 67–8)

Consider, too, Davies Giddy's speech against Samuel Whitbread's bill for the establishment of parish schools in 1807 where Paine's assertion that "monarchical and aristocratical government requires ignorance" is proven correct:

> However specious in theory the project might be of giving education to the laboring classes of the poor, it would, in effect, be found to be

prejudicial to their morals and happiness; it would teach them to despise their lot in life ... instead of teaching them the virtue of sub-ordination it would render them factious and refractory ... it would enable them to read seditious pamphlets ....[33]

Was Giddy alluding to Paine's *Rights of Man* both as a product of working-class education and a "seditious" influence at that— particularly since it had already been censored for 15 years? Moreover, in addition to recommending and providing for edu-cation, Paine would also set aside 20 shillings to each of 50,000 women or young couples with newborn infants as well as a sum allotted to the defrayment of funeral expenses for those dying at a distance from friends and family.

At best, the idea of education for the poor was a controversial one, but one which Paine took for granted. However, perhaps that which clearly distinguishes his plans from other schemes for public welfare is a markedly less judgmental mode of allocation whereby the provisions constitute a right rather than charity or a reward for good behavior. Burgh, for instance, drew the tradi-tional distinction between the deserving and undeserving poor, believing it a "good regulation, that the idle poor should lose their right to public charities and lawful settlements, and be sent to the plantations, when they come to want, instead of the alms-house"; every parish should keep "a register of every inhabitant, man, woman, and child" so that "Whenever any person becomes, through idleness or wickedness, a nuisance in the place where he lives, complaint ought to be made ... to the magistrate" (I, 54). In contrast, Paine sought to provide resources to all who required it. All told, Paine calculates the costs of educating 630,000 children at £4 each a year as £2,520,000: although it is worth pointing out that the actual amount stands at £3,024,000 due to a mathema-tical error in Paine's calculation.[34]

Equally bold is Paine's far reaching insights on the challenges faced by the elderly—particularly at a time when the latter were perceived to be generally disregarded; foreigners, including Wende-born himself, were apt to observe that "In no country do poverty and old age seem to be considered as greater evils than here ... but old age, though accompanied with sufficient fortune, is not withstanding, too often neglected" (I, 418). Care for the elderly was often balanced between the family and community, with the parish determining the level of allocations; moreover, the sense that poor relief should serve a moral purpose—as is evident from Burgh's remarks—and that parish monies should only be granted to those in absolute need suggests that not all elderly persons were "automatically entitled to relief" (Ottaway, 183). Perhaps Paine, in his capacity as a member of the town vestry at Lewes, had become aware of the shortcomings of a localized system of relief. Estimating that those over 50 comprise 1/16 or 1/17th of the population, numbering approximately 420,000 people in a population of 7 million, and that a third (140,000) are needy, he proposes £6 a year for those between the ages of 50 and 60 and £10 for those over 60:

> At fifty, though the mental faculties of man are in full vigour, and his judgment better than at any preceding date, the bodily powers for laborious life are on the decline. He cannot bear the same quantity of fatigue as at an earlier period. He begins to earn less, and is less capable of enduring wind and weather; and in those more retired employments where much sight is required, he fails apace, and sees himself, like an old horse, beginning to be turned adrift.

> At sixty his labour ought to be over, at least from direct necessity. It is painful to see old age working itself to death, in what are called civilised countries, for daily bread.

Paine's generosity becomes especially apparent when his provisions are compared with actual provisions for the elderly, ranging from 5.7p. to 30p. per week, with an average between 14p and 26p. Such would have meant £2 4s. to £6 10s. a year—substantially less than Paine's minimum of £6 for those in their 50s and £10 in their 60s. It is also worth noting that his scheme provides considerably more to those in their 60s than that at Terling. If there are in fact even more impoverished elderly people, he adds darkly, "society, notwithstanding the show and pomposity of government, is in a deplorable condition in England" (268). Again, he emphasizes this support as a right rather than a privilege—in much the same way that Winstanley posited sustenance on the commons as a right—by reiterating it within three paragraphs: that funds should be treated "not as a matter of grace and favour, but of right" and "not of the nature of a charity but of a right." Funds were to be provided to a wide swathe of the elderly, including "husbandmen, common labourers, journeymen of every trade and their wives, sailors, and disbanded soldiers, worn out servants of both sexes, and poor widows" as well as "middling tradesmen" and those of "every class of life connected with commerce and adventure." It is telling that he grants lifelong provisions for newly discharged military personnel at 3 shillings a week—even if he only accounted for a total of 30,000 soldiers in the army, a slim fraction of the actual number in 1791 (i.e., in 1710, the number was already 139,000).[35]

Since each Briton already paid £2 11s. 6p. a year in taxes and thereby £154 10s. cumulatively, why then should the funds they receive after the age of 50 not serve as "a legal interest of the net money he has paid?" Here, we approach the concept of Social Security. Rather boldly, Paine dramatically pits the lives of the poor and middle-class elderly against those of the wealthy and powerful:

> Is it, then, better that the lives of one hundred and forty thousand aged persons be rendered comfortable, or that a million a year of public money be expended on any one individual, and him often of the most worthless or insignificant character? Let reason and justice, let honour and humanity, let even hypocrisy, sycophancy and Mr. Burke, let George, let Louis, Leopold, Frederic, Catherine, Cornwallis, or Tippoo Saib, answer the question. (269)

What is to be inferred, of course, is that the lives of these supposed crowned heads and other worthies are no more important than those of the masses. The few should not profit at the expense of the many: a point which must have rankled Paine's aristocratic readers, leading to the proscription of *Rights of Man*.

Indeed, what is also striking is Paine's understanding of circumstances leading to poverty, even if he does not address the causes of poverty in small towns and rural areas. Perhaps reflecting back on his own sights and experiences in London as a young man in his early twenties, he reveals a rare awareness not only for those similarly situated with few definitive resources for employment, but also those raised in the city by "dissolute parents," frequently without "any means of a livelihood." Hunger can prove a threatening challenge for both groups, such that "a day, even a few hours" can often cause "the crisis of a life of ruin," circumstances which, in turn, contribute to the "little thefts and pilferings that lead to greater." Here, Paine envisions an employment center imbued with features of a workhouse, but with few of its punitive features: an edifice that can hire and house as many as 6,000 people in need of work. The £40,000 to be spent on this project he hypothesizes would certainly be more practical than the £20,000 in taxes which support the already wealthy Duke of Richmond. Again, Paine juxtaposes the lives of ordinary Britons to the elites, professing outrage at their privileges: "It is horrid that any man, more especially at the price coals now are, should live on the distresses of a community; and any government permitting such an abuse, deserves to be dismissed," particularly when the fund is "said to be about twenty thousand pounds per annum." It is here that Paine arrives at one of his most poignant and sublime passages that concludes with another dig at the affluent:

> By the operation of this plan, the poor laws, those instruments of civil torture, will be superseded, and the wasteful expense of litigation prevented. The hearts of the humane will not be shocked by ragged and hungry children, and persons of seventy and eighty years of age, begging for bread. The dying poor will not be dragged from place to place to breathe their last, as a reprisal of parish upon parish. Widows will have a maintenance for their children, and not be carted away, on the death of their husbands, like culprits and criminals; and children will no longer be considered as increasing the distresses of their parents. The haunts of the wretched will be known, because it will be to their advantage; and the number of petty crimes, the offspring of distress and poverty, will be lessened. The poor, as well as the rich, will then be interested in the support of government, and the cause and apprehension of riots and tumults will cease.—Ye who sit in ease, and solace yourselves in plenty, and such there are in Turkey

and Russia, as well as in England, and who say to yourselves, "Are we not well off?" have ye thought of these things? When ye do, ye will cease to speak and feel for yourselves alone.

In many respects, this passage can be said to represent the culmination of centuries of thought on the rights of sustenance for all, from Gratian and Godfrey of Fontaine to the rebels of 1549 and the Diggers, all of whom variously contemplated the right to survive and to share commodities "which Nature the parent of us all, would have common." Only then can political and social orderliness prevail.

No less bold is Paine's attempt at a more egalitarian form of taxation where the affluent would shoulder a greater burden of taxes. Although the concept of proportionate taxation was far from new—after all, earlier monarchs had always raised funds or coerced loans from their wealthiest subjects, Paine's scheme was nonetheless a relatively unprecedented and comprehensive one for the 18th century: even if Adam Smith suggested that subjects should support their government "as nearly as possible in proportion to their respective abilities," specifically in terms of "the revenue they enjoy" and the French Constituent Assembly of 1789 proclaimed in the Declaration of Rights that while all citizens must pay taxes, they should pay "in proportion to their faculties."[36] Paine begins by proposing the eventual reduction of the duty on hops, candles, soap, and windows. Unlike Burgh who desired a poll tax to replace excise and customs in order to reduce costs for the vast majority of people (a plan which Smith opposed as "direct taxes upon the wages of labour" especially when "levied upon the lower ranks of people" 464), Paine attempts to supplant the commutation tax with a tax on income earned from property rather than luxuries; as he observes, it is more meaningful to tax the means of acquiring luxuries rather than the goods themselves. Again, Paine's plan was by no means the first proposal for progressive tax—but rather the first to explore it on so thorough a scale: earlier in the century, Sir Matthew Decker had proposed a tax on pitched houses, with 500,000 of 1,200,000 houses to be exempted from taxation (i.e., those inhabited by the "inferior classes of people", Sinclair, Pt. 3, 154) with a duty of

£10 on average, "varying according to the wealth of the possessor," while others had advanced schemes where individual income would be taxed through assessment of housing, equipage, number of horses and servants (Sinclair, Pt. 3, 155) This is why, according to Paine, burdens must be shifted "to where it can best be borne," and justice restored "among families by a distribution of property" with overgrown influence from primogeniture "extirpated." Because "the richest in every nation have poor relations, and those often very near in consanguinity," limits should be set on the accumulation of property by bequest, allowing it to pass in another line of the family: it is an idea that resembles James Harrington's plan for all large properties to be distributed evenly among children in any given family and to have no more than £2,000 derived from landed income. Paine's reasoning also shares certain affinities with Ogilvie's plan of 1781, particularly where the latter asserts:

> The desire of transmitting their estates to a long series of descendants, arises very naturally in the minds of men, who have enjoyed ample possessions under the protection of a well constituted government ... It might be entitled however to more praise, as proceeding from a liberal spirit ... as highly favourable to the general welfare, if, instead of securing superfluous opulence to one favoured line of representatives, the plan ... had for its object, to diffuse a moderate competency among a numerous tribe or family of descendants, and to provide, that no one of the whole race shall be reduced to penury ... Both these intentions might be combined in the same scheme, by securing the present rent of the entailed estate to the lineal heir, at all events, and giving at the same time to all other descendants of the entailor, or of his ancestors, a right when any lease fell vacant, (the leases not exceeding three lives) to claim possession of it in full property, at the last rent.[37]

Not less important from Paine's perspective is the simple fact that the accumulation of physical property amounts to "a waste of national property" with the "great extent of [private] parks and chases" particularly when "the annual production of grain is not equal to the national consumption." Indeed, Paine's rationale for a land tax is comparable to Ogilvie's belief that "the gross amount of property in land is the fittest subject of taxation" and can "be made to support the whole expence of the public" (Ogilvie, 207). Note, however, that Paine does not go as far left as Thomas Spence who proposed that land be held in common for all by local parishes.

Under Paine's plan, however, the tax becomes progressively steeper until £23,000: if the land tax for the thirteenth thousand already offers scant profit to the owner, standing at 10s. per pound, it becomes even steeper at the 23rd thousand where the tax reaches 20s. per pound. As such, the owner of an estate earning more than £23,000 will only net roughly £10,630 after taxes. When an estate reaches such a size, it becomes more profitable to divide it into five estates of £4,000 and one of £3,000, so that the total amount of taxes will only be £1,129 which is 5% of £23,000, instead of the full amount of £10,630 when held by one landowner. Given the scarcity of such estates, Paine concedes, there is arguably little gain to be reaped by the government; instead, he explains, the object is not so much the produce of the tax but the idea of justice since for too long, "the aristocracy has screened itself too much, and this serves to restore a part of the lost equilibrium." However, there are also definitive benefits: firstly, younger siblings and relations of wealthy heirs will attain some degree of economic security. Secondly, because all will have a share in the family wealth, there will be no need for "useless posts, places and offices." Once more, Paine returns to his complaints on the lack of tax burdens borne by the aristocracy, adding that commutation "ought to have been at the expense of those for whom the exemptions from those services were intended" but was imposed on a less well-off set of people. It was not until 1796 that Paine would arrive at a scheme that most closely approximates the concept of Social Security. Deeming it necessary to "remedy the evils and preserve the benefits that have arisen to society by passing from the natural to that which is called the civilized state," he proposed a scheme in *Agrarian Justice* (1797) where a "national fund" would be created by which £15 would be paid to everyone at the age of 21 in addition to an annual sum of ten pounds per annum to all those at 50 years of age, "as a compensation in part, for the loss of his or her natural inheritance, by the introduction of the system of landed property."[38] However, it is worth noting, as Malcolm Chase observes, that Paine's scheme for progressive taxation in *Rights of Man* is actually more radical in scope than that in his later work with its focus on death duties.[39]

Paine begins to wrap up his schemes for social and economic justice by returning to the poverty suffered by the very young and old, stating that "There are two classes of people to whom the laws of England are particularly hostile, and those the most helpless; younger children and the poor" (282). Much of what follows, apart from his summary of monies to be distributed to needy families and the elderly poor, focuses on the redistribution of monies: here, Paine provides for 252,000 families at the rate of £4 per child under 14 and an additional £250,000 for the education of 1,030,000 children. That Paine was not altogether certain of the amounts becomes clear ten pages later, where he makes slight revisions, £5 to 104,000 families, £7 each to 100,000 families, £8 to another 100,000 families and £10 to 50,000 poor and widowed families, all per family per year. There would be a further £4 per family for each child under fourteen with an addition of £250,000 for 1,030,000 children, £6 for all people between the ages of 50 and 60, and £10 for those over 60. (Note that in this revision Paine provides for 354,000 families rather than 252,000 as previously noted.) Not unlike the rebels of 1381 (who chafed at the limits on wages decreed by the Statute of 1351) or Ogilvie,[40] Paine criticizes the limits imposed on wages and prohibition against collective bargaining.[41] Why should workers not have every right to determine their wages—just like law-makers do in leasing out farms and houses? Especially with inflation and rising taxes? Indeed, like Ogilvie who remarked that "These lower classes have only the labour of their hands for their commodity," Paine wondered "why is that little, and the little freedom they enjoy to be infringed"—especially when laborers had families to support? As such, it was only fair for wealthy landowners to be subjected to limits on their income "of not less than twelve thousand a-year, and that of property they never acquired (nor probably any of their ancestors), and of which they have made so ill a use" (282). Perhaps emboldened by his fame, Paine would also revive the issue of the excise officers' pay, demanding an increase of £20 to the salary. Not least did he also resume his criticisms from Part 1 of the discrepancy between wages earned by ordinary ministers and those of bishops, questioning whether it be right that "there ought to be an income of twenty or thirty pounds to one man, and a thousand to another" (284).

From proposals for the alleviation of poverty and the increase of ordinary wages, Paine turns his attention to the political problems which he holds responsible for the destruction of public welfare. Here, Paine begins by pointing out the general corruption in politics: William Pitt the Younger could only appear less unscrupulous than his immediate predecessors, Lord North and Sir Charles James Fox in the Fox–North Coalition (1783). But alas, Paine sighs, as Pitt's seeming "ignorance of vice" and "apparent candour" were delusive. Instead, Pitt increased taxes while "ransacking Europe and India for adventures" (286). Paine obviously disapproved of Pitt's endeavor to centralize British control in India and his engagement in the Triple Alliance with Prussia and Holland in 1788 for the purposes of forcing Spain to yield its control over the western coasts of North and South America. Interestingly, even though Pitt was successful in narrowly averting national bankruptcy by stimulating trade and reducing the debt contracted from the war in America substantially from £243 million to £170 million between 1786 and 1792, Paine does not mention it.[42]

In short, a new system of government is required since a change of ministry accomplishes little as Pitt proves himself scarcely better than the much-hated Fox–North coalition:

> All this seems to show that change of ministers amounts to nothing. One goes out, another comes in, and still the same measures, vices, and extravagance are pursued. It signifies not who is minister. The defect lies in the system. The foundation and the superstructure of the government is bad. Prop it as you please, it continually sinks into court government, and ever will. (286)

For Paine, Pitt has done little but continue the legacy of William III and "its handmaid the Hanover succession" (286). The only way discreditable dealings can be completely eradicated is by axing the monarchy and thereby taking away "the power of making war into the hands of foreigners" (287).

From here, Paine returns to taxes and the amelioration of hardship, thereby resuming his thread on necessary change. He proposes taxing the interest on the national debt—for instance, taxing it a half penny in the pound in the first year, a penny the second, etc.—while removing a given tax (e.g., a tax on wagons or female servants). Eventually, poor-rates, taxes on windows, and the commutation tax will all be eliminated such that stockholders of the national debt will also find relief. At the same time, the poor will be unburdened "and all discontent will be taken away." This is where we find one of Paine's most memorable quotes:

> When it shall be said in any country in the world, my poor are happy; neither ignorance nor distress is to be found among them; my jails are empty of prisoners, my streets of beggars; the aged are not in want, the taxes are not oppressive; the rational world is my friend, because I am the friend of its happiness: when these things can be said, then may that country boast its constitution and its government. (288)

A more peaceful society can only be accomplished by tending to the needs and wants of the poor. Through "reason and discussion," there should be few public disturbances because "The poor, in all countries, are naturally both peaceable and grateful in all reforms in which their interest and happiness is included. It is only by neglecting and rejecting them that they become tumultuous" (289). Even today, as we will see in the Conclusion, Paine's words are far from fulfilled, especially when neoliberal Western governments continue to slash public spending while prison populations explode and military spending rises amidst a general angst and insecurity.

It is perhaps not surprising that Paine returns to address the idea of revolution. Clearly, since general welfare is so wanting across Europe, revolution is necessary—with Britain no exception.[43] Again, he points out the lack of true representation, repeating his mistaken point that less than one-hundredth of the population are enfranchised. (As mentioned earlier, the real number was about one-sixth.) It is equally notable, however, that he believed the French revolution to be a distinguished by "reason and common interest" and of relatively "quiet operation," largely resolved by "reason and discussion."[44] Indeed, he reiterates his trust in the powers of both as he states a few paragraphs later that "reason and discussion will soon bring things right." Even more strikingly, Paine intimates that this new mode of revolution as witnessed in France is itself revolutionary: "reason and discussion, persuasion and conviction, become the weapons in the contest, and it is only when those are attempted to be suppressed that recourse is had to violence" (292). This point is repeated towards the end where he states: "Formerly, when divisions arose respecting governments, recourse was had to the sword, and a civil war ensued. That savage custom is exploded by the new system, and reference is had to national conventions. Discussion and the general will arbitrates …."

While Paine does not suggest explicitly that money spent on wars should be diverted to the public, he proceeds to recommend the reduction of navy forces in France and England by 90%. After all, what can be more foolish than "building navies, filling them with men, and then hauling them into the ocean, to try which can sink each other fastest?" For Paine, peace costs little, but is "attended with infinitely more advantage, than any victory with all its expense": even if "court governments" relied on war for taxation and other sources of profit. Here, too, Paine calls for an end to empires, calling for Spain to liberate South America, while comparing the behavior of the British in the East Indies to that of the "Goths and Vandals" (291). Paine's optimism for change resurfaces in the next paragraph as he imagines that "the iron is becoming hot all over Europe" as "the insulted German and the enslaved Spaniard, the Russ and the Pole, are beginning to think. The present age will hereafter merit to be called the Age of reason": the latter of which would form the title of his next work. Indeed, one may even wonder if Paine's final turn to the idea of religious toleration in the final paragraphs of the chapter may have signaled his intents for *The Age of Reason*. The practice of religion in the old, reformed world, Paine reiterates, has been "very improperly made a political machine" in order "to prevent the nation turning its attention to subjects of government" (294). Religion, then, is yet another distractor—just like war.[45]

As noted in Part 1 of *Rights of Man*, Paine associates the old world and the establishment with perversion and unnaturalness. The conclusion is no different as Paine uses his metaphor of a budding spring:

> It is now towards the middle of February. Were I to take a turn into the country, the trees would present a leafless, wintery appearance. As people are apt to pluck twigs as they walk along, I perhaps might do the same, and by chance might observe, that a single bud on that twig had begun to swell. I should reason very unnaturally, or rather not reason at all, to suppose this was the only bud in England which had this appearance. Instead of deciding thus, I should instantly conclude, that the same appearance was beginning, or about to begin, every where; and though the vegetable sleep will continue longer on some trees and plants than on others, and though some of them may not blossom for two or three years, all will be in leaf in the summer, except those which are rotten ... It is, however, not difficult to perceive that the spring is begun.

Here, it is the vegetation that do not grow leaves which prove rotten. To remain barren during the "political summer" is similarly a sign of human stagnation. Although it is difficult to determine if future revolutionaries had Paine's imagery in mind, it is striking that the Revolutions of 1848 were variously referred to as "Spring of Nations," "People's Spring," and "Springtime of the Peoples"—names that may have in turn inspired the moniker, "The Arab Spring," of 2011.

NOTES

1 Algernon Sidney, *Discourses on Government*, ed. Thomas G. West (Indianapolis: Liberty Fund, 1990, 1996) p. 91.
2 See Book XXIII, Chap. 29. *The Spirit of the Laws* in *The Complete Works of M.de Montesquieu*, Vols. 1–4 (London, 1777) 2. http://oll.libertyfund.org/titles/montes quieu-complete-works-vol-2-the-spirit-of-laws

3 See Part 1, https://www.marxists.org/reference/subject/economics/rousseau/inequality/cho1.htm#s1

4 James Mackintosh makes a comparable point on the legislative power of propertied elites in *Vindiciae Gallicae*: "The accumulation of that power which is conferred by wealth in the hands of the few, is the perpetual source of oppression and neglect to the mass of mankind ... They necessarily in all countries administer government, for they alone have skill and leisure for its functions. Thus circumstanced, nothing can be more evident than their inevitable preponderance in the political scale. The preference of partial to general interests is however the greatest of all public evils. It should therefore have been the object of all laws to repress this malady, but it has been their perpetual tendency to aggravate it." https://oll.libertyfund.org/titles/mackintosh-vindiciae-gallicae-and-other-writings-on-the-french-revolution

5 *Discourse on Inequality*, Part 2. See: https://www.marxists.org/reference/subject/economics/rousseau/inequality/cho2.htm

6 [John Scott], *Observations on the Present State of the Parochial and Vagrant Poor* (London, 1773) p. 34.

7 R. Potter, *Observations on the Poor Laws on the Present State of the Poor and on Houses of Industry* (London, 1775) p. 31.

8 Fred. Aug Wendeborn, *A View of England towards the Close of the Eighteenth Century* (London, 1791) p. 117.

9 *The Complete Writings of Thomas Paine*, Vols. 1–2, ed. Philip Foner (New York: Citadel Press, 1945) 2, 536.

10 Thomas Paine, *Agrarian Justice* in *Complete Writings* 1, p. 610.

11 Table 1 is taken from John Sinclair, *History of the Public Revenue of the British Empire*, Pt. 3 (London, 1790) pp. 291–3.

12 Sinclair tallies this partial sum as £5,627,672, but the amount is as stated above. Similarly, the entire sum is £19,591,885 rather than £19,591,285 as written by Sinclair.

13 Gerrard Winstanley, *Complete Works of Gerrard Winstanley*, Vols. 1–2, ed. Thomas N. Corns, Ann Hughes, and David Loewenstein (Oxford: Oxford University Press, 2009) 2, p. 303.

14 M.J. Daunton, *Progress and Poverty: An Economic and Social History of Britain* (Oxford: Oxford University Press, 1995) p. 526.

15 *Federalist Papers*, #34 https://avalon.law.yale.edu/18th_century/fed34.asp.

16 The idea of individual farms and cottages would be echoed by Mary Wollstonecraft in her reply to Burke, *Vindication of the Rights of Men*.

17 Emmanuel Joseph Sieyès, *An Essay on Privileges* in *Political Writings Including the Debate between Sieyès and Tom Paine*, ed. Michael Sonenscher (Indianapolis: Hackett, 2003) p. 71.

18 James Burgh, *Crito*, Vols. 1–2 (London, 1767) 2, pp. 93–4.

19 Paine notes that the land-tax in 1646 was £2,473,499. The year that actually corresponds to that amount is 1696. See John Sinclair, *The History of the Public Revenue of the British Empire, Part 3* (London, 1790) p. 7.

20 M.J. Daunton, *Progress and Poverty: An Economic and Social History of Britain, 1700–1850* (Oxford: Oxford University Press, 1995) p. 528.

21 William Ogilvie, *An Essay on the Right of Property in Land* (London, 1781) pp. 81–2.

22 This is adapted from the table, Net Receipts of the Public Income, in *British Historical Statistics*, B.R. Mitchell (Cambridge: Cambridge University Press, 1988) pp. 575–6.

23 Thomas Piketty, *Capital in the Twenty-first Century*, trans. Arthur Goldhammer, Kindle Edition (Cambridge, MA: Harvard University Press, 2017) p. 162.

24 Cited in Andy Wood, *The 1549 Rebellion and the Making of Early Modern England* (Cambridge: Cambridge University Press, 2007) p. 35.

25 See also John Brewer, *The Sinews of Power: War, Money, and the English State* (London: Unwin Hyman, 1989), pp. 29, 40.

26 Brewer notes that the navy "was thus one of the largest single employers of civilian labour in 18th-century England" and that "Naval ships and shipbuilding operated on a scale quite unlike that of civilian industry and commerce" as "Capital and labour were deployed in a manner that was beyond the resources of the merchant or manufacturer." The costs of feeding the navy were no less important (35–6).

27 It is worth noting that the Catholic inclinations of Charles II were partly responsible for a closer and less hostile relationship between England and France.

28 Pitt the Younger actually allocated about 7.5 million to the army and navy.

29 Paine was not the first to defend Tyler; Oliver Goldsmith had already done so in his *History of England*, stating: "The insurrections of the barons against their King, historians talk of with no great animosity; the insurrection of the plebeians against the barons, in the present case, is branded with all the virulence of reproach. The punishment of the insurgent barons, is generally styled cruelty; the punishment of men who fought for native freedom, is called justice; but we must be contented with such misrepresentations of facts, till philosophers can be found to write history." See *An History of England, in a series of letters from a nobleman to his son*, Vols. 1–2 (London, 1764) 1, 142.

30 As recent historians have demonstrated, amounts allocated to the poor could vary markedly, particularly between the north and south of England. According to Susannah R. Ottaway, many elderly people in the south were granted pensions which provided all or most of their needs. In the north, pensions were smaller and often intended as supplements. See Ottaway, *The Decline of Life: Old Age in 18th-century England* (Cambridge: University of Cambridge Press, 2004) p. 4.

31 Writing in 1784, Wendeborn also assumed the population of England to be near 7 million. He seems to have had a lower estimate for the number of the impoverished, with one million so poor "it must be supported by the rest; that four millions earn only as much as is requisite for their necessities" (121).

32 Paine may have heard from Thomas Jefferson a plan to establish public schools in Virginia proposed not long after the writing of the Declaration of Independence. In a letter to John Adams on Oct. 26, 1813, Jefferson recollects a bill he

proposed not long after the signing of the Declaration for "the general diffusion of learning." He "proposed to divide every county into wards of 5. or 6. miles square, like your townships; to establish in each ward a free school for reading, writing and common arithmetic; to provide for the annual selection of the best subjects from these schools who might receive at the public expense a higher degree of education at a district school." http://press-pubs.uchicago.edu/foun ders/documents/v1ch15s61.html

33 Quoted in Clyde Chitty, *Education Policy in Britain* (London: Palgrave Macmillan, 2014) p. 5.

34 There is a minor error in Paine's calculations. Paine writes: "Admitting England to contain seven millions of souls; of one fifth thereof are of that class of poor which need support, the number will be one million four hundred thousand. Of this number, one hundred and forty thousand will be aged poor ... There will then remain one million two hundred and sixty thousand, which at five souls to each family, amount to two hundred and fifty-two thousand families, rendered poor from the expense of children and the weight of taxes.

The number of children under fourteen years of age, in each of those families, will be found to be about five to every two families; some having two, and others three; some one, and others four: some none, and others five; but it rarely happens that more than five are under fourteen years of age, and after this age they are capable of service or of being apprenticed. Allowing five children (under fourteen years) to every two families,

The number of children will be 630,000

The number of parents, were they all living, would be 504,000."

This does not add up to 1,260,000, but rather 1,134,000. Note that Paine probably forgot that he derived the number of families by assuming each unit to be made up of 5 people: namely, 2 parents and 3 children. The actual numbers of parents and children should be:

children 756,000

parents 504,000.

35 The total number of soldiers—30,000—can be inferred from addition of the annual pay of 15,000 disbanded soldiers and the additional annual pay of 15,000 sixpence per week.

36 Jean-Pierre Gross, *Fair Shares for All: Jacobin Egalitarianism in Practice* (Cambridge: Cambridge University Press, 1997) p. 122.

37 William Ogilvie, *An Essay on the Right of Property in Land* (London,1781) p. 131.

38 Paine explains their injustice by stating that "But the landed monopoly that began with it has produced the greatest evil. It has dispossessed more than half the inhabitants of every nation of their natural inheritance, without providing for them, as ought to have been done, an indemnification for that loss, and has thereby created a species of poverty and wretchedness that did not exist before."

39 See Malcolm Chase, "'The Real Rights of Man': Thomas Spence, Paine, and Chartism" (*Miranda*, 2016) para. 8. He states: "Its most eye-catching proposal, for old age pensions, simply repeats without much elaboration remarks he had made in the second part of *Rights of Man*. Its fiscal proposals, concentrating as

they do on death duties, are arguably less radical in scope and intent than the progressive taxation Paine had earlier proposed in *Rights of Man*." https://journals.openedition.org/miranda/8989

40 Ogilvie writes: "It would be injustice and oppression, therefore, in any one order to impose restrictions on any other, respecting the price they may demand for their peculiar commodity. This injustice, however, certain higher orders have attempted, tho' generally without success, to put in practice, on various occasions, against their inferiors; against hired servants, day labourers, journeymen, and artists of various kinds, by prescribing limits to the wages they are allowed to ask, or to receive. These lower classes have only the labour of their hands for their commodity ...." (202–3).

41 J.C.D. Clark suggests that Paine "cannot easily be located within what was once pictured as a tradition of 'working-class' activism that later found fulfilment in trade unions" (90). However, his conjecture is not altogether accurate as Paine's activities for the excise officers and this line from *Rights of Man* indicate. Paine obviously believed in the usefulness of unions.

42 Pitt reduced duties on tea, alcohol, and tobacco from 120% to 25% in order to make smuggling less appealing: in actuality, Pitt was more conservative than North in matters of taxation. Interestingly, Pitt would also reduce the number of government employees as well as sinecures: the latter, however, continued to be an object of criticism through the first two decades of the 19th century. Pitt also put an end to the means of influence implicit in tendering for loans while public accounts were held to stricter review. All told, given the quadrupling of trade between America and the British empire and the sharp reduction in debt, Britain was also able to procure low interest rates for borrowing: again, this gave it all the advantage over France. Modern historians, however, have also credited Pitt's predecessor, North, for the improvement. For further details on Pitt and the economy, see John Ehrman, *The Younger Pitt: The Years of Acclaim* (London: Constable and Co., 1969, 1984) pp. 277, 318.

43 Just as in the *Address and Declaration at the Thatched House Tavern*, where Paine states, "As Englishmen, we also rejoice, because we are immediately interested in the French Revolution," he notes in *Rights of Man* "Of all nations in Europe, there is none so much interested in the French revolution as England" (289).

44 Note again the Winstanley-like emphasis on "common." Paine's trust in the powers of discussion may have been informed by his experiences with the radical democratic societies held across England. See Jon Mee, *Print, Publicity, and Radicalism in the 1790s: The Laurel of Liberty* (Cambridge: University of Cambridge Press, 2016) pp. 24, 40. He suggests that Paine only began to openly endorse universal male suffrage in August 1792 with his publication of *Letter Addressed to the Addressers* after his involvement with the London Corresponding Society and the Society for Constitutional Information during the spring and summer of 1792.

45 The ideas in John Lennon's "Imagine," written nearly 180 years later, appear to align with Paine's. Imagine there's no countries/ It isn't hard to do/ Nothing to kill or die for/ And no religion, too/ Imagine all the people living life in peace,

https://genius.com/John-lennon-imagine-lyrics. Lennon's ideas on religion, as recorded in an interview, also bear a distinct resemblance to Paine's: "But still, the concept of imagining no countries, imagining no religion—not imagining no God, although you're entitled to do that, too, you know? Imagine no denominations. Imagining that we revere Jesus Christ, Mohammed, Krishna, Melanippe, equally—we don't have to worship either one that we don't have to, but imagine there's no Catholic/Protestant. No Jew/Christian. That we allow all ... we allow it all—freedom of religion for real, I mean. For real. Just imagine it? Would it be terrible?" See: http://www.beatlesarchive.net/john-lennons-last-inter view-december-8-1980.html

CONCLUSION

This Republic had its beginning, and grew to its present strength, under the protection of certain inalienable political rights—among them the right of free speech, free press, free worship, trial by jury, freedom from unreasonable searches and seizures. They were our rights to life and liberty.

As our Nation has grown in size and stature, however—as our industrial economy expanded—these political rights proved inadequate to assure us equality in the pursuit of happiness.
We have come to a clear realization of the fact that true individual freedom cannot exist without economic security and independence.

Franklin Delano Roosevelt, January 11, 1944

A great nation is judged not by how many millionaires and billionaires it has, or by the size of its military budget. It is judged by how well it treats its weakest and most vulnerable citizens. A truly great nation is one that is filled with compassion and solidarity.

Bernie Sanders, *Our Revolution*, 2016

To say that Paine's *Rights of Man* left a significant impact on the reading audiences of the 1790s would be an understatement.

During 1791 itself, there were already eight editions and 50,000 copies sold in Britain. The French were sufficiently impressed to grant honorary citizenship to Paine and appoint him as a representative for Pas-de-Calais. In his native country, however, reactions were considerably more divided despite its bestselling status, with many reformers and radicals celebrating it enthusiastically on one hand and propertied elites (including members of the government)—taking alarm on the other. Let us take a step back to reflect on Paine's ideas in *Rights* and analyze immediate reactions to his work. Which aspects did they admire? Denigrate?

Rights of Man, Part 1, as we have already seen, was still not altogether removed from traditional Whiggism. Although Paine sought the eradication of hereditary government and titles by contending for natural rights, rather than relying on Saxon rights as did his contemporaries, John Cartwright and Granville Sharp, he had not quite embraced universal suffrage. Instead, Paine clung to the traditional view—one akin to Burke's—that those owning more property should enjoy more political privileges. Moreover, whatever his criticisms of monarchy, he did not object to the idea of a constitutional monarchy in France and refrained from disparaging Louis XVI and his wife, Marie Antoinette. It is telling too that while Paine expressed some awareness of the injustice faced by the poor and middling classes, he barely addressed the economic challenges faced by either class in England and France in any detailed fashion. Paine, in other words, had not ventured beyond the pale, which may explain why he was not charged with seditious libel as in the case of Part 2—apart from the fact of its pricing: at a relatively steep three shillings, it would have been out of reach for most ordinary readers. No doubt too that Pitt hesitated to give any additional publicity to Paine's already notorious text. Instead, he chose to commission a highly derogatory biography from George Chalmers.

It is not until the writing of Part 2 that Paine finally departed from Whiggism. Delving into the ills of monarchical government, he extolled republican government, elevating it over monarchies and simple democracies alike. Representative governments, according to Paine, could better fulfill people's needs than any type of hereditary government by avoiding fruitless wars of conquest or lineal disputes for peaceful trade. Without a wasteful royal court bent on war and conspicuous display, Paine explains, a republic can steer money into improved standards of living for its people—particularly the poor and elderly. Although not all of the ideas in Chapter 5 are novel as we have seen, it was Paine who explored these schemes in fuller depth: thereby fusing the rights rhetoric of the Levellers with the collective communitarianism of the Diggers. No less did Paine challenge the wisdom of establishing foreign empires most thoroughly and radically by suggesting that European countries pool together military resources rather than retain individual forces: an idea which broadly anticipates NATO. As such, the simultaneous alignment of his ideas on representation, progressive taxation, welfare, reduction of military resources, not to mention his denial of a British constitution, made him one of the boldest and most daring political thinkers of the 18th century—even if he did not explore, say, women's rights or the abolition of slavery.[1]

Radical ideas aside, the fact that *Rights of Man*, Part 2 was priced at a mere six pence made the sales even more spectacular than those of Part 1, with sales estimated to be around 200,000.[2] As W.A. Speck notes, this mass production was unprecedented. The fact that the Society for Constitutional Information and the Corresponding Societies helped distribute the pamphlet while organizing discussions and debates played a substantial role in popularizing the work itself to the extent that Pitt fired off a proclamation against "divers, wicked and seditious writings" on May 21, 1792. How did other contemporaries view *Rights of Man*?

Despite its phenomenal popularity, it received mostly negative reviews, with the exception of *The Analytical Review*, and responses in the form of pamphlets that veered between rage and contempt: even when opinion on the French revolution itself was divided, with some defending it (e.g., Brooke Boothby's *Observations on the Appeal from the New to Old Whigs and Mr. Paine's Rights of Man* and the anonymous *Cursory Remarks on Paine's Rights of Man*) and others deprecating it. Perhaps not surprisingly, critics vehemently disagreed with Paine on the subject of the British constitution, with many insisting on its existence and some claiming it as the best. In *Letters to Thomas Payne*,[3] the anonymous writer insisted that every nation with a government had a constitution while that of *Considerations on Mr. Paine's pamphlet on the Rights of Man* upheld the British constitution as "nearly perfect" and one "still better in practice than in theory" by providing its citizens with "a more perfect degree of liberty and security" than any other nation:[4] he was also quick to point out that the French did not select special delegates for creating a new constitution but merely convened those who were already part of the three Estates (48). John Quincy Adams would make similar points in his rebuttal, *Answer to Pain's* [sic] *Rights of Man.* [5] Those who complained about the inadequacy of representation were no less inclined to defend the Constitution, including the writer of *Letters* who acknowledged that "our representation in Parliament is very defective" (23) and that of *Cursory Remarks on Paine's Rights of Man* who longed for a "more equal representation in Parliament".[6] Some, including Sir Brooke Boothby, went as far as to maintain in Burkean fashion that "The members of the House of Commons are not the representatives of Rutlandshire and Yorkshire, but representatives of the nation."[7] In turn, some criticized Paine's historical claims, with the *Letters to Thomas Payne* and *An Answer to Pain* (25–6) denying that the constitution arose out of the Conquest (27) and *The Republican Refuted* going further by contending that copyholds and charters were not derived from William the Conqueror but rather the Saxons.[8]

Likewise, Paine's criticisms of hereditary government, privilege, and primogeniture came under fire. Some, including the anonymously penned *Considerations on a Pamphlet by Mr. Paine*, pointed out that nobles did not enjoy special privileges apart from being judged in the House of Peers—a significant advantage nonetheless—and moreover, that inequality was not so much connected with birth, but with wealth.[9] Similarly, Boothby argued that peers and commoners were treated equally before the law (149). However, neither explanation was entirely correct: peers enjoyed a special privilege for their first crime while penalties for libel against the aristocracy were severe. Many pamphleteers, not unlike Joseph Priestley some thirty years earlier, also maintained that the wealthy were best equipped to govern, given their wealth and education: a view that was shared by the authors of *Letters to Thomas Payne* (47); *The Republican Refuted* (76), and *A Short View of the Rise and Progress of Freedom in Modern Europe*. As the author of *A New Friend on an Old Subject* pointed out, the aristocracy was not only "brought up in the study of treaties, politics, and history" but were also "impressed from their earliest infancy with worthy notions of the importance of their duty."[10]

Many argued against the dismantling of primogeniture, even if they felt uncomfortable with the exclusive privileging of the heir. Some believed that inequality between siblings was generally mitigated as most parents found some way to provide for the heir's sisters and younger brothers. The author of *The Republican Refuted* denied that primogeniture was "materially injurious to the community," since "the industry of the younger son, and the dissipation of the elder ... speedily bring the rentals of both to an equality" (78). Of course, neither fact entirely discredits Paine since some parents did practice primogeniture uncompromisingly: his friend, Mary Wollstonecraft, had complained of such treatment in her own family. As for titles, nearly all found them innocuous at worst and inspiring at best. The writer of *New Friend on an Old Subject* feared that "the aged members of society" would "lose the chief stimulus to their exertions" by being unable to "transmit the rewards of their good offices" to their children (24–5) while the author of *Letters to Thomas Payne* claimed that the abandonment of primogeniture "would destroy commerce with its demands on extensive capital" (48). The last point was similarly underscored in *Slight Observations upon Paine's pamphlet*, which also praised titles for inciting men "to glorious deeds" so that "hereditary nobility conferred upon the father, is an example of emulation to the son" served "as a check upon his vicious propensities."[11]

Paine's conceptualizations of an ideal society and government would be equally lambasted. Although *Rights of Citizens* was published prior to the publication of Part 2, the writer obviously agreed more with Rousseau than Paine when claiming that "Nature leads to the unequal division of property ... Savage life is the infancy of the human species, and civilization its maturity": inequality, in other words, was to be expected in a civilized society. In *Reason of Man*, John Jones discerned a contradiction in Paine's opposition between government and society: if "common interest without government produces security," why was it that government becomes necessary "to restrain the vices of society?"[12] Others, not unlike Alexander Hamilton, questioned the peaceful nature of commerce: in *Cursory Remarks on Dr. Priestley's Letters to Mr. Burke, and Strictures on Mr. Paine's Rights of Man*, the writer pointed out how "a *prevailing spirit of commerce*" (45) frequently provoked war. In turn, some criticized Paine's tallying of taxes over the centuries. *An Answer to the Second Part of Rights of Man*, for instance, observed that the dramatic increase in the price of wheat between 1500 and 1666 accounted for the steep rise in taxes over the same period. He would also complain that Paine's annuities for those over 50 could render such workers and their children "idle"; moreover, he feared that it was not only "unjust to expect such a contribution from the wealthy and industrious" (53–4) but that the price of labour would increase because workers would "become more indifferent to whether they obtained employment" and "more exorbitant" in their demands for higher wages (54–5). Finally, no less marked were criticisms of Paine's writing. The author of *Cursory Remarks on Dr. Priestley's Letters* grumbled that Paine has "attempted to destroy our language, that he might with more ease juggle us out of our constitution" (60). But if Boothby huffed that "He writes in defiance of grammar, as if syntax were an aristocratical invention," he would also pay Paine a backhanded compliment when comparing him to Burke: Paine "exposes some of the toryisms of *The Reflections* with a good deal of spirit and success in his rough plebeian way; and the contrast between the polished redundancy of the one, and the quaint vulgarity of the other is not unpleasant" (117). Indeed, with the popularity of Paine among radicals, Pitt would commission Hannah More to write *Cheap Repository Tracts*, designed to disseminate conservative views, but written in Paineite style.

Whatever popularity Paine enjoyed with the radicals went no further. Although it is difficult to measure influence, the rise of Church and King mobs, quietly stoked by local gentry and magistrates certainly discouraged radicalism. Few scholars today are able to determine if lower-class support was won over by the promise of free food and drink that accompanied the burning of effigies of Paine or independent motivation. Whatever the case, the resulting proscription would last for nearly a century with the display of any portrait of Paine declared illegal.

I THE LEGACY OF *RIGHTS OF MAN*, 1800–1900

In October 1805, the cranky John Adams complained to Benjamin Waterhouse that no man "had more influence on its inhabitants or affairs or the last thirty years than Tom Paine … A mongrel between pig and puppy, begotten by a wild boar on a bitch wolf."[13] Yet, for all that, it is challenging to discern the direct imprint of Paine on the political movements which succeeded him over the following centuries. Despite the fact that Jeremy Bentham adopted Paine's ideas on hereditary government and universal suffrage after 1809—while early socialists such as Robert Owen mostly ignored Paine's ideas,[14] neither utilitarians nor socialists particularly heeded his views on natural rights either; Bentham, of course, had famously dismissed natural rights as "nonsense upon stilts" and "bawling on paper" even though he concurred with Paine on universal male suffrage and hereditary government while harboring a distrust of the establishments, famously referring to them as the "sinister elite."[15] The likes of Henry Hunt, Major John Cartwright and even William Cobbett himself—the man who dug up Paine's bones in order to have them publicly interred in England—would increasingly distance themselves from him.[16] It is as such that J.C.D. Clark has recently concluded that "In neither utilitarianism nor socialism did natural rights play a central role."[17] In order to understand the apparent loss of Paine's influence and oversight of his ideas, however, it is important to examine some of the chief causes, with the most obvious being the continued censorship of Paine's texts through the early decades of the 19th century. It is also important to remember that those who desired reform naturally feared that any reference to Paine would suffer a similar proscription. Certainly, liberal Anglicans and Dissenters attempted to keep a prudent distance from Paine for fear of being tarred with the "atheist" brush after the publication of his *Age of Reason:* a work that ignited even more controversy than *Rights* as Paine criticized organized religion and the veracity of the Bible. Those who admired Paine unreservedly, as the radical Richard Carlile recounted, felt they had little choice but to hold their celebrations of Paine's birthday secretly (Roberts, 107).

But perhaps a more compelling reason might be the sheer rapidity of economic changes as Britain underwent industrialization at a faster rate than other nations. By the tail end of the 18th century, prospects of independent livelihoods for unskilled and semi-skilled laborers had dwindled drastically, leading them to flock to larger towns and cities for work at mills and mines. The growing use of mechanization combined with the loss of independence made inevitable changes in the lifestyles and living standards of workers, thereby presenting a radically transformed universe. If pre-industrial laborers had once enjoyed some control over their hours and weekly schedules, factory and mill owners now exerted far more in the name of discipline: changes which disrupted the personal lives of workers and their families. The very fact of the Luddite and Swing riots in rural areas hinted at harder years ahead as the progress of agricultural mechanization threatened more job losses. At the same time, wages dropped for semi-skilled workers and artisans. In Bolton, for instance, the wages of a handloom weaver fell precipitously from 30s6d to 5s6d. New labor laws had a negative impact on shoemakers, carpenters, and tailors, with the repeal of apprenticeship laws in 1813–15. Not least disturbing was the growing distance between workers and their employers: workers no longer shared meals with their employers as the latter sought higher standards of living and to distance themselves from their perceived inferiors. As such, it would have appeared to some that while age-old hierarchies of wealth and power remained, many of its more compassionate and paternalistic aspects vanished.

In light of these startling changes, it is hardly fortuitous that by 1830, radicals no longer followed Paine in criticizing the burdens of taxation and hereditary government, but viewed them as only a few of many problems. For writers like Thomas Hodgskin, the terms had changed entirely. Capitalists now "inherited" the power over all the "labouring classes" formerly wielded by the "ancient tyrant of the soil," necessitating a shift from "reproaches ... on the feudal aristocracy" to "capital and capitalists," namely, a new "oppressive aristocracy which is founded on wealth" and "profit." Similarly, by 1838, the Chartist journalist Bronterre O'Brien dismissed the critiques of the "evils of taxation" central to the arguments of "Mr. Cobbett, and his predecessor, Paine" as outdated, referring to it as "delusion," for "the profits realized on Capital" is "greater than all the other burdens put together."[18] At the same time, Chartists veered closer to the more radical Thomas Spence than Thomas Paine in their thoughts on landed property.[19]

Nonetheless, Clark's claim that "the old idea of a transformation in natural rights theory at the end of the 18th century, involving the liberating emergence of ideas of 'human rights', is now problematic" (15) is not altogether accurate. Although Paine remained an unnamed bogey for the first few decades of the 19th century, his memory and legacy were not completely extinguished. This began with William Cobbett's own affirmation of Paine's belief that government was the chief cause of economic hardship. A few historians have gone so far as to suggest that the Luddite riots were partly influenced by readings of Paine; for just as the radical W.T. Sherwin extolled Paine for shaping a new conceptualization of political reform that began from bottom to top rather than top to bottom, Chartists subsequently invoked Paine in their demands for an expansion of suffrage to all men since the Reform Bill stopped short of the ideal. It was then, as Matthew Roberts explains, that Paine was no longer the preserve of a miniscule minority, but became a part of the national working-class movement with thousands of supporters (Roberts, 120). Even if O'Brien dismissed Paine's relevance to a rapidly industrializing Britain, many of his fellow Chartists would express admiration for the older radical, adapting Paine's message for the new times while transforming his rhetoric of rights into a rhetoric of class. Universal suffrage now meant not only enfranchisement, but also social emancipation.[20] Even O'Brien himself grasped the importance of Paine's call for a political convention (qtd. in Battistini, 94) as another writer in *The Poor Man's Guardian* held it "bad policy ... to attempt to obtain favour in the eyes of a plundering aristocracy by depreciating the RIGHTS OF MAN."

Meanwhile, in the young American republic, Paine suffered a somewhat similar fate. As Harvey Kaye explains, many Americans were swept up by the Second Great Awakening while the "nation's governing elites" cooperated "in suppressing or marginalizing the story of his radical life and labors" (117). Paine was championed by many who belonged to the working classes, becoming an inspirational figure for the workingmen's movement of the 1820s: for just as in Britain, disputes between employers and laborers began to take precedence. (Suffrage, on the other hand, was not as significant an issue in the young republic since many states had already tossed aside property qualifications.) Not unlike radicals across the Atlantic, Frances Wright, and Robert Dale Owen (son of Robert Owen) paid tribute to Paine in their demands for anti-monopoly legislation, laws against imprisonment for debt, and most of all, public education. Thomas Skidmore, for instance, used the democratic lessons of Paine as a critique of social hierarchies even if he disagreed with Paine's ideas in *Dissertations on Government* which argued against the repeal of the bank charter and the expansion of print money in 1786. As Matteo Battistini notes, "By reading Paine, post-revolutionary generations of journeymen and workers understood that the conditions of poverty and political exclusion from which they suffered were not irrevocable, but were dependent on government and society."[21] Finally, it is worth noting that even though Henry George did not cite Paine in his *Progress and Poverty: An Inquiry into the Cause of Industrial Depressions and Increase of Want with Increase of Wealth* (1879), his text would nonetheless vindicate Paine's ideas on the problems deriving from the inequality of land ownership (Kaye, 169).

II BACK TO THE FUTURE: THE RELEVANCE OF *RIGHTS OF MAN* IN THE 21ST CENTURY

In light of these 19th-century criticisms, it might seem that *Rights of Man* would be even less pertinent today despite the proliferation of representative governments across the world and the widespread adoption of progressive taxation and public welfare schemes. Apart from his premature prediction of the demise of hereditary government in seven short years, Paine would probably be greatly astonished to learn that in many respects, the U.S. and Europe have reversed places in spite of the retention of constitutional monarchies in the latter: with the most socially egalitarian nations—Sweden, Norway, and Denmark—maintaining not only a higher degree of public services (e.g., universal health care, tuition-free public universities) but also enjoying greater social mobility and democracy than the U.S.[22] Paine might smile wryly at the fact that the U.K. itself has nearly surpassed the U.S. in terms of social mobility and democracy. He would be even more shocked to learn that the U.S. spends more on the military than any country on the planet while cutting public services in the interests of "fiscal responsibility," with the presidency acquiring yet more authority over the last 16 years. One can only imagine his reaction at the thought of being quoted by conservatives from Ronald Reagan to the Tea Party in praise of "small government" for the purposes of reducing taxes on the wealthy. In short, how can Paine possibly instruct us more than two centuries later in the age of post-industrialization and the cyber-age?

Nonetheless, if we scratch beneath the surface, we will find that Paine has been vindicated to a much larger degree than imagined and that his fundamental analysis of the relationships between society and government remains as prescient as ever: as a matter of fact, *Rights of Man* could arguably be even more applicable today with the amplification of some of the problems which he identified in 1791–2. Certainly, the popular uprisings which took place around the world between late 2010 and early 2012, all seemingly sequenced on the heels of one another, can be construed as a manifestation of the world revolution so eagerly awaited by Paine 220 years after the publication of *Rights of Man*. With the student protests over rising tuition fees in the U. K. triggering the Arab Spring in Tunisia, and the Arab Spring itself (which had spread to other parts of the Middle East) partly informing the public union protests in the American Midwest,[23] all prior to the worldwide arrival of Occupy Wall Street during the fall of 2011, revolution can be said to travel both east and westwards with numerous commentators noticing a vague yet unmistakable mirroring of public sentiment in various parts of the world.

At the most basic level, these uprisings can be viewed as a reprisal of the many against the few, not unlike the Peasants' Revolt of 1381, the 1549 Rebellion, the English Civil War, and the French revolution—if only because so few world leaders have chosen to learn from the past. As the Middle East expressed outrage at overt repression and oppression, many in the West felt no less frustrated at their governments for ostensibly going through the motions of democracy while ignoring the voices of the many. Economist Joseph Stiglitz has observed of his conversations with young people from around the world that regardless of the political grievances in the Middle East and the West, there are shared themes and a basic perception that the economic and political system has failed the majority of people:

> That the young would rise up against the dictatorships of Tunisia and Egypt was understandable. The youth were tired of aging, sclerotic leaders who protected their own interests at the expense of the rest of society. They had no opportunities to call for change through democratic processes. But electoral politics had also failed in Western democracies. U.S. president Barack Obama had promised "change you can believe in," but he subsequently delivered economic policies that, to many Americans, seemed like more of the same.[24]

In other words, the messages conveyed by the Arab Spring, the public union protests in the Midwest, and Occupy Wall Street, converged even if emanating from seemingly disparate local circumstances. These actions can be said to attest to the truth of Paine's words that "Whatever the apparent cause of any riots may be, the real one is always want of happiness. It shows that something is wrong in the system of government."

Perhaps the most basic question is how did Paine's adopted country end up at this juncture, illustrating the truths contained in *Rights of Man*? How did his vision for a democratic, egalitarian world remain yet unfulfilled in spite of universal suffrage and the apparent replacement of hereditary privilege by meritocracy?

To realize just how ironic this reversal is, let us look more closely at his remarks from a letter to his friend, Kitty Few Nicholson, dated January 6, 1789. Here, he writes:

> A thousand years hence ... perhaps in less, America maybe what England now is! The innocence of her character that won the hearts of all nations in her favor may sound like a romance ....
> When we contemplate the fall of empires and the extinction of nations of the ancient world, we see but little to excite our regret than the mouldering ruins of pompous palaces, magnificent monuments ... But when the empire of America shall fall, the subject for contemplative sorrow will be infinitely greater than crumbling brass or marble can inspire. It will not then be said, here stood a temple of vast antiquity ... but here, ah painful thought! the noblest work of human wisdom ... the fair cause of freedom rose and fell!

As we have seen in Part 2, Chap 1 of *Rights of Man*, Paine extolled the young republic for its relatively egalitarian character and its prudent use of public money; it was a country where "the poor are not oppressed, the rich are not privileged" and taxation low "because their government is just." That these assertions are no longer applicable to 21st-century America, however, is proven by research corroborating the allegations of a rigged economy launched by Occupy Wall Street and recent presidential candidate Bernie Sanders. Instead, the litany of political and economic ills in America has come to resemble those which Paine associated with 18th-century England including decreased social mobility, rising inequality, especially in the form of childhood poverty, financial hardship for the elderly, stagnating wages, and shrinking public services. How did this happen? And what can *Rights of Man* teach us?

What is perhaps most ironic in the rise of inequality and political oligarchy in the U.S. is the role of trade and commerce: activities which Paine assumed would improve the general welfare of any nation. Although money and property have always played a role in American government—a fact that can be easily gleaned from the writings of the Federalists—the importance of both surged at various points: namely, the Gilded Age, and more recently, the period dating from the mid-1970s. With Jimmy Carter's initial moves towards deregulation and the destruction of unions, developments which were accelerated by Ronald Reagan's further privileging of corporate interests, the philosophy of a "free market" replaced the democratic socialism of Franklin Delano Roosevelt who famously acknowledged that "true individual freedom cannot exist without economic security and independence." In other words, corporations had become the new aristocracy of 20th-century America. Co-opting Paine's arguments on the virtues of a small government, Reagan and the Republicans lowered taxes on corporations and the wealthiest citizens in addition to deregulating the markets and further dismantling unions—all while blaming minorities and immigrants. But even as Democrats criticized Reagan and his successor, George H.W. Bush, for creating a state of inequality, many broadly reaffirmed Republican economic practices despite adopting a class-conscious, pro-worker rhetoric. In addition to passing NAFTA, begun under Bush, Bill Clinton continued to deregulate Wall Street throughout his two terms from 1993 to 2000. Indeed, a recent study has found that despite the modest protections and benefits offered to ordinary citizens by the government, domestic and foreign policies (regardless of party) have almost always been already powerful business and economic interests with the exception of the period between 1940 and 1975 (Joseph, 69–70). The Iraq war of 2003, which allowed many in the oil and gas sector as well as the military industrial complex to reap sizable profits, probably serves as one of the most notorious examples of foreign policy dictated by business interests: one has only to recall the string of names it earned during the course of action to glean a lack of political purpose. Similarly, the no-strings attached bank bailouts following the financial crisis of 2008 are widely claimed to be guided by Wall Street interests: particularly when the bailouts, as separately noted by Robert Reich, Joseph Stiglitz, and other economists, were offered to the bankers who took unscrupulous risks rather than members of the populace who suffered the effects of a deregulated housing market.[25] The same might be said for the legal provision of 2003 that prohibited government from bargaining for prices on drugs which was, in effect, a gift of some $50 billion or more per year to the pharmaceutical companies (Stiglitz, 47–8). Neither drug pricing or the bailouts, however, are surprising given the power of lobbyists. The fact that there are about 2.5 lobbyists for every U.S. representative explains why Congress was easily dissuaded from imposing adequate regulation—to say nothing of the existing practice of "regulatory capture" by which leaders of various corporate sectors (e.g., telecom, banking, securities, etc.) wield their political influence to appoint people sympathetic to their interests to regulatory agencies.

Equally significant in the growing influence of oligarchical power is the role played by wealthy voters as they proved more inclined than ever to "buy" politicians. Again, it is not difficult to discern distinct similarities in the relationship between modern political representatives and their donors with that between the 18th-century M.P. and his aristocratic patron, since property—rather than people—once again were the subjects of representation. Here, one must note that in comparison with other Western nations, the lack of limitations on campaign spending and contribution in the U.S. had already long encouraged a "pay for play" mentality prior to the passing of Citizens' United in 2010, not to mention the rise of the super PAC that served to raise additional venues for funding the high costs of advertising on television, radio, and the internet.[26] Indeed, the comparison of relationships between 18th-century English M.P.s and the aristocracy with present-day American political representatives and the 1% may be more apt than imagined for just as members of Parliament were largely drawn from the class of the propertied elites—roughly the top 1–5%—the median minimum net worth of today's senators and House members was $511,000 at the beginning of 2018, that is, roughly five times the median net worth of an American household, which the Federal Reserve pegged at $97,300 in 2016. As one writer has recently commented, "The financial disparity between those who try to govern and those who are governed is almost certainly even greater than that."[27] In short, higher members of governments are more attuned to the interests of the 1%, precisely because they belong to those ranks themselves.

With foreign and domestic policies slanted to favor corporations and Wall Street, inequality naturally widened as salaries for workers in the manufacturing sector declined sharply from the late 1970s and C.E.O. compensation rose exponentially. Rather than earning a mere 20 to 40 times as in 1950 to 1980, in the 1990s, C.E.O.'s earned roughly 300 to 1,000 times as much as the average employee—arguably greater than the difference between a bishop and a parish minister (250–333x) as deplored by Paine and his contemporaries. Some may argue that since present-day inequality does not arise from entirely arbitrary advantages such as hereditary privilege (i.e., bishops were generally younger sons from aristocratic families), there is less sense of injustice. A growing number of economists, however, have come to question this premise, observing that the assumption of superior performance is too frequently used as an excuse for excessive inequality—with some, including Thomas Piketty, going so far to question the relationship between accomplishment and pay:

> The most convincing proof of the failure of corporate governance and of the absence of a rational productivity justification for extremely high executive pay is that when we collect data about individual firms ... it is very difficult to explain the observed variations in terms of firm performance. If we look at various performance indicators, such as sales growth, profits, and so on, we can break down the observed variance as a sum of other variances: variance due to causes external to the firm .... (Piketty, 422)

While those making more than $500,000 a year have seen their remuneration multiply (and those above $1 million a year rising even more rapidly), those lower down on the scale have only seen theirs inch up slightly in the 1990s and 2000s (Piketty, 395). A comparably substantial growth has been mirrored in compensation for presidents of colleges and universities over the last three decades as they earn somewhere between 100 and 300 times as much as adjunct instructors who teach more than 50% of university courses. Perhaps our system is just as riddled with what Paine referred to as "mental levelling" (202) when modern C.E.O.s and university presidents all but enjoy the privileges of a king who "can do no wrong," by remaining almost impervious to discipline.

At the same time, inequality loomed even larger as taxes on the wealthiest declined after 1980. Even though the top rate imposed by Clinton—39.6%—was higher than Reagan's and George H.W. Bush's, it was nonetheless significantly lower than the rates of the 1960s (above 90%) and 1970s (70%). Taxes on capital gains (forms of income received disproportionately by the rich) were lowered further to 20% in 1997 and then to 15% under Bush while interest on municipal bonds was not even taxed while thresholds for estate tax were raised: the latter can be said to represent the very reverse of what Paine desired. As such, not unlike the aristocracy and nobility of late 18th-century England and France—the literal and figurative 1% of their day—the richest 1% of Americans earned more while enjoying overall tax rates lower than those of Americans with more moderate incomes.[28]

Conversely, as the fortunes of the upper decile improved after 1980, the wages and living standards of the middle and lower classes had already begun to decline in the mid-1970s.[29] Recent research by the Economic Policy Institute has confirmed that legislation played a role in destroying unions, slowing the rise of the minimum wage, and implementing a monetary policy that prioritized low inflation over full employment—all of which pulled the balance of power away from workers and towards their employers.[30] Although the period of 1940–80 can hardly be said to have been ideal or perfect in terms of general equality, given the prejudice and systemic discrimination faced by ethnic minorities and women, it was one that witnessed real wage growth and substantial social mobility, as well as an expansion of public services and infrastructure—due in large part to the populist ideals and policies implemented by Franklin Delano Roosevelt. The rules sanctioned by the National War Labor Board, the government agency that approved all wage increases in the United States from 1941 to 1945, were instrumental in raising the incomes of the bottom 90% by endorsing raises only for the lowest paid workers while systematically freezing managers' salaries in nominal terms.[31] Equally noteworthy was a minimum wage that was used to lift lower wages in the 1950s and '60s, attaining its maximum level in 1969 at $1.60 an hour (or $10.10 in 2013 dollars, taking account of inflation between 1968 and 2013), at a time when the unemployment rate was below 4% (Piketty, 388–90). According to the Economic Policy Institute, the hourly wages of median-wage workers from 1979 remained stagnant, rising just 6%—less than 0.2% per year until 2013. Indeed, according to the Pew Research Center, after adjusting for inflation, today's average hourly wage has approximately the same purchasing power as it did in 1979. Moreover, in 2018, just 38% of jobs nationwide pay enough to afford a middle or upper class life for a dual income-earning family with two children ($45–80,000) while 32% of jobs pay a living-wage (between $27,000 and $45,000 for a single, childless adult); and 30% pay what we call a "hardship" wage (under $27,000 for a single, childless adult).[32] The fact that a minimum wage fails to cover rent anywhere in the country[33] while nearly half of Americans cannot cover for a $400 emergency has been an equally grave problem.[34] All told, the living standards of the bottom 90%, and particularly the bottom 50% have declined as the upper decile's share has increased from 30–35% of national income in the 1970s to 45–50% in the 2000s (Piketty 366–9).

Ironically, then, the New World came to outstrip the Old World in terms of inequality, with the top decile in Britain taking 40%, in France and Germany 35%, and less than 30% in Sweden (Piketty, 408): the differences appear all the more stark when benefits and public services are taken into account. It is worth noting that the U.S. spends far more per capita on health care than any other nation—almost $10,000 per man, woman and child—for far fewer services; bypass surgery, for instance, costs far more in the U.S. than in Australia.[35] Health outcomes are also worse in the United States than in nearly all other advanced industrial countries despite higher per capita spending (Stiglitz, 97). In general, America's poor have a life expectancy that is almost 10% lower than that of those at the top (Stiglitz, 15). At the same time, infant mortality in the U.S. is worse than in some developing countries, and worse than in Cuba, Belarus, and Malaysia. This may be perhaps be attributed to poor child care: the U.S. ranks near the bottom when it comes to spending on child care and pre-school. Among member nations of the Organization for Economic Co-operation and Development, 84% of 4-

year-olds are enrolled in early education, versus just 69% in the
U.S. (Sanders, 257). Meanwhile, only 3% of the federal budget is
spent on K-12 education while 20% is spent on the military.[36] At
the other end of the scale, where university education is concerned, the U.S. charges some of the highest tuition and boarding
fees in the world with many students shackled by debt for years,
sometimes decades, after graduation. The obstacles placed in the
way of education appear all the pronounced when coupled with
the fact of the high rate of incarceration in the U.S.: one that is
even higher than that of China—thereby making it the highest in
the world (Stiglitz, 15). As pundits and politicians frequently
opine on the deterioration of family life, the U.S. is the only
advanced economy that does not guarantee its workers some
form of paid family leave, paid sick leave or paid vacation time
(Sanders, 236–7). Neither do we find much improvement when we
approach the last decades of life. Although there are over 65s who
choose to work, there are at least as many who do so out of
need.[37] Indeed, far from recalling Paine's belief that "At sixty his
labour ought to be over … It is painful to see old age working
itself to death" (267), both Republican and Democratic politicians have sought to cut Social Security (in addition to Medicare)
or raise the age for retirement since the 1990s.[38]

The state of American public infrastructure is hardly better.
Despite a general awareness of the near terminal state of the elec-
tric grid, little has been done to confront the problem even as it
ranks at a relatively low 24, right below Barbados. Access to
broadband and speed are anything but outstanding as both rank
around a mediocre 15 (Sanders, 249). Arguably worse is the state
of our roads and bridges, which the American society of civil
engineers has deemed to be at near-failing (D+) level: one-third of
roads are in poor or mediocre condition while a quarter of bridges
are functionally obsolete due to the extreme underfunding of
maintenance. (As a designer of bridges, Paine would probably be
horrified.) At the same time, passenger and freight networks are
also outdated (Sanders, 246). All told, Europe spends more than
twice our gross share of GDP on infrastructure and China four
times as much. But perhaps our lack of public investments is not
entirely surprising given our highly uneven wealth distribution

according to Stiglitz. As he suggests, the more divided a society becomes in terms of wealth, the more reluctant the wealthy are to spend money on common needs because they can purchase their own parks, private schools and universities, personal security, and health care (Stiglitz, 93). In turn, it is no less striking too that just as the poor were disenfranchised in 18th-century England and France, Republicans have also effectively disenfranchised minorities and low-income voters by means of gerrymandering and voter-ID laws: by doing so, the desires and needs of the latter go unheeded.

Perhaps that is the true reason for the popularity of shows like *Downton Abbey* amongst the top decile as well as new numerous adaptations of *Pride and Prejudice* in the 1990s and 2000s and yet another remake of *The Great Gatsby* in 2013, with economists noting that present-day capital, measured in years of national income, is returning to levels not witnessed since the "hyperpatrimonial societies" of *ancien-regime* France or Belle Epoque Europe (Piketty, 147, 215, 331). Much like *ancien-regime* France, the top 10% possesses as much as 50–60% of the national income (Piketty, 330), particularly since between 1977 and 2007, the richest 10% appropriated three-quarters of the growth while the richest 1% alone absorbed nearly 60% of the total increase of U. S. national income in this period. On the other hand, the rate of income growth is less than 0.5% per year for the bottom 90% (373). The lack of social mobility is also reminiscent of 18th- and 19th-century Europe: in the U.S., those at the bottom have a good chance of staying there, as do those at the top, and much more so than in other countries.[39]

Not least, this inequality and advantages of the wealthy can be said to be further aggravated by the very real fact of hereditary privilege even if it is not so obvious as in 18th-century Britain.[40] Instead, it continues to operate, but covertly, particularly for those in the upper decile. One might note, for instance, how members of the so-called meritocracy enjoy hereditary advantage in school and college where sons and daughters of alumni or politicians, celebrities, and tycoons get a leg up in admissions. The mechanics of nepotism include not only a son or daughter following the same path but can also involve the parent handing his position directly on to his or her offspring.[41] Even more interesting is the way nepotism persists in politics. A child of a senator is 8,500 times more likely than any other child to become a senator: in contrast, s/he is "only" 1,895 times more likely to become a famous C.E.O. if born to a C.E.O. and 1,639 times more likely to win a Pulitzer Prize if born to a Pulitzer Prize winner. It is thus most ironic that the U.S.—rather than Europe— has forgotten Paine's derision for hereditary privileges in the academic, corporate, and political spheres. It is perhaps as such that cultural historians have compared the present era to late 18th-century France, with Thomas Frank observing that "Inequality is what we say when we describe how the relationship of the very wealthy to the rest of us has come to approximate the relationship of Louis XVI with the peasants of eighteenth-century France" (7).

Paine's words ring true again when we consider the lack of overall happiness in his adopted country and other parts of world where inequality has become a looming issue, especially where the misdeeds and crimes of the .01% go largely unpunished.[42] According to the Pew Research Center, the level of political dis- content in the United States has been generally growing from 1958 to the present. Today, 19% of Americans trust government to do the right thing; 74% think most elected officials put their own interests ahead of the country's; 57% are frustrated with government and 22% are angry (EIU, 15). The report further observes a "growing gulf in the values held by political elites and ordinary people" that led to the election of Donald Trump in 2016. This helps explain why the Economist Report now classifies the U.S. as a flawed rather than a full democracy, one that ranks at 25 below Norway, Iceland, Sweden, New Zealand, Denmark, Canada, Ireland, Finland as well as the U.K., Japan, and Chile. If Paine attributed the cause of riots to a "want of happiness" this indicates that "something is wrong in the system of government, that injures the felicity by which society is to be preserved," James Gilligan has noted more recently that "Worldwide, the most powerful predictor of the murder rate is the size of the gap in income and wealth between the rich and the poor" while "the most powerful predictor of the rate of national or collective violence—war, civil insurrection, and terrorism—is the size of the gap between income and wealth between the rich and poor nations" (qtd in Joseph, 46). In addition, as Stiglitz suggests, decreased wages and standards of living as well as persistent underinvestment in public services and education are often accompanied by malnutrition, drug abuse, and deterioration in family life, all of which have adverse effects on health and longevity (Preface, 15). Modern society, as described by Peter Joseph, has become a "competitive game" that "is about survival and well-being": one which poses not only the threat of loss, but also "makes loss and suffering inevitable for a large percentage of players" (85). Perhaps that's why dystopic fiction such as *The Hunger Games* has thrived alongside *Downton Abbey* in 21st-century America—just as the Gothic novel, with its oppressive aristocrats and ecclesiastics—flourished in 1790s England.

American dissatisfaction with elitist government likewise reinforces Paine's own observations on the British government of his period. Today, it is worth pointing out that both parties of government are hesitant to serve the people—most notably in their reluctance to address, let alone implement, a system of Medicare for all or make public universities tuition-free even though such aims are desired by over 60% of Americans regardless of party;[43] as such, we clearly have a situation described by Paine where "we now see … the curious phenomenon of a nation looking one way, and the government the other—the one forward and the other backward," with governments proceeding "By precedent" and nations "by improvement" (2:4). This apparent lack of public awareness on the part of the government brings to mind Paine's advice that "there ought to be … a method of occasionally ascertaining the state of public opinion with respect to government" (289). All told, the policies followed by Reagan, the Bushes, Clinton, Obama, and Trump, many of which have ignored the needs of the vast majority of Americans, might prove Paine's very point that "All this seems to show that change of ministers amounts to nothing. One goes out, another comes in, and still the same measures, vices, and extravagance are pursued" because "The defect lies in the system" (286). Or, as Thomas Frank has recently put it:

> So we bounce on, from government by one group of affluent people to government by a different group of affluent people. Consensus-minded centrism yields to authoritarianism, which will self-destruct in time and allow the consensus-minded another chance, which they will inevitably fumble, and so on. When will it all end? When the People finally come back for their Party. (Frank, 246)

It is little wonder that the idea of a political revolution as initiated by Bernie Sanders during his campaign of 2016 has garnered great attention not only in the US but in Europe.

By contrast, countries which suffer less inequality such as Sweden, Norway, Denmark, and Finland score higher on the happiness metric.[44] As Frank puts it, "the more equal a society is in terms of income, the more stable, healthy, and happy that society will be" (180). It is no coincidence either that not only do Scandinavian citizens enjoy a higher degree of social mobility and markedly less social inequality but also lay claim to a higher level of democracy. "Most people feel they are part of the democracy and have a shared experience in society," said Karl Ove Moene, Professor in Economics and leader of the research team at the Centre of Equality, Social Organization, and Performance at the University of Oslo. "Norwegians recognize our politicians as regular people, not some sort of elite."[45] Press freedom ranks among the highest in the world.[46] Here, too, incarceration rates are among the lowest in the world.[47]

At the end of the day, *Rights of Man* remains as relevant as ever—and particularly in the United States. After all, as Paine concluded, "The question is not whether those principles [of *Rights of Man*] are new or old, but whether they are right or wrong" (296). His longing for a world without "ragged and hungry children, and persons of seventy and eighty years of age, begging for bread" and a time when "the number of petty crimes, the offspring of distress and poverty, will be lessened" remains patently unfulfilled as the affluent grow even wealthier while the poor sink deeper into poverty; no less so than in 18th-century England, "a great portion of mankind" still exist "in a state of poverty and wretchedness."[48] Political representatives would do well to remember that "Whatever the form or constitution of government may be, it ought to have no other object than the general happiness": and that whenever "it operates to create and increase wretchedness in any of the parts of society, it is on a wrong system" (237). Perhaps instead of providing yet more advantages to the wealthiest and powerful while contemplating yet more tax cuts for the most well-off and cuts to Social Security, Medicare, and Medicaid, these representatives might also do well to ask themselves "Is it, then better that the lives of one hundred and forty thousand aged persons be rendered comfortable, or that a million a year of public money be expended on any one individual, and him often of the most worthless or insignificant character?" And finally, perhaps the 1%—those "who sit in ease, and solace yourselves in plenty"—might ask themselves whether it is time for reform. For it is as true in 2020 as it was in 1792 that:

> When it shall be said in any country in the world my poor are happy; neither ignorance nor distress is to be found among them; my jails are empty of prisoners, my streets of beggars; the aged are not in want; the taxes are not oppressive; the rational world is my friend, because I am a friend of its happiness: When these things can be said, there may that country boast its Constitution and its Government.

But with the rise of the populism on the left—as well as the right[49]—and a growing consensus among them on the dearth of democratic representation, social and political equity as well as the overrepresentation of monied interests, an observation from Paine's public letter to the Citizens of the United States is slowly unfolding itself before the world: "There is too much common sense and independence in America to be long the dupe of any faction, foreign or domestic."[50] Perhaps a political summer is truly at hand.

NOTES

1 In "The Limits of Revolutionary Radicalism: Tom Paine and Slavery", *Pennsylvania Magazine of History and Biography* 123:# (1999) pp. 177–99, James V. Lynch observes that "Intellectually, Paine was antislavery, but he rarely transformed his thought into visible and public action" (180). In a letter, Paine suggested that

the most effective way of abolishing slavery would entail former slaves "taking their own part" (191). The implication seems to be that without direct knowledge or experience of slavery, he would not be able to write as persuasively. One may wonder if this is also why he did not write about women's rights. With his friend Mary Wollstonecraft writing her *Vindication of the Rights of Woman*, he may have felt that he would not be able to make a stronger case.

2 W.A. Speck, *A Political Biography of Thomas Paine* (London: Pickering & Chatto, 2013) (Kindle Edition) Loc 2882 of 7222.

3 *Letters to Thomas Payne in answer to his late publication on The Rights of Man by a member of the University of Cambridge* (London, n.d.) p. 15.

4 *Considerations on Mr. Paine's Pamphlet on the Rights of Man* (London, 1791) p. 50.

5 John Quincy Adams, *Answer to Pain's [sic] Rights of Man* (London, 1793) p. 28.

6 *Cursory Remarks on Paine's Rights of Man* (London, 1792) p. 16.

7 Sir Brooke Boothby, *Observations on the Appeal from the New to the Old Whigs, and on Mr. Paine's Rights of Man* (London, 1792) p. 212.

8 Charles Harrington Elliott, *The Republican Refuted in a series of letters of biographical, critical and political strictures* (London, 1791) p. 51.

9 Here, it is also worth noting that research by such modern economists as Thomas Piketty has claimed that wealth in 18th-century France and Britain was primarily derived from inheritance.

10 [Frederick Hervey] *A New Friend on an Old Subject* (London, 1791) p. 24.

11 *Slight Observations upon Paine's Pamphlet, principally respecting his comparison of the French and English Constitutions* (London, 1791) p. 32.

12 John Jones, *The Reason of Man: With Strictures on Paine's Rights of Man* (London, 1792) p. 14.

13 See: https://founders.archives.gov/documents/Adams/99-02-02-5107

14 Harvey Kaye suggests that Paine's writings made Owen a deist while convincing him that people could improve themselves when freed from oppressive institutions. See Kaye, Thomas Paine, *Thomas Paine and the Promise of America: A History and Biography* (New York: Hill and Wang, 2006) p. 126.

15 Qtd. in H.L.A. Hart, *Essays in Jurisprudence and Philosophy* (Oxford: Clarendon Press, 1983) p. 182.

16 Matthew Roberts, "Posthumous Paine in the United Kingdom, 1809–1832: Jacobin or Loyalist Cult?" in *The Legacy of Thomas Paine in the Transatlantic World*, ed. Sam Edwards and Marcus Morris (London: Routledge, 2018) pp. 107–31, p. 114.

17 J.C.D. Clark, *Thomas Paine: Britain, America, and France in the Age of Enlightenment and Revolution* (Oxford: Oxford University Press, 2018) p. 411.

18 Qtd. in *Class and Conflict in Nineteenth-century England: 1815–1850*, ed. Patricia Hollis (London and New York: Routledge, 1973, 2016) p. 12.

19 In "'The Real Rights of Man': Thomas Spence, Paine, and Chartism" (Miranda, 2016) para.6. Malcolm Chase states "It was Spence's agrarian thought that more commonly informed theory and practice in the early labour and radical movements. This is evident even in the writings of Paine's indefatigable disciple Richard Carlile." See: https://journals.openedition.org/miranda/8989

20 Matteo Battistini, "'Revolutions are the order of the day': Atlantic fragments of Thomas Paine, *c.* 1819–1832" in *The Legacy of Thomas Paine in the Transatlantic World*, ed. Sam Edwards and Marcus Morris (London: Routledge, 2018) pp. 89–104, p. 93.

21 Battistini, pp. 89–104, p. 89.

22 In *Framed*, Sanford Levinson writes: "One might, for example, define democracy as the relatively unimpeded ability of political parties that gain the support of electoral majorities to work their will, even if constrained by certain substantive constitutional norms protecting a set of privileged rights. But then one should recognize that the five modern monarchies mentioned above are considerably more 'democratic' than the modern United States with regard, for example, to the degree that their parliaments represent the majority of the population." See *Framed* (Oxford: Oxford University Press, 2012) p. 80. The five monarchies are Britain, Denmark, Norway, Spain, and Sweden (78).

23 See, for instance: https://www.motherjones.com/politics/2011/02/egypt-madison-ians-pizza/

24 J.E. Stiglitz, *The Price of Inequality: How Today's Divided Society Endangers Our Future* (New York: W.W. Norton & Co.). Kindle Edition. Preface. See also Peter Joseph, *The New Human Rights Movement: Reinventing the Economy to End Oppression* (Dallas, TX: BenBella Books, 2017), Kindle Edition. He states: "the Arab Spring protests registered frustration with overt oppression in the shape of dictatorship and elitism" (35).

25 Robert Reich states "Bailing out Wall Street's bad debts when millions more Americans can't pay their bills is like bailing out a rowboat springing more leaks when the ocean is rising. Many of the average taxpayers being asked to take on Wall Street's bad loans are the same people whose incomes are dropping, which means they're struggling to pay their debts and potentially creating even more bad loans." See: https://www.marketplace.org/2008/09/24/business/fallout-financial-crisis/we-need-main-street-bailout-too.

26 Super PACs cannot make contributions to candidate campaigns or parties, but may engage in unlimited political spending independently of the campaigns. Unlike traditional PACs, they can raise funds from individuals, corporations, unions, and other groups without any legal limit on donation size.

27 David Hawkings, "Wealth of Congress: Richer than Ever, but Mostly at the Very Top." See: https://www.rollcall.com/news/hawkings/congress-richer-ever-mostly-top. See also, Levinson, *Framed*, p. 137.

28 After the Trump tax cuts of 2018, this phenomenon has become even more exacerbated: https://www.nytimes.com/interactive/2019/10/06/opinion/income-tax-rate-wealthy.html

29 See: https://getpocket.com/explore/item/this-cartoon-explains-how-the-rich-got-rich-and-the-poor-got-poor

30 See: https://www.epi.org/publication/what-labor-market-changes-have-generated-inequality-and-wage-suppression-employer-power-is-significant-but-largely-constant-whereas-workers-power-has-been-eroded-by-policy-actions/

31 Piketty, p. 476. All quotations and references from Piketty are drawn from this edition.

32 See the report from The Third Way, "The Opportunity Index: Ranking Opportunity in Metropolitan America," Oct. 30, 2018: https://www.thirdway.org/report/the-opportunity-index-ranking-opportunity-in-m etropolitan-america. Note that some of the largest corporations take advantage of welfare by paying their workers so little that they must rely on public assistance: for instance, McDonald's and Walmart. As Peter Joseph puts it, both are able to do so because "the state is subsidizing the wages, effectively saving these big corporations responsibility and money by taking tax dollars from the public" (151).

33 See: https://www.cbsnews.com/news/minimum-wage-doesnt-cover-the-rent-a nywhere-in-the-u-s/?fbclid=IwAR33BUNdRbxV9_Fa1BtMhF-uGp DZxbBK1FokEyNSJNxr8FNVfaJOocO5b8o

34 The figures from the Economic Policy Institute, and Pew Research National Employment Law Project are taken from https://www.usatoday.com/story/m oney/personalfinance/2017/10/06/why-half-of-americans-cant-come-up -with-400-in-an-emergency/106216294/

35 Bernie Sanders, *Our Revolution: A Future to Believe in* (New York: Thomas Dunne, 2016) p. 326. All quotations and references from Sanders are drawn from this edition.

36 See Erik Kain, "Do Americans Care More About War than Education?," https:// www.forbes.com/sites/erikkain/2011/04/17/do-americans-care-more-about-wa r-than-education/#5cc44d146aa1. "Problems in education are compounded by inequality. The gap in test scores between rich and poor American children is roughly 30–40% wider than it was 25 years ago" (Stiglitz, 32). Only around 9% come from the bottom half of the population, while 74% come from the top quarter (Stiglitz, 19, 83).

37 See Paula Span, "Of Retirement Age, But Remaining in the Work Force," http s://www.nytimes.com/2016/08/02/health/retirement-working-longer.html. "Then there's the troubling fact that many older people have no choice; they hold onto their jobs not because they cherish them, but because they lack alternative income." Also, see: https://www.cbsnews.com/news/the-coming-storm-entering-retirement-broke-and-bankrupt/

38 See chapters 5 and 7 of Thomas Frank, *Listen, Liberal: Or, What Ever Happened to the Party of the People?* (New York: Metropolitan Books, 2016). To varying extents, Clinton, George W. Bush, and Obama considered cutting or privatizing Social Security. More recently, there has been chatter of Trump cutting both in order to pay for tax cuts passed in 2017, largely for the benefit of the wealthy and corporations.

39 Stiglitz suggests that if the U.S. were really a land of opportunity, the life chances of success—of, say, winding up in the top 10%—of someone born to a poor or less educated family would be the same as those of someone born to a rich, well-educated, and well-connected family. But that's not the case at all.

40 See: https://www.theatlantic.com/magazine/archive/2018/06/the-birth-of-a-new-am erican-aristocracy/559130/?utm_source=eb

41 See: https://www.nytimes.com/2015/03/22/opinion/sunday/seth-stephens-davido witz-just-how-nepotistic-are-we.html and https://abcnews.go.com/2020/story?id= 124321&page=1. There have even been apologists for nepotism: https://www.thea tlantic.com/magazine/archive/2003/07/in-praise-of-nepotism/302753/

42 Economist Intelligence Unit, "Democracy Index 2016: Revenge of the 'Deplor-ables'." See: http://www.eiu.com/Handlers/WhitepaperHandler.ashx?fi=Dem ocracy-Index-2016.pdf&mode=wp&campaignid=DemocracyIndex2016

43 See cnbc.com/2018/08/28/most-americans-now-support-medicare-for-all-and-free-college-tuition.html: https://www.cnbc.com/2016/08/01/over-60-of-america ns-back-tuition-free-college-survey-says.html. The article further clarifies that "Seventy-seven percent of people ages 18 to 29 supported tuition-free college while roughly half of people 50 and older did." See also: https://www.inside highered.com/quicktakes/2017/01/13/poll-bipartisan-support-free-college-states

44 https://www.forbes.com/sites/alicegwalton/2018/04/03/nordic-coun tries-continue-to-rank-high-in-happiness-while-america-falls/#3bf8f22023fa

45 https://www.huffingtonpost.com/entry/norway-best-country-to-live_us_5a 6059c7e4b046f0811d0235

46 See: https://nordic.businessinsider.com/the-nordics-have-the-worlds-best-free dom-of-press-2017-4/. Finland, Norway, Denmark, and Iceland rank in the top four in 2018. The U.S. and U.K. rank at 18 and 19, respectively.

47 "U.S. incarceration rates are the highest in the world, about 10 times those throughout Scandinavia, which are among the world's lowest." https://www.thea tlantic.com/international/archive/2013/09/why-scandinavian-prisons-are-sup erior/279949/. In particular, the lowest incarceration rates are Iceland, Japan, Finland, Sweden, Netherlands, Denmark, Norway, and Slovenia. https://www.sta tista.com/statistics/300986/incarceration-rates-in-oecd-countries/

48 It is worth noting that while Bernie Sanders seems to come closest to Paine's ideas, presidential candidate Andrew Yang has actually invoked Thomas Paine's *Agrarian Justice* in his discussion of a Universal Basic Income (UBI).

49 Conservative pundit Tucker Carlson has stated: "Our economic situation, and the plight of the white working class, is the product of a series of conscious decisions that the Congress made." https://www.vox.com/2019/1/10/18171912/ tucker-carlson-fox-news-populism-conservatism-trump-gop

50 Thomas Paine, "To the Citizens of the United States of America," Letter 1 in *The Complete Writings of Thomas Paine*, Vols. 1–2, ed. Philip Foner (New York: Cita-del Press, 1945) 2, pp. 908–912, p. 910.

INDEX